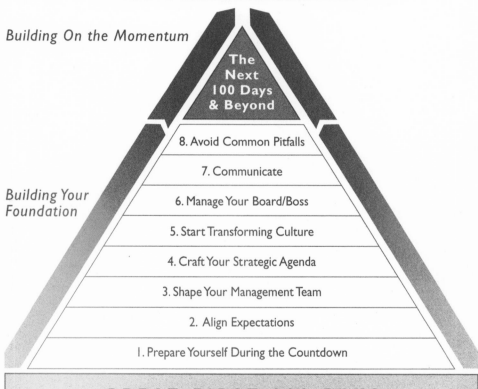

GREAT PERFORMANCE

Building On the Momentum

The Next 100 Days & Beyond

Building Your Foundation

8. Avoid Common Pitfalls

7. Communicate

6. Manage Your Board/Boss

5. Start Transforming Culture

4. Craft Your Strategic Agenda

3. Shape Your Management Team

2. Align Expectations

1. Prepare Yourself During the Countdown

GREAT FIRST 100 DAYS

YOU'RE IN CHARGE—NOW WHAT?

"Clarity, wisdom, good judgment—all ring like a clanging bell in Citrin/ Neff's recipe for getting out of the starting gate FAST! If you are heading into a new leadership role, read this book before you begin if you want to finish in triumph."

—Jack Valenti, retired president and CEO,
Motion Picture Association of America

"Take it from somebody who's been there: *You're In Charge—Now What?* asks all the right questions and tracks down all the right answers from the people who ought to know. Best of all, authors Thomas Neff and James Citrin tell the compelling, often dramatic stories of leadership transitions in ways that make the book come alive."

—Dick Parsons, chairman and CEO, Time Warner Inc.

"*You're in Charge—Now What?* may be the best how-to leadership book I've ever read. It ranks right up there with *Good to Great*. I think it has terrific insights and powerful tips for any leader at any level in any business. I was taking notes and making commitments in the first hundred pages!"

—George H. Conrades, chairman and CEO, Akamai Technologies

"When you really need to hit the ground running, *You're in Charge— Now What?* should be your bible. With astute observations and compelling real-life stories from executives who have managed to keep their stride to the top echelons of business, Citrin and Neff offer the ultimate blueprint for success. A must-read for anyone entering into a leadership role at any level."

—Peter Chernin, president and COO, News Corporation

"This book is a must-read for anyone about to begin a new managerial job. Combining detailed research with fascinating stories of success and failure in the crucial first hundred days, Citrin and Neff provide indispensable advice for CEOs and first-line managers alike."

—Sydney Finkelstein, professor of strategy and leadership,
Tuck School at Dartmouth, and author of *Why Smart Executives Fail*

"Neff and Citrin bypass the quicksand of clichés of other taking-charge books to reveal the genuine lessons of successful first strides and candid fateful missteps in the earliest days of new leadership missions. The secret road maps used by many prominent leaders are revealed for the first time. They offer powerfully useful suggestions that new bosses can immediately translate into actions to ensure mastery of their own fresh leadership frontiers."

    —Jeffrey Sonnenfeld, associate dean, Yale School of Management

"Taking charge demands a fast start and a clear agenda, and drawing on the gritty advice of those who've brought both, Thomas Neff and James Citrin have written the playbook. For making good and fast decisions in the first days of fresh responsibilities, *You're in Charge—Now What?* will ensure the right start when it really counts."

    —Michael Useem, director, Wharton Center for Leadership and Change, and author of *The Leadership Moment*

"Neff and Citrin have distilled hundreds of interviews into a set of valuable advice and practical suggestions for new leaders at all levels. *You're in Charge—Now What?* will resonate with everyone who's in or about to start a new leadership job."

    —Jon R. Katzenbach, founder and managing director, Katzenbach Partners, and author of *Why Pride Matters More Than Money: The Power of the World's Greatest Motivational Force* and coauthor of *The Wisdom of Teams: Creating the High-Performing Organization*

"Citrin and Neff's *You're in Charge—Now What?* resounds with the authentic voice of leaders who launched and led high-stakes, front-page, often risky organizational beginnings. The book is rich with lessons leaders can use today to create the new organizational and personal compacts required to deliver remarkable results and keep their promises through strategic personal planning, self-management, tough and tender conversations, rituals, processes, and confrontations. In their own words, remarkable, gutsy leaders offer a proven guide and compass to avoid the gaffes, gaps, and potholes inherent in any leader's first hundred days. No leader should be without this book, because every day offers the opportunity to relaunch a dream with a deadline."

—Roger Fransecky, Ph.D., president, The Apogee Group

YOU'RE IN CHARGE— NOW WHAT?

YOU'RE IN CHARGE— NOW WHAT?

THE 8 POINT PLAN

THOMAS J. NEFF & JAMES M. CITRIN

WITH CATHERINE FREDMAN

CROWN
BUSINESS
NEW YORK

Permission to use "Gary Kusin's First 100 Day Plan" granted by the author.

Permission to use a memo titled "On Becoming an Associate" by Ron Daniel granted by the author.

Excerpts from pages 111–114, 138, and 165 and the chart of IBM's Required Behavioral Change on page 206 from *Who Says Elephants Can't Dance? Inside IBM's Historic Turnaround* by Louis V. Gerstner. Copyright © 2002 by Louis V. Gerstner. Reprinted by permission of HarperCollins Publishers Inc.

Published in the United States by Crown Business, an imprint of the Crown Publishing Group, a division of Random House, Inc., New York.
www.crownpublishing.com

Crown Business is a trademark and the Rising Sun colophon is a registered trademark of Random House, Inc.

Library of Congress Cataloging-in-Publication Data

Neff, Thomas J.
You're in charge—now what? : the 8 point plan / Thomas J. Neff and James M. Citrin, with Catherine Fredman.
Includes bibliographical references and index.
1. Executive ability. 2. Leadership. 3. Strategic planning. 4. Corporate culture. 5. Organizational change. I. Title: You are in charge—now what?. II. Citrin, James M. III. Fredman, Catherine. IV. Title.
HD38.2.N44 2004
658.4—dc22   2004019876

ISBN 1-4000-4865-6

Printed in the United States of America

Design by Robert Bull

10 9

First Edition

To the memory of my parents, Elizabeth and Wallace Neff.
TJN

To Patty and George Sarner, the world's best in-laws,
for their eternal love and support.
JMC

CONTENTS

YOU'RE IN CHARGE—NOW WHAT?

INTRODUCTION

Recently our friend Matt Mannelly was sitting at the Dunkin' Donuts in New Canaan, Connecticut, jotting some notes on a piece of paper. Standing on line, we wondered how his job search was going. When we sat down at Matt's table, he gave us the wonderful news that he had just closed a deal late the previous night to become president of Cannondale Bicycles.

After well-deserved congratulations, we asked when he would be starting. "In *two hours,*" he replied.

Given that Matt was jumping into his new role with almost no time to prepare, he was happy to hear about our three-year research project studying a hundred of the best and worst leadership transitions and the key lessons about how to get off to the right start. While he intuitively knew that he had a unique window of opportunity to make a positive first impression later that morning, Matt had not developed a precise plan for what he was going to do when he showed up. We suggested that he consider such fundamental questions as:

- Who are you going to meet with first, and what are you going to say?
- How is your appointment being announced internally and externally?
- Have you prepared a formal presentation for employees and the management team?
- Did you review your day and meeting agenda with the board?

These kinds of details are often overlooked, creating the impression that you are disorganized or out of sync with the person who hired you. We also pointed out to Matt that while he is going to be focused on getting his message *out,* the managers he meets are likely going to be seeing and hearing something altogether different. "They will be sizing up your every word, move, and expression to see if they will grant you their respect," we told him. "And they will be thinking, 'Will this new president be good or bad for me?' " We also suggested that in his earliest conversations and communications, he should find a way to share the reasons why he took the job, his own personal and professional background, his expectations of the management team and employees, and potentially an assessment of the company's competitive positioning, as well as initial thoughts about a vision for the future. These were just some of the questions and issues he had to be ready for on his first day.

Matt had in fact thought about many of them, but he had not focused at all on some of the others. There were at least two potential traps into which he had been heading unaware before our conversation. So with the help of coffee and doughnuts we spent the next hour sharing highlights of what many of the most prominent business leaders did that resulted in the very best and worst leadership transitions. One we talked about in detail was Paul Pressler.

• • •

There was a lot of apprehension on September 26, 2002, when Gap Inc. announced that Paul S. Pressler, chairman of Walt Disney Parks and Resorts, would become the company's new chief executive. People were asking, "Who is this guy? What does he know about retail, fashion, and apparel? What will he do when he shows up?"

Pressler had a major challenge as CEO, and he was committed to getting off to the right start so he could lay the foundation for the company's long-term success. The world's largest specialty-apparel retailer, with its Banana Republic, Old Navy, and Gap divisions, had lost touch with its customers, resulting in twenty-nine straight months of declining same-store sales. Profits had evaporated, replaced by ballooning debt that had been steadily downgraded to junk status. And morale among the employees was at a low point.

But in his first hundred days, and in the two years that followed, Pressler found just the right combination of words, decisions, and actions to get the company back on track and create the momentum that has propelled Gap Inc. to an accelerating revitalization. You will see threads of what Pressler did in his early days and how he did them woven throughout this book: Get set to learn, listen well, set proper expectations, read the culture, build trust, lead by example, set the appropriate direction, and communicate effectively. His actions, in fact, followed eight key steps:

1. He prepared himself well during the "countdown period." In the three-week period between his announcement and his start date, Pressler talked to former Gap Inc. managers as well as analysts and shareholders. Then he loaded up his luggage with every strategy document and piece of historical information the company could assemble and took off for a week in Hawaii. Each day he lugged reports and binders to the beach and immersed himself in the financials and planning work. By the time he was set to start, he had defined the challenges facing the company and thought out his initial approach to dealing with them (and realized that his Armani-crammed closet would have to make room for the Gap blue jeans he would wear to the office). "You never feel like you have enough time to prepare," says Pressler. But he quickly adds, "I suspect that more time would not have given me much better skills to come into the job." He also jointly agreed with his family that it would be best for all if his wife and children remained in their southern California home and schools for several months while he dug into his new San Francisco–based role, avoiding a double dose of upheaval.

2. He set and aligned proper expectations. Pressler did not come out guns blazing with aggressive financial objectives or predictions. Nor did he make big promises that might later be undermined through underdelivery. Rather, with his managers, employees, and board of directors, Pressler set and aligned everyone's expectations by listening exceptionally well and communicating what he expected of himself and the company in a way that people could understand and buy into. Pressler's process was as important to this as the specific expectations he set. He conducted one-on-one interviews with the company's top fifty managers, asking each one the same six carefully considered questions to get their insights about the business, to solicit their advice, and to see what themes emerged. He and the Gap Inc. communications department also created a weblog for all the company's employees, posting all of his activities and what he was learning. As a result, "people saw that I was genuinely engaged and was willing to listen before I talked about where we needed to go or communicated a vision or approach," Pressler says. "And that put people at ease. More important, people felt very connected to the learning experience *I* went through, and all these folks in the field who felt underappreciated began to feel that they were significant. I wasn't making promises or changes as much as being a listening post."

3. He shaped his management team. Pressler was deliberate about making top management changes, focusing his early efforts on building the leadership group into a true team. He held regular off-site meetings with an outside facilitator, starting about a month after he joined the company. "We talked about the strengths and weaknesses of the company and the competition and the challenges facing us," he states. "I gave them feedback from all the interviews I had done with our top fifty managers, and they validated and refined what I found. It was at that point that I shared my observations about some fundamental needs of the business, what I called our 'enabling backbones.' " Eventually he moved to biweekly meetings that were more tactical, focusing on the day-to-day fundamentals about what was going on in the organization. He made a couple of specific changes in the top management team, most notably recruiting a new chief financial officer with whom he had worked at Disney.

4. He crafted his strategic agenda. Pressler recognized that it would be premature in the first hundred days to develop a comprehensive strategic plan—and even if he did, it might be wrong. But he knew that in an organization of 165,000 employees, he needed to find a way to set a direction and motivate the people. So using all the learning from the countdown period and his early listening, he developed a "strategic agenda" that established some fundamental principles and goals. This agenda centered on using customer insights and data to drive the business, refocusing on Gap Inc.'s core customer base, focusing all employees on company-wide objectives, improving the logistics and inventory-management systems to reduce costs and free up cash, and making the company a great place to work. These themes were specific enough to provide focus but general enough that all areas of the company could begin applying them in ways that made sense to them. He ultimately developed a more detailed strategic plan just over a year into his tenure.

5. He started to transform the corporate culture. With expectations properly set, his management group starting to work as a team, and a strategic direction in hand, Pressler was able to work on transforming the Gap Inc. corporate culture. In fact, as with all of the eight key components of his hundred-day plan, he did not approach this particular step in a serial fashion. He actually *started* to transform the culture from day one, building on his efforts throughout his first hundred days, and the hundred days after that. His top fifty management interviews, his novel weblog communications device, his leadership team building, his examples of realistic optimism and high energy level, and most important, his active listening started to resurrect the more action-oriented, empowering, and high-spirited culture at the company. Over time Pressler has been able to help Gap Inc. shift from a top-down "merchant-centric" culture to a more team-oriented culture rooted in consumer research, focused marketing, and efficient operations.

6. He established a productive working relationship with his boss. As with his management team and employees, Pressler set the stage for working well with the company's board of directors by being straightforward, communicative, and organized and by listening well. Gap Inc. had had only two CEOs in its entire history. As a first-time CEO, Pressler did not pretend to be an expert in working with a board, and his disarming candor about being a neophyte was exactly the right approach. The board was thrilled at the prospect of starting a partnership based on mutual openness and respect. "Later on, when I started to present strategy to them, they were very dynamic and engaged," Pressler says.

7. He communicated exceptionally well. In addition to all the listening and learning and questioning and synthesizing that constitute effective communication, Pressler was also creative in how he communicated. Pressler's weblog, or online journal, he had to introduce Pressler and remain visible to the company's employees. It also sent the message about what he stood for and what was important. The site, which gathered something of a minicult following, tracked his travels and store visits, showed interactions with store managers, salespeople, and customers, and provided a communication mechanism for employees to share their thoughts in return. Right from the start Pressler demonstrated that he was a real person, had a sense of humor and a passion to listen and learn, and was maniacally focused on Gap's most important constituency, its customers. "What I did during my first hundred days sent a clear signal that I was going to listen before we talked strategy or made any major decisions. I built a constituency by allowing people to see that I had a clear communication plan and it bought me time," he says.

8. He resisted the powerful temptations that trap many new leaders. Pressler felt many pressures, both from within the company and externally, to make changes fast, to be decisive, and to set bold visions. But he recognized that these were seductive traps. He did not allow himself to be portrayed as a savior, he most certainly did not attempt to be a know-it-all, and he made sure to keep open to the torrent of data and information that flows into any leader when they start a new role. He remained steadfast to his agenda of listening and learning, working with his management team, spending time on the sales floors and in the stockrooms at various company stores, and describing his discoveries, thoughts, and ideas to the management team and the company's employees at large.

"The first hundred days are critical," Pressler concludes of his start at Gap Inc., "because you set a very strong tone about how you want to run the company. The organization is assessing every move, every word, what you say and what you don't say. I'm not sure that if you stumble in the first hundred days it's fatal, but it's a major opportunity missed and would take you a lot of time to recover."

THERE IS NOT JUST ONE FIRST HUNDRED DAYS

No matter what your profession is, what level you are at, or whether you work as part of a large corporation, a small company, a not-for-profit organization, or as an individual practitioner, you can expect to experience numerous "first" hundred days over the course of your career. The average professional with thirty-five years of experience today has held six or seven different jobs. A fast-track manager will switch jobs within a company every two and a half to three years, not even counting other significant career transitions, such as heading up important projects or taking on an additional functional responsibility. That is assuming that you stay at the same company, a prospect that is less and less likely. Our research shows that professionals with only ten years of work experience today have already worked for an average of four companies and are projected to etch another six on their résumé throughout the remaining course of their careers.

This trend is likely to persist as companies continue their rigorous cost-management and efficiency drives, making "reductions in force" standard operating procedure. The constant streamlining will, in turn, continue to erode individuals' sense of loyalty to a company, encouraging them to branch out in their career development and job searches.

Each new leadership role will demand that you adjust to a different culture, operating process, support system, and management style within the organization. Every shift in the work environment requires a fresh start and a new response. The bottom line is this: Both you and the workforce at large are going to have many first hundred days over the years to come.

General Electric's chairman and chief executive officer, Jeffrey R. Immelt, concurs. "I've not only had a lot of first hundred days over the course of my GE career," points out Immelt, who held eight different jobs at GE over the course of twenty-one years, "I've had a lot of first hundred days since becoming CEO!" After winning a grueling three-way horse race to succeed legendary GE chief Jack Welch, Immelt served an eight-month apprenticeship and took the top job on September 7, 2001. Four days later the world changed: "I had the first hundred days of dealing with global terrorism, the first hundred days of international discourse and government intersecting with business as it never has before, the first hundred days when I was CEO-designate, and the first hundred days as CEO. Every manager and every CEO is going to have many first hundred days, simply because of the world we now live in."

No matter what your present level of leadership, the first hundred days of a new job holds both a unique window of opportunity and a heightened state of risk. The opportunity comes from the fact that a leadership transition is a time of maximum uncertainty, when all assumptions are up in the air and open to change. As the new leader, you're generally given the benefit of the doubt. "I think it's your one chance to ask stupid questions," says Robert Eckert, chief executive of Mattel, who had an exceptional first hundred days.

The opportunity also derives from the fact that people *expect* a new leader to bring about change. The decisions you make during those first three months are in some ways less likely to be challenged, internally or externally, because there's both a presumption and an expectation that you will do things differently. It's a honeymoon period in which your authority and the permission to act are still rooted in your appointment rather than in the results you've achieved.

But because you are under a spotlight, the decisions you make and how you make them will label you as either rash or purposeful, firm or indecisive. The actions you take, who you consult, how you manage the decision-making process, and what you say will categorize you as either inclusive or authoritarian, fair or arbitrary, a visionary or a cautious bureaucrat, a good listener or closed-minded. The impression you make and the signals you send will either motivate people to pledge their loyalty or allow them to sit on the sidelines, or worse, impel them to turn against you.

Richard Parsons, chairman and chief executive officer of Time Warner, compares the period to quick-drying cement. While the cement is still wet, you can shape and mold it into a sturdy foundation that will shape and support your next hundred days, and the hundred days after that. But once the cement dries, any mistake costs more time, energy, and money to dig up and rework.

WHERE DID "THE FIRST HUNDRED DAYS" COME FROM?

The special significance of the first hundred days as a concept dates to Franklin Delano Roosevelt's first term as president of the United States.* It was March 1933, and the country was in crisis. The Great Depression had wrecked the economy, almost every bank was closed, one in every four people was unemployed, and the very survival of democratic capitalism was in doubt.

During FDR's first three months in office, he proposed, and Congress enacted, a sweeping program to bring recovery to business and agriculture, relief to the unemployed and to those in danger of losing farms and homes, and regulatory reform, especially through the establishment of the Tennessee Valley Authority. According to Arthur M. Schlesinger Jr.'s *The Age of Roosevelt: The Coming of the New Deal,* in his first hundred days "Roosevelt sent 15 messages to Congress, guided 15 major laws to enactment, delivered 10 speeches, held press conferences and cabinet meetings twice a week, conducted talks with foreign heads of state, sponsored an international conference, made all the major decisions in domestic and foreign policy, and never displayed fright or panic and rarely even bad temper."

Within a hundred days of Roosevelt's inaugural proclamation "We have nothing to fear but fear itself," America had a sense of renewed

* Mark Ronovitch, archivist at the FDR library in Hyde Park, New York, believes that the actual term *First Hundred Days* might have come from Napoleon, as he had described his return from one hundred days of exile in Elba in 1815. But it clearly became popularized by the beginning of Roosevelt's New Deal administration in 1933.

hope and confidence, a feeling that the business of the country was in good hands. The agenda that Roosevelt unveiled during those first three months shaped public policy not just during his own tenure in office but throughout the twentieth century. And the speed at which he accomplished it became the yardstick by which every subsequent U.S. president has been measured, for better or for worse.

Today, more than seventy years later, this special time period has woven its way into our popular culture. A Yahoo.com search for "The First Hundred Days" turns up 89,600 references!

THE TOUGH NEW ENVIRONMENT

Today's job pressures start at the CEO level and trickle down, resulting in more and more "first hundred days" experiences at every level throughout an organization. According to Harvard Business School professor Michael Watkins, each year more than *half a million* management positions turn over in *Fortune* 500 companies alone. Even when a new appointment goes to an internal candidate with long tenure, the imperative to deliver a strong takeoff is no less compelling—or daunting.

Until recently, corporate executives were cut more slack. They were confident about staying in the job as long as they wanted and being able to make their mark. That has all changed.

Every leader, no matter how popular or how self-confident, is vulnerable in a way that earlier leaders were not. New CEOs today go into the job aware that they have to prove themselves to their boards of directors and shareholders and knowing that they don't have as much time to do it. Mistakes count more in this charged atmosphere, and the trigger is pulled earlier, heightening the sense of urgency to get off to a fast start and get it right the first time.

Consider the findings from the influential Booz Allen Hamilton annual CEO succession study. In 2002 and 2003 three to four times as many chief executives around the world were removed for poor performance as in 1995. The authors summarized pessimistically, "At some juncture, the prospect of forced dismissal will seem so likely that it will hang like a cloud of misery over a chief executive, undermining his or her ability to perform."

Insiders do not have a home-field advantage. Twenty years ago, fewer than 15 percent of *Fortune* 500 companies brought in a CEO from the outside, according to a study by Margarethe Wiersema, professor of strategic management at University of California Irvine's Graduate School of Management. Today that figure is nearly 40 percent. "And when it came to replacing dismissed, as opposed to retiring CEOs, companies chose outsiders an overwhelming 61 percent of the time," she writes.

No one is safe from the turbulence roiling today's work environment.

But you can maximize your own professional success by ensuring that in your first hundred days and in the many subsequent first hundred days that you will encounter, you get off to the right start. And that is the goal of this book.

OUR RESEARCH FOUNDATION

Our research foundation is based on a study of more than a hundred of the most visible leadership transitions, the vast majority of which took place over the past five years. We conducted in-depth interviews with more than fifty chief executives who took the top job within the past three years. We spoke at length with numerous board directors, divisional presidents, human resources chiefs, and other functional leaders. And we reviewed more than seventy-five secondary sources, including articles, books, and specialized studies. More specifically:

• We called on a CEO roster ranging from the heads of established multinational corporations like Gillette and Procter & Gamble to dynamic startups, like Imaginova and GlobalSpec, to important educational institutions and not-for-profit organizations like Harvard University, the U.S. Olympic Committee, and Outward Bound.

- We interviewed CEOs who had ascended through the ranks and were promoted to lead great companies like General Electric and UPS, as well as those who had been recruited from the outside, at companies such as Mattel, AT&T, and 3M.

- We brainstormed with brave souls who parachuted into companies in crisis, like Tyco International, America Online, and Adelphia, as well as those who inherited more prosperous and stable situations, like Amgen and Intuit.

- We examined cases where an executive's succession had been planned for a few years, like John Hancock, and those where the top job came up for grabs and was filled in matter of weeks, like The Home Depot and Yahoo!

- We evaluated chief executives whose first hundred days heralded a strong performance, like Kinko's and Avon, and also those whose tenure was cut short in a dramatic fashion, like Ford and Bertelsmann.

- We interviewed corporate board members and succession committee chairs from companies such as Lucent, Hewlett-Packard, Boeing, and Motorola to get their insights on winning and losing scenarios that they've been involved with and witnessed from their perspective as the boss's ultimate boss.

- And we spoke with some of those most directly impacted by all of these CEO successions—divisional presidents, functional executives, and human resources leaders.

FOR CEOS AND NEW MANAGERS OF ALL STRIPES

The lessons learned from our research are not restricted to chief executives. To be sure, the CEO position is different from other jobs within a company. Any other position comes with some form of support network and the knowledge that there's always at least one more person who has the final say. The CEO role is an order of magnitude higher in terms of intensity and responsibility around what needs to be done. "There's a feeling that this is it, this is where the ultimate decisions are made and the heavy responsibility of making the right decisions most of the time weighs on you," says Jacques Nasser, former head of Ford Motor Company, who learned many of these lessons the hard way.

Yet because a similar sense of responsibility is shared by anyone in a leadership position, we found that the lessons were valid across the entire management spectrum. Lew Platt agrees. "Almost everything applies in varying degrees," says the former head of Hewlett-Packard and current chairman of Boeing. "There's nothing that different about the CEO job except the incredible demands it makes on your time, that you largely give up your personal life, and that everyone watches what you do. If you're a manager elsewhere in the organization, that's not always the case. But the mechanics are pretty much the same."

While this book is not at all exclusively about—or for—new CEOs, we have concentrated on CEOs for two reasons. First, they've had a lot of successful "first hundred days" experiences, by the very nature of their careers. Robert Nardelli, for example, held eleven different leadership positions as he moved through GE's leadership pipeline before taking charge at The Home Depot in December 2000. Other people, like Norman Blake, former head of the U.S. Olympic Committee, and John Read, president of Outward Bound USA, were chief executives at a series of different companies before moving into the not-for-profit sector.

Second, the lessons from CEO leadership transitions can be directly extrapolated to almost any new management situation. It will come as no surprise to you that getting off to the right start is just as important if you are a new professional, a project leader, a department manager, a division president, or the CEO. And while some of the specific do's and don'ts for CEOs are unique to their role, most essential things like setting expectations, developing a vision, establishing a management process, creating priorities, building your management team, and doing an exceptional job on your earliest projects apply equally to anyone in a new leadership role.

When Ron Daniel was the managing partner of McKinsey & Company from 1976 to 1988, he sent a memo to new recruits when they started, entitled, "On Becoming an Associate." His advice is still memorable all these years later: "Recognize the necessity of getting off to a good start in the firm. Your first few engagements are critical. During these studies, you can establish an internal clientele for yourself—that is, by performing in an outstanding way, your reputation will be quickly established in your office and even the firm." (We've incorporated Ron's memo in the Appendix of the book.)

This is especially important because whenever you assume a new role, you're in what Max DePree, former CEO of furniture company Herman Miller and author of *Leadership Is an Art,* calls "a temporary state of incompetence." Even if you think you know a company—or a department or a division—before you take over its leadership, think again. As GE's Immelt reminisces, "I worked for this place for twenty-one years before I got the CEO job and there were still things that shocked me when I took over."

The knowledge gap is even wider for outsiders. "Anyone coming into a new situation is faced with the fact that they often have to do the most at the point they know the least. You may have previous experience and you may be smart and have insight into how things work, but you know the least about the actual company you're engaged in at the same time you have to set things in motion," says AOL chairman and CEO Jonathan F. Miller, himself recruited into the company from the outside.

All of this underscores the need to have the right attitude and your own agenda to handle your first hundred days. "*Agenda* is the right word—it's not a plan or strategy," insists Immelt. "It's what you stand for, what you're focusing on." What is the right attitude? It is "Congratulations, you got the job, now you have to earn it," says Lloyd Braun, former chairman of ABC Entertainment and a new executive at Yahoo. You will generate goodwill and support by reaching out for others, listening, trying to be helpful, and committing to show others that you were the right choice for the job.

Time is also a more scarce resource than you may realize. Assuming that a new leader works six days a week and fourteen hours a day, barely twelve hundred *hours* are available throughout the course of the first hundred days. New leaders need to spend as much time as possible absorbing, listening, learning, establishing relationships, and making decisions and can't afford to waste a single hour. During their earliest days they will be barraged with phone calls, speaking requests, and thousands of e-mails from eager employees, suppliers, vendors, and advisers of all types trying to establish influence and gain professional advantage based on gaining their favor and entering into their good graces at a vulnerable moment in time. They need to be intensely focused on the important issues; otherwise they will bog down in a morass of minutiae that probably won't matter in the long run. Setting an agenda helps keep this all on track, and clearly communicating that agenda helps keep the organization on track, too.

THE GOAL OF THIS BOOK

The goal of this book is to provide you and those you work with all that you need to build your own agenda and plan. Through numerous examples, we will demonstrate how to get in mental, emotional, and physical shape for your hundred-day sprint. We'll show what initial steps to take to shape that quick-drying cement. We'll explore how to begin to assess and shape your management team, and we'll show you how to set your strategic agenda. We'll also detail how to assess and start to transform the culture inside an organization, as well as establish productive working relationships with your boss or board of directors, as well as other outside constituents. We'll show you how communication is one of the central aspects of leadership in the early days and beyond. Last but not least, we'll detail the most common pitfalls that trap new leaders and how you can avoid them.

While the first hundred days are often conducted at a breakneck pace, it is essential to realize that they are really just the first leg in a much longer race. Successful leaders know that they have to learn to channel the adrenaline rush of the hundred-day sprint into the discipline and endurance to deliver sustained excellence throughout the marathon. Your first hundred days will be a testing period in which people will push to see what you will and won't do. You will also be testing your own limits and resolve and doing so for those around you.

To put the first hundred days into their proper context, we developed the framework on the following page in the image of a pyramid to house our 8 Point Plan for getting off to the right start. As we hope to make clear in the chapters to come, there are a series of key actions that you can follow, building layer upon layer of the pyramid, to achieve a great first hundred days. Doing so will then maximize your opportunity to achieve successful long-term performance.

We hope to accelerate your learning curve and reduce the anxiety that is standard issue for all leaders as they get set to start a new assignment. A key tenet of leadership is that one of the most important roles of the leader is to define reality. The first hundred days of a new regime both distill and display your management style in that new reality.

Let's start by getting you prepared for the race.

THE FIRST HUNDRED DAYS PYRAMID

GREAT PERFORMANCE

Building On the Momentum

The Next 100 Days & Beyond

Building Your Foundation

8. Avoid Common Pitfalls

7. Communicate

6. Manage Your Board/Boss

5. Start Transforming Culture

4. Craft Your Strategic Agenda

3. Shape Your Management Team

2. Align Expectations

1. Prepare Yourself During the Countdown

GREAT FIRST 100 DAYS

ONE

THE COUNTDOWN

PREPARING FOR THE RACE BEFORE YOU REACH THE STARTING LINE

When does a race begin? At the starting line, when you are taking your last deep breath in anticipation of the starter's gun? Earlier that day, when you follow the rituals that focus your mind on the race ahead? Or weeks or months in advance, when you construct the training program that will enable you to meet and manage the upcoming trial?

WALK IN WITH A "STRATEGIC PROCESS"

Everyone's countdown period to a new leadership position is different, depending on whether they come into a new position from inside their organization or were recruited from the outside, whether they are entering a company in crisis or in a stable environment, and whether they are jumping right into a new job from an already demanding one or have the luxury of some free time for additional preparation.

But all countdown periods share a common goal: to learn as much as possible about the new world you're about to enter so that you can figure out how to best explore and navigate your way through it. To accomplish that, says Dave Peterschmidt, CEO of the Internet security firm Securify and former CEO and COO respectively of Internet pioneers Inktomi and Sybase, "You shouldn't expect to walk into a new leadership job with an established strategic plan. Rather, you should walk in prepared to lead a strategic *process*."

This is a process of multiple dimensions. You're clearing and focusing your thoughts so that you can diagnose the challenges and opportunities of the new situation. You're identifying key constituencies and starting to forge alliances and build new relationships. You're attempting to flush out biases while distilling valuable information from people who have key insights into the company. You're thinking about all that needs to be done in the context of your own skills and experience. You're considering the strength of the managers who will soon make up your team, and you're hypothesizing about where the holes are likely to be. Simultaneously, you're preparing yourself emotionally for a major life transition and taking steps to get your family and support infrastructure ready to run without you for a period of time.

THE VALUE OF PREPARATION

By now, just about everyone knows that Lance Armstrong is the record-breaking six-consecutive-times winner of the Tour de France, one of the most grueling endurance contests in the world. His success is based not only on his extraordinary athletic ability, supernatural lung capacity, and ferocious competitive drive fired by his heroic conquering of cancer, but also on the intensive time and energy he invests in preparing for the race. In his memoir, *It's Not About the Bike,* Armstrong discusses the importance of building the right team, learning the course, and ensuring that he and his support staff have the right training, the proper conditioning, and the best equipment to go for the win. He literally memorizes the entire 2,106-mile course, diligently researching every conceivable permutation of wind, weather, and temperature affecting each curve and straightaway.

No serious athlete walks into a competition without prior preparation. It should be no different when you are approaching a challenging new business assignment. You too are entering a race. If you are not sharp and at the top of your game *before* the starting gun fires, you will squander a golden opportunity and diminish your chances of achieving your goals.

"The countdown establishes the foundation to maximize your chances for success," says Dan Schulman, CEO of Virgin Mobile USA. "The days leading up to the point when you actually take the job are some of the most important to being successful. Day one on the job better not be 'day one' where you're working on your action plan; it should be well under way by the time you get there."

SPEND TIME IN THE RIGHT WAYS

Establishing and maintaining the right priorities is one of the greatest challenges a new leader faces. One of your goals during the countdown period is to try to shape events before they shape you.

Let's assume you work an average of six days a week and fourteen hours a day. That means that a finite 1,204 hours are at your disposal during the first hundred days. How should you allocate your time and energy to achieve the greatest return on this scarce resource? Which areas should you focus on, and which can you afford to put on the back burner? Effective planning will help you invest your available time wisely.

During our research, we asked leaders which actions they rated as the most important for getting off to the right start. Topping the list were five items:

1. **Absorb information.**

2. **Define the company's challenges.**

3. **Establish credibility and win employees' trust.**

4. **Assess the senior management team.**

5. **Prepare yourself emotionally.**

While all five of these items are critical—and are addressed in the chapters that follow—the last one is frequently neglected. New leaders are often so anxious to jump into their new role that they jump right in, or they put their personal life on autopilot. Yet a solid emotional foundation is in large measure a precondition for achieving the other objectives, as they can't be achieved without preparing oneself for the difficult and intense period ahead. Psychologists maintain that you cannot truly open a new chapter in life until you close the previous one. People need a sense of closure before they can possibly be ready to listen, learn, and lead. Simply recognizing this fact and following the intuitive knowledge that you need some type of break or "interstitial" time before moving into a new role will help get you ready.

Based on these five priorities for the countdown period, we have extrapolated ten guidelines to optimize your countdown period. (See Conclusion at the end of this chapter.) They range from sifting through the avalanche of information to hone in on the most critical issues, to developing strategies for building people's trust, to ensuring that you are in the best possible physical, mental, and emotional shape to meet the challenges ahead.

GET SET TO LEARN

Preparing yourself for a new job requires understanding how the company operates, where it has been, where it is headed, how the management team works, and where your own abilities fit into the mix—all of which require an incredibly steep learning curve. As GE's Jeff Immelt points out, "You never get a job because of what you know. It's about how fast you learn and how much you can adapt."

Bob Nardelli, a former colleague of Immelt's at GE and now CEO of The Home Depot, adds, "You really have to immerse yourself" to get up to speed. The countdown period offers you the chance to take whatever due diligence process you've already started and dig a little deeper.

Jim Kilts, the first outside CEO at Gillette in seventy years, had six weeks between acceptance and his start date in February 2001. The once high-flying maker of Mach3 razors, Duracell batteries, and Oral-B toothbrushes had missed its earnings for fourteen consecutive quarters. Sales and earnings had been flat for five years. Two-thirds of Gillette's products were losing market share, and Gillette's value dropped 30 percent between 1997 and 2000. Investor enthusiasm for the formerly hot stock had dwindled.

During his countdown period, Kilts launched an exhaustive investigation with a handpicked team composed of the former heads of strategy and public affairs at Nabisco, where Kilts had most recently been CEO, a financial expert and several financial analysts with whom he had brainstormed with over the years. They scoured the public information—past annual reports, Wall Street research, the business press, and industry reviews. "We tried to evaluate Gillette as we would look at a competitor," Kilts recalls.

It was important to Kilts to learn the industry's opinion of Gillette before he was exposed to the company's own interpretation: "I tried to absorb all the key things that I could about how the outside world looked at the company before I read any of the internal reports."

Then he went on the road. Before showing up for his day one in the office, he traveled with Gillette salespeople. He visited stores, inspected warehouses, and dropped in at manufacturing plants. He spoke with suppliers, pored over consumer feedback reports, picked the brains of board members, and chatted with retail customers. That is how he discovered Gillette's dirty little secret.

To hit their numbers each quarter, Gillette's salespeople habitually resorted to a business practice known as trade loading: offer a cut-rate deal, rearrange product packaging, do anything to make a sale to a retailer to stock inventory. While trade loading isn't illegal, it is not a sustainable strategy because you are in essence borrowing from the future to pay for the present and devaluing your products in the process. Major retail customers, the chain stores selling Gillette products, knew that the company was desperate to make its numbers and came to learn that all they had to do was wait until the last week of the quarter to order so that they could cut the best possible deal.

Gillette found itself trapped in a downward spiral. In a pamphlet Kilts produced entitled "Escaping the Circle of Doom," he pointed out that businesses get in trouble by setting overly ambitious objectives, such as increasingly unrealistic sales growth targets; then, in trying to meet those targets, making bad decisions, which lead to further misses, which lead to more bad decisions. Gillette compounded its circle-of-doom problems by allowing its spending and overhead to grow out of control. The company had become the fastest bill-payer in the industry and the slowest collector of receivables. As part of its lack of financial discipline and poor information systems, sales results were not tallied every day or even every week—merely at the end of each quarter.

Only after his analysis was far along did Kilts speak with people from inside the company. "I had one dinner with the CFO and the acting CEO," he recalls. "We didn't talk about the detailed business issues but rather about how the company was feeling—the people issues that you couldn't get a feel for from the outside. That was the only meeting I had with inside managers from the company before I actually showed up."

When the time to start finally arrived, Kilts blew in like a hurricane. "My first board meeting was two days after I got here. Within the first hour of meeting me, they heard my philosophy plus my analysis of the company." They also heard how he planned to remedy the situation, a strategy he and his team had brainstormed and thought through during the prior six weeks.

Most people do not have the benefit of Kilts's six weeks of full-time preparation or his dedicated team to get up to speed. And there are serious risks to coming into a new situation with your action plan too well developed. (You can be wrong; and even if you're right, you may not achieve the necessary buy-in.) But in Kilts's case, he had close enough prior experience, self-confidence, and ample time and resources to devote to the process. The key lesson is to use whatever time and resources you *do* have from the point at which a new opportunity becomes plausible until you actually start to learn.

THE APPRENTICE

Insiders who ascend in an orderly progression and have time before taking on their new responsibilities may have an enviable opportunity: to serve as an apprentice to a leader during a transition period.

After a highly public succession contest, Jeff Immelt was selected to take the reins from the world's most celebrated CEO, Jack Welch, on Thanksgiving weekend 2000. "We all staggered across the finish line," says Immelt, referring to the two other candidates in the race, former colleagues Jim McNerney (now CEO of 3M) and Bob Nardelli. Immelt was exhausted from the ordeal, conducted while he was running GE Medical Systems. The thought of stepping into Welch's position on January 1, with only thirty days of preparation, seemed ludicrous. "I didn't have any perspective," Immelt recalls. "Before I became chairman-elect, I had only been to one board meeting."

To compensate, Immelt began an eight-month apprenticeship with Welch as his mentor. "Once I was named, Jack let me run the company and was here to coach. This was the chance to have dinner with him and talk about things with the guy who understood the company better than anyone in the world."

Immelt spent those eight months meeting customers, employees, and investors, "each day, every day," he said. "I spent lots of time on the businesses I didn't know. It was getting my hands around the culture, the people, the values—what was going to be different, what was going to be the same. I needed that time because of the mass of the company. It gave me the opportunity to pick his brain on a bunch of stuff that I'd always wanted to ask him but didn't have the venue to do it. And it allowed me to get reloaded emotionally, get energized, and think about where I wanted to go with the company. Then, when he was ready to retire, I was ready to go."

Of his apprenticeship, Immelt concludes, "It was like having a running start."

MEET WITH SMART OBSERVERS

Other newly appointed leaders similarly recall turning to their predecessors for advice, training, contacts, and mentoring—even for making personal introductions to important clients, key shareholders, useful industry sources, and other constituents. The idea, for most in this type of situation, is to step into the outgoing CEO's shoes with the understanding that the actual dance steps will be up to them.

Mike Eskew had close to a year before becoming the chief executive of package delivery giant UPS. He describes his training period as a collaboration between himself and outgoing CEO Jim Kelly. Together they planned ways in which Eskew could make the most of the interim period. "I spent a lot of time in Washington, D.C., talking to public affairs people to understand who the key lawmakers were. I started to meet a lot of customers to give them a feel for who I was. And I made it a point to visit each of the board members before I became CEO, to ask them about their thoughts, concerns, and ideas. I had been named vice chairman about a year earlier, so people expected that I would step into this job and knew I had the background. It was not a shock for anyone."

At medical products company Baxter International, incoming CEO Harry Jansen Kraemer and outgoing CEO Vernon Loucks forged a productive partnership that ensured a smooth transition. Kraemer had worked for the company for sixteen years and had served as president for one year and as CFO for nearly five years before that. Loucks's plan was for Kraemer to serve two apprenticeships, one before taking on the responsibilities of chief executive and one before becoming chairman a year later.

"Until I became CEO, I spent 99.9 percent of my time internally," Kraemer explains. "Becoming the CEO meant I had a lot to learn on the external side—the elevated visibility, more demands on my time from a political perspective visiting congressmen and supporting health care initiatives. Vern started almost immediately introducing me to different groups. He took me to Washington, D.C., a couple of times; he took me to the Business Roundtable, the Healthcare Leadership Council, and told me the key people to get to know. He had been with Baxter for thirty-five years and had been the CEO for twenty, and he knew everybody. He told me, 'Harry, here are some good contacts for you. You're going to have a lot more demands on your time, so here's how I would rank them given your background.' He had laid out what needed to happen before he retired and definitely mentored me through that process."

While effective for getting off to the right start, the early mentorship by Loucks and Kraemer's ability to improve the company's cash flow could not be sustained. Following months of disappointing earnings, a lagging share price, and downward revisions to earnings estimates, Kraemer resigned from Baxter in January 2004.

DRAFT A HUNDRED DAY AGENDA

With the information and insights that you've gathered in place, you can then turn to the most concrete deliverable of the countdown period: drafting a hundred day agenda. "It almost goes without saying that the notion of having a clear agenda and a message is critical, but I'm shocked at how infrequently it happens," comments Jeff Immelt. *Agenda* is the right word. You cannot possibly have enough insight yet to craft a detailed plan or an in-depth strategy. But you should certainly have a clear idea of what you believe, the key issues that you are going to be focusing on, and some form of organizing framework for the key actions you will want to take.

Several days before Bob Eckert began his job as CEO of Mattel, he wrote down his goals for the first hundred days. Eckert's agenda is not so much unique as representative of a straightforward, solid approach that works in many different situations.

"I listed the five constituencies that I thought were important and the goals I had for each one and the plan of attack. The constituencies were: (1) senior management, (2) employees, (3) customers, (4) investors, and (5) the board of directors. My goal for the rank-and-file employees, for example, was to provide visibility and initiate dialogue, and I planned to do that through daily informal group lunches in the cafeteria and walk-arounds in the building. For senior management,

BOB ECKERT'S COUNTDOWN
TO A SUCCESSFUL START AT MATTEL

How do you get set to go when you're moving into a new industry or area? These nine recommendations will help.

1. **Call on customers.** Without being overly direct, you can learn how the industry is viewed.

2. **Watch consumers.** For consumer goods manufacturers or retailers, time spent in the store pays huge dividends.

3. **Find retirees.** Alumni know more about the industry and the company's culture than anyone else.

4. **Read everything.** The Internet makes it easy to find obscure books and articles. I read anything that any analyst had written in the past few years. I looked through the periodicals and I found a book—*Toy Wars*—that is mostly about Hasbro but has some insights into Mattel that were very helpful.

5. **Talk to a mentor.** Even though he or she may not know the prospective industry well, your mentor does have an objective opinion of your abilities and capacity to adapt.

6. **Phone a friend.** I had better results getting input from a few friends than most of the *Who Wants to Be a Millionaire* callers do.

7. **Keep notes from every conversation.** When you have time to reflect, these notes can help you put together the puzzle pieces of the new job or industry.

8. **Write down your goals for the first hundred days.** What do you plan to bring to the new company? What knowledge can you transfer from your former industry? What do you need to learn quickly? How will you do it?

9. **Commit fully.** Always look forward, instead of being distracted by the could-haves, would-haves, and should-haves of your old job.

my goals were to engage them in the business, demonstrate inclusive leadership, and begin to identify gaps and organizational needs. I planned to start with an informal two-day off-site meeting to talk about business issues and build camaraderie, and I wanted to schedule that during my first two weeks.

"That plan of action included the three components I believed would get Mattel back on track: Build brands; cut costs; develop people. I had that all on one sheet of paper and referred to it every couple of days to remind me."

WHEN YOU ARE A CANDIDATE

Many of the leaders we interviewed for this book put together an agenda for their first hundred days: some did so during the countdown period after they accepted the new job, and some actually did so while they were finalist candidates for the position. In fact, occasionally we advise hiring managers or board search committees to ask the two or three finalist candidates to draft a strategic agenda for their first hundred days as part of the final selection process. When done right, this not only helps determine who the ideal candidate is, it also accelerates the planning process to help the new leader get off to the fastest start possible. One of the elements we've included in the Appendix is the single best First Hundred Day Plan done by a CEO candidate during a search process, written by Gary Kusin, CEO of Kinko's.

THE VISION THING

How necessary is it for the new leader to formulate a vision statement?

Many people in business and the media have long been enamored of vision statements from high-profile leaders; others are cynical as to their value. In leadership transition situations, employees are under-standably anxious to hear a road map for the future and what it will mean for them. Similarly, customers, suppliers, and investors all want to know whether they will need to readjust their own plans. But craft-ing a vision statement in the countdown period—and even in the first hundred days—may be not just premature but a waste of time. The most immediate concerns are generally whether the new leader is credible, what he or she stands for, and what tactical and operating actions need to happen. Discussions about "where we want to be in five years" typically ring hollow early on.

So the art is to find the right balance between setting a direction and keeping practical.

"The word *vision* is often misused and is a nebulous thing," points out Virgin's Dan Schulman. However, he adds, "You can and should nail down what you are trying to create and what the goals and objec-tives are. At Virgin Mobile we knew from the very beginning that we weren't trying to create a niche industry player of half a million sub-scribers. We were trying to create a multibillion-dollar company from scratch. Understanding what that goal would entail helped inform every decision, from investments to people to systems infrastructure. Our longer-term objectives were very important when we were think-ing about the second- and third-order decisions that needed to be made to achieve that."

During his countdown period Paul Pressler was initially con-cerned enough about the need for a vision for Gap Inc. that he put it on his "to think about" list while in Hawaii, preparing for his new role. But he came to realize that it was not necessary after all. As part of his countdown curriculum, Pressler read *Who Says Elephants Can't Dance?*, Lou Gerstner's firsthand account of the turnaround he led at IBM. Gerstner had kicked off a controversy when, at his first major press conference, he announced, "There's been a lot of specu-lation as to when I'm going to deliver a vision of IBM, and what I'd like to say to all of you is that the last thing IBM needs right now is a vision." What the company needed, he went on to tell the stunned crowd (who didn't seem to recall anything else from his speech), "was a series of very tough-minded, market-driven, highly effective strategies for each of its businesses—strategies that deliver performance in the marketplace and shareholder value." (More on the Gerstner story can be found in Chapters 3 and 4.)

Pressler says, "This was very inspiring and gave me a little bit more confidence to say that it doesn't all have to happen right away. It convinced me that I could go with that line about not needing a vision for a while."

What Pressler did instead was formulate an agenda for his first hundred days as CEO. The backbone would be one-on-one meetings with Gap Inc.'s fifty top executives, at which he would ask each executive the same five questions:

- What about Gap Inc. do you want to preserve and why?
- What do you hope I do?
- What are you concerned I might do?
- What are you concerned I might *not* do?
- What is your most important tool for figuring out what the consumer wants?

Pressler correctly recognized that the process of asking these questions would accomplish three objectives simultaneously. It would (1) build a foundation of trust with each manager, (2) help him make important personnel assessments, and (3) gather input for developing the company's strategy going forward.

As it turned out, the answers to these questions would also compel fundamental changes in planning Gap Inc.'s product lines. Even more important, the question-and-answer sessions conceived during Pressler's countdown period would, he claims, "make clear what the culture of the organization was. From there it was an easy framework to figure out what needed to change and what needed to be preserved."

ASSESS WHAT YOU NEED TO KNOW

The countdown period is the ideal time to assess not just the situation but your own skills. Do you have the knowledge and the network necessary to meet the challenges you've identified? Be brutally honest; your success depends on it. When you find a gap, do not hesitate to call for help.

When Anne Mulcahy was selected as the president and CEO-in-waiting of Xerox in May 2000 (she became CEO in August 2001 and chairman in January 2002), she had already built an excellent reputation within the company, spending sixteen of her twenty-four years at Xerox in sales before becoming the head of human resources and chief of staff for former CEO Paul Allaire. She is the first to admit that this was not the track record of a potential CEO. She did not have an MBA and had never sat on the board of directors. In a *Fortune* magazine article (June 23, 2003), Mulcahy said, "I never expected to be CEO of Xerox, I was never groomed to be CEO of Xerox. It was a total surprise to everyone, including myself."

With the company on the skids—in 2000 Xerox had $17.1 billion in debt and $154 million in cash, its stock had fallen from $63.69 a share to $4.43, and it was shedding market share like an oak tree in November—Mulcahy knew she had to acquire financial acumen fast. She tapped her director of corporate financial analysis to give her "Balance Sheet 101." He taught her about debt structure, inventory trends, and the impact of taxes and currency moves so that she could understand what would generate cash and how each of her decisions would affect Xerox's $30 billion balance sheet. Every night she took home binders of study material, then crammed over the weekend. "It was an unusual situation for the finance director—tutoring the CEO," Mulcahy recalls. "But there wasn't a lot of time for false pride."

Similarly, when Terry Semel became chairman and CEO of Internet bellwether Yahoo! in May 2001, he had a twenty-one-year track record building Warner Bros. from an $850 million single-revenue-

stream company operating in one country into an $11.5 billion diversi-
fied entertainment and consumer products powerhouse with operations
in fifty-five countries. While the parallels of this to Yahoo! were compelling—the company was at a crossroads needing to focus on building
some core capabilities and a viable profit-generating growth strategy—
there was one very important thing Semel lacked: knowledge of and experience with the Internet. Semel's turnaround of Yahoo! could never
have been accomplished without the mentorship of cofounder and
Chief Yahoo! Jerry Yang. Even prior to Semel's formal start date, Yang's
enthusiastic and patient coaching on how the Internet worked and
Yahoo!'s place within the industry was formative. And Semel's embrace
of the legendary entrepreneur enabled a true partnership to be forged.

Gary Kusin realized that it wasn't a teacher that he needed when
he took over as CEO of Kinko's; it was a partner. "As I was doing my
due diligence, I saw lots of conflicting data and got lots of conflicting
stories about what was going right and what was going wrong in the
company. I felt the best thing to do would be to strip this thing down.
And it was very important that in doing that I could have someone
whom I trusted who could do that for me while I got out and got to
know the company and all of the various stakeholders firsthand."

Kusin turned to Dan Connors, a former Bain consultant who had
led strategic planning at Kusin's previous company. Kusin made
bringing Connors with him a condition for taking the job at Kinko's:
"I wanted to bring him in for the simple reason that I'd want him to
lead the strategy work while I could dig in very quickly on all the
other fronts."

SELECT A SOUNDING BOARD

Counselor or confidant, finding someone to act as a sounding board
is essential. Sooner or later during the countdown period and most
assuredly in the first hundred days, you are going to be hit with a surprise. And it is usually not a pleasant one.

That's why you need someone to bounce ideas off of, someone who understands the context of the challenges you're facing, who can hold up a mirror to warn you of your shortcomings but has your best interests at heart. A confidant is a leader's secret weapon, and the countdown period is the time to think about who that person or persons are going to be. For many people, it is a spouse or a friend outside the organization. For others, it is a trusted colleague. For top executives, the head of human resources often plays that role (and a good HR chief loves being the top management adviser). A confidant may just as easily be a consultant or a banker or an executive coach. Or in the case of a new CEO recruited from outside the company, it is often a member of the board's search committee or even the executive search consultant who led the recruitment.

There is no rule that says you can only have one confidant. Some business leaders assemble a network of advisers to serve as a sounding board to provide support at key decision times.

Scott Flanders, CEO of $1 billion Columbia House, the world's largest direct marketer of music, videos, and DVDs, was a chief executive at age thirty. After an early career as a tax accountant, he rose up through the trade publishing field, becoming president of Macmillan Publishing Company and then founding an Internet firm called Telstreet before being recruited to Columbia House. Over his career, Flanders has cultivated a small brain trust on which he has drawn over the past decade. His network includes several of his former bosses, the human resources chief of a major corporation, and a business consultant he has worked with for almost twenty years. Flanders has relied on input from his advisers to make decisions, including whether to accept the offer to join Columbia House when it was a joint venture of Sony and Warner Music, whether to pursue a leveraged buyout for the company, and how to structure the board of directors for the now privately owned company. (Columbia House went private in a major LBO led by the Blackstone Group in mid-2002.)

Selecting a sounding board is not a new idea, but that does not make it any less valuable. Napoleon Hill, the renowned motivator and author, described the concept of a "master mind group" in his influential book, *Think and Grow Rich,* back in the 1930s. Working closely for twenty years with industrialist Andrew Carnegie in the later years of his life, Hill concluded that one of the keys to Carnegie's success was creating a small group of trusted people to serve as his personal network. The job of the "master mind group," according to Hill, is to help you think through important issues, challenge you, and support you.

In your countdown period and beyond, you will surely benefit from having a confidant or group of advisers to help you address the business issues as well as the emotional and psychological challenges that lie ahead. Many of the most successful business leaders we know have achieved their success by drawing on the power and support of a group of talented people who are invested in their development and accomplishments.

PREPARE YOUR PERSONAL SUPPORT TEAM

Planning to take on a new leadership role is not only about preparing yourself. It requires thinking about how your new phase will impact your family and other members of your personal support team. You need them to understand and buy into what will be necessary for your new assignment. This is always a delicate balancing act, recognizing that for a period of time things will be out of whack, requiring more effort on their parts as well as yours, until you can all reach a new equilibrium.

When Ed Breen, the president of Motorola, decided to accept the Herculean challenge of turning around the $36 billion scandal-ridden Tyco International, he sat down with his three teenage children and said, "Dad's going to boot camp."

His family was already used to the obligations demanded by Breen's current job and his previous one as CEO of General Instrument Corporation. But Breen rightly anticipated that the intensity of the Tyco situation would be at a much higher level. "The way I laid it out to the family was, we'll be together on weekends, but don't expect to see me during the week," Breen recalls. Even so, he was torn. "You just can't disconnect yourself from their life."

As a leader, you have become used to answering to the needs of a constellation of corporate constituents. But it is self-evident that your family is at a minimum an equally important stakeholder in your career. The farther up the leadership ladder you ascend, the more difficult the balancing act usually becomes.

This is especially true during your first hundred days, when job-related demands become all-consuming. When Patricia Russo took over from Henry Schacht as the CEO of troubled Lucent Technologies in January 2002, she made sure that her family was prepared. "I told my husband and kids that they needed to consider this a twenty-four-seven job. Not that I would be working a hundred percent of the time, but that when you have this kind of responsibility, you need to be available a hundred percent of the time. In this kind of job, you simply cannot be disconnected."

STRIKE THE BEST POSSIBLE BALANCE

Ironically, because taking on a new leadership position is so taxing, there is a certain advantage to leaving your family behind—that is, relocating solo, with the family following later—in the early days, while you get your bearings. That way you can work long hours without distraction, have dinners or late meetings with new colleagues to get to know them better and build trust, and assimilate in the evening all the information and input you've gotten during the day.

The notion of a few months' lead time is not alien to many families of executives who have traveled or relocated during their careers. "If the company needs you tomorrow but the school year doesn't end tomorrow or you have no home at the new location, less disruption actually occurs when the family stays behind for a few months—though the separation is never easy," explains Dan Kerpelman, who has relocated thirteen times in fifteen years. "Equally important, the reprieve from day-to-day family obligations enables total focus on the new job. This factor is critical because it enables full concentration on establishing your agenda during the vital initial days." His latest relocation, however, was the toughest. Kerpelman had been based in Paris, France, in his previous position as general manager of the diagnostic X-ray business at GE Healthcare when he was tapped to become president of Kodak's Health Imaging Group, based in Rochester, New York—and due to personal family needs, he was forced to leave his family behind for close to a year. Kerpelman visited whenever he could. "The need to travel globally for business meant that I could make a stop on weekends from time to time."

Technology helped, too. He and his family used private e-mail accounts for instant messaging and sent short text messages over their cell phones.

The extra calendar time gained by not having to spend during-the-week time with his family allowed Kerpelman to work at an extreme pace and get off to a great start at Kodak. However, not seeing his wife on a daily basis and not being able to attend his kids' soccer games and school plays understandably created an emotional hole during the prolonged absence. "I missed them all the time," he recalls. By the time the family was successfully reunited in their new home in Rochester, Kerpelman, who had by then become a natural and core member of the Kodak top management team, was able to strike a new and positive work-family balance.

While Kerpelman's case of transatlantic separation is extreme, the routine demands of a new job can be almost as taxing in preventing you from spending time with your family. Dan Schulman learned this lesson during a brutal four-hour daily commute to his previous job as CEO of Priceline.com. "Getting up at four-thirty every morning and getting home at nine at night the first six months wasn't a problem, because I was operating on adrenaline," he says. "But after that it really started to wear. You can't get by on the adrenaline rush long term."

Keep in mind also that it's *you* who gets the thrill of the adrenaline rush; your spouse and family can see that you're engaged and excited. But it is they who have to deal with your physical absence and your mental distraction. The more demanding your new position, the more difficult it will be for your spouse and family. "It will put a huge strain on your marriage," warns Kevin Sharer, whose own marriage broke up soon after he became CEO of Amgen.

That's why Gary Kusin literally asked his family for permission to "check out" for a few months when he signed on at Kinko's. Ed Breen adds, "If they don't buy into it, you can't deal with that pressure. You've got enough other things going on to also deal with a family situation."

Cammie Dunaway found another way to handle a disruptive relocation when she joined Yahoo! in June 2003 as chief marketing officer, responsible for leading the company's worldwide branding efforts and driving its product-marketing initiatives. A seasoned executive with nearly twenty years of marketing experience, Dunaway had most recently spent thirteen years at Frito-Lay Company, supervising such prominent brands as Doritos, Chee-tos, Lay's, Ruffles, and Rold Gold Pretzels. She, her husband, and their five-year-old son were very happy living in Dallas, and when she accepted the position, they knew they would have to relocate to northern California. But rather than uproot the family all at once, Dunaway moved up solo for sixty days, a move she says was critical for helping her get off to the right start. "I am a big believer in balancing an intense professional life with a healthy and fulfilling family life, especially with a five-year-old," Dunaway says. "But when you're a new CMO at a new company in a new industry, the first couple of months is *not* the time for balance." She adds that once you get your grounding, start building relationships, and begin to establish priorities, then it's the right time to come back all together.

Whether or not there is a relocation involved in accepting a new top leadership position, the key to preparing your support team is to strike the best possible balance. The best way to do that is to find a way to be able to focus on the new task at hand intensively and without guilt while postponing for a period of time your normal family responsibilities.

This provides a double benefit. On the work front, it allows you invaluable time to assimilate the torrent of information you have received, and it affords you the time to get to know key managers on a more personal level. Often the strategic and personnel insights garnered outside the office during these informal get-togethers cannot be replicated by meetings during the day. On the home front, this also allows for continued stability of the family unit. Among the major stresses in life are starting a new job, selling and buying a home, moving to a new community, leaving friends behind, making new ones, and finding and starting at new schools. The idea of doing all of this simultaneously can be overwhelming. At some point soon you will need the support of your family. So if you possibly can, get settled in your new position and then resume your family responsibilities so that they too can get started on their new journey.

GET IN SHAPE FOR THE RACE

There are few things more distressing than seeing a friend who had been a picture of fitness and vitality descend into lethargy and gluttony after the intensity of starting a new job. Nowadays work can and will suck up every spare moment unless you fight hard to prevent it. This problem is exacerbated in the first hundred days as you are operating on adrenaline to establish your bearings, figure out how to get things done in the new organization, make progress on key priorities, and work hard to make strong first impressions. It is all too easy, therefore, during the early days of your new role to put off the hard work of getting or staying in good physical shape. But rather than procrastinate and wait for your next new year's resolution to get back in shape, it is a better idea to use your countdown period to do so in the first place.

Dan Schulman is on the board of Symantec, an Internet security software company whose CEO, John W. Thompson, printed a T-shirt that Schulman finds particularly pertinent. On the back it reads, *This is the most important quarter of the year,* and on the front it reads, *Always.* "That's true," says Schulman. "This is a race that doesn't have a finish line."

That is why you have to get in shape for it—not just by establishing an emotional equilibrium yourself and with your family but by making sure that you have the physical stamina to perform at your peak day in and day out for the sprint that is your first hundred days. "You have to take care of yourself, otherwise it becomes a slippery slope," cautions Jon Miller, chairman and CEO of AOL.

Miller practices karate every morning before tackling issues at the office. Others keep a daily date with the StairMaster. Dan Stone had been involved with the Leukemia and Lymphoma Society's Team in Training, an endurance sports training and fund-raising program, and had already participated in a hundred-mile bike ride before becoming chief executive of Space Holdings (now Imaginova), parent company of leading space-related media properties, including website Space.com, trade newspaper *Space News,* and software publisher Starry Night. He continued his training program while on the job and completed his second century ride six months later. Cycling is an integral part of his ability to perform on the job. "I start with a bunch of problems on my mind, and after ten miles, I've solved many of them in a much more creative way than if I were sitting at my desk," he says. "It's a support system for the stresses of the job."

The first hundred days are the sprint phase in what is truly a marathon, a race that will include many first hundred days. Knowing that beforehand gives you the opportunity to step up your fitness routine during the countdown period.

New leaders looking back at their early days in the job frequently say that they were quite unprepared for its emotional and physical toll. That's why it's vitally important to use the countdown period to make additional deposits into your personal "bank account," so that you and your family will have plenty of reserves to draw on in the tough period ahead.

TAKING IT TO A NEW LEVEL

Just about everything we've said so far applies to a leader at any level. The basic advice holds true, regardless of whether you're taking your first managerial steps or have climbed to the top rung of the leadership ladder. "The way you choose people, motivate people, set the strategic agenda—that's really all the same stuff," says Lew Platt, chairman of Boeing and former CEO of Hewlett-Packard. Looking back on his first management job—running a maintenance organization at HP—he recalls, "I can honestly say the techniques I used to motivate people, to get them committed, were no different as CEO than as head of maintenance."

But each time you add a few more zeros to the number of people you're managing, you enter a new zone. And the challenges, complexities, and expectations are magnified exponentially when you move into the top leadership position and add increasingly diverse constituencies.

Becoming a chief executive means dealing with a set of demands that are of a different magnitude than any other job. Most people view it as a logical progression and promotion, says former Ford CEO Jacques Nasser. "It's much more than that. It's a change of life experience.

"There's a tremendous difference in the sense of responsibility and ultimate decision-making. There's an intensity around what needs to be done, a feeling that this is it, this is where the decisions are made, and the heavy responsibility of making the right decisions most of the time weighs on you."

Anne Mulcahy was promoted to the corner office at Xerox during some of its darkest days. "Nothing spooked me as much as waking up in the middle of the night and thinking about ninety-six thousand people and retirees, and what would happen if this thing went south," she noted in *Fortune* magazine.

"That sense of stewardship," agrees Chris Lofgren, CEO of

transportation giant Schneider National, "that's what hit me hardest within the first month or two. Nothing in particular happened. There was just this recognition that Don [Schneider, the outgoing CEO] spent decades building the company, and as a leadership team, we have a huge responsibility to make sure that when we turn this over to others, we leave it in as good a shape as he left it for us."

When you're managing a division or a department or a project, you've got someone above you to whom you can refer—or defer—the big decisions. You frequently may not have to be the one who says no. But as the top executive, there's no longer a single individual who can take the heat for you. "You have lost for the first time the relationship where you have a boss whom you can get help from and talk to in an open way," says Lew Platt. "And everybody looks at you because you're now the face for the organization."

That's the biggest difference between being the head of a division of a company and becoming the CEO. Every heartbeat, every murmur, gets reported on, whether it's about the company, about you, or about things that are happening in your life. Everything becomes open season. That's yet another aspect of the job to get prepared for during the countdown period.

THE INSIDER'S ADVANTAGE . . . AND DISADVANTAGE

Are the countdown period and subsequent first hundred days made easier if you've been promoted from within the company? The answer is both yes and no.

If you're an insider picking up the reins, your intimate knowledge of the company and its culture gives you a running start. You know how things work, who makes them work, and which buttons to push to get them to work; you can probably pinpoint trouble spots and the people who cause them. You also have a network of trusted colleagues within the company whom you can rely on to give advice and get things done. These are important assets on which to build.

But the advantages of being an insider are counterbalanced by two major drawbacks. First, you cannot possibly have the clarity and fresh perspective of an outsider. Longtime habits and perceptions may blind you to inefficient processes or misplaced assumptions. Without even realizing it, you may have fallen into the "that's not how we do things around here" trap, which cuts off the possibility of doing things differently. By contrast, when you are new to a company or an industry, you have the ability to ask "dumb" questions—questions that ultimately and frequently turn out to be not so dumb after all. Asking these questions can get you unvarnished feedback and provide you the ability to test underlying assumptions in new ways.

To illustrate, consider the case of Dave Calhoun, one of the top executives at General Electric. Over the course of his twenty-five-year GE career, Calhoun has been CEO of five different multibillion-dollar divisions: GE Plastics Asia, GE Transportation, GE Lighting, GE Employers Reinsurance, and finally the $11 billion GE Aircraft Engines division. Calhoun told us, "When you are new to a company and an industry, you have the unique opportunity to ask the dumbest questions—and get the *best* answers," he says. "You listen and then act on what you heard. If you are great about following through, you have the chance to really make a positive impact." This strategic process of Calhoun's has long been his modus operandi in taking over new businesses, as he believes deeply that it is the optimal way for a new leader to not only get up to speed quickly but to turn a leadership transition into a major opportunity for improvement. Calhoun shared a concrete example of how he has put this into action. "During the period when GE began its intense drive into services, our aviation business was expanding its service shop footprint all around the world, investing millions in facilities [service shops] and often bumping into our good customers, who do their own service work. I asked the apparently naïve question, 'Why do we do that? Don't our customers already have a footprint?' I then was able to go deeper with questions such as 'Why don't we collaborate with them, as we do in the rail business—their labor, our technology?' The result: more to invest in technology development, less in facilities; more margin for all."

The second drawback to entering a new leadership position as an insider is that you typically have less "permission" to shake things up. When an insider is appointed to a new leadership position, the organization may not have the expectation that a new direction is called for. This is precisely why an insider was appointed in the first place, presumably. But change always accompanies a new leadership appointment, regardless of where the new leader is coming from. The challenge for insiders is that they may find themselves forced to behave in ways that run counter to what they've grown up believing—and what their colleagues expect of them. These expectations can make subtle changes appear drastic, and if radical measures are necessary, they become that much more difficult to make. Furthermore, business decisions can turn overly personal, especially when colleagues with whom you've worked for years need to move on—for their sake and that of the company.

Outsiders taking on a leadership role in a new organization face a different set of opportunities and challenges. The very act of appointing an outsider signals that change is on the way. By no means does this implicitly guarantee an organization's acceptance of change; nor does it ease the burdens of implementation. But a newcomer is generally granted a honeymoon period, allowing him or her to get up to speed with the company's business and culture.

Though you have gained a reputation from your work in other companies (especially if you are a high-profile executive), you are still a stranger within your new organization, and as such, you face the critical task of reestablishing your credibility. Rest assured, everyone will have done a Google search on you and will be watching with laser precision to see whether you will fit into the organization or trigger the organization's institutional antibodies and be rejected. As an outsider, you bear much of the onus of helping your employees get to know you, so you have to think about how to reach out early in your tenure and how much time you wish to invest in this activity. Last but not least, you have to find people within the organization you can trust and depend on, while considering who you can tap in your own network to come join you.

How an Insider Can Think Like an Outsider

When Alan Lacy was selected to be the chief executive of retail giant Sears in December 2000, the company's former chief financial officer and six-year Sears veteran was greatly concerned about these very issues that surround insularity. "From an internal successor's perspective, you can grasp the opportunity to move quickly, because you have the lay of the land and understand how the organization works. This can help you get things done faster than someone coming in from the outside. But you also have to challenge yourself and ask, 'Gee, if I had come in from the outside, what are the things I would want to approach differently or take some time on?'

"When I got the job, I felt I had to do two things at once consciously. I knew I should take full advantage of my inside knowledge to make progress quickly on the stuff I was familiar with. And because I had *not* been deeply involved in the core business—I had done essentially everything but run the core business in my previous six years—and had seen people try superficial fixes that did not fix our core, I needed to take the time to come up with the right substantive strategy."

So time is exactly what Lacy took. Selected to the top spot in December 2000, he did not officially become CEO until October 1, 2001. During this extensive countdown period he assembled a team of internal people and also called in an outside consultant. "We locked ourselves into a room for nine months, figuratively speaking, working through what the right thing was for the company to do, and by July 2001 we had formulated a plan."

His advice to leaders coming into new positions from the inside: "I would take the opportunity to make yourself an outsider. Having an outside facilitator can help with this—he or she can bring in a third-party perspective and independent facts or research that might be different from what you have at the top of your mind or readily at hand."

COMPLETING THE COUNTDOWN

The get-ready process varies from person to person and from situation to situation. The common denominator is that this is the period in which you create the conditions for deep learning and credibility building so that you can start your new job with maximum effectiveness and momentum.

"The result of Gary [Kusin] spending that time up front is that he understood the difficulties ahead for Kinko's," recalls George Tamke, partner of the private equity firm Clayton, Dubilier & Rice and chairman of Kinko's when the company was majority-owned by that firm. "The worst thing in the world that could happen when you're bringing in a new CEO is that they do not have an appreciation for the challenges that they're facing and they wake up one morning in the job and say, 'Holy cow! What have I just done?' That is awful. It's like a bad acquisition; it takes an enormous amount of time to fix and get squared away." In retrospect, although there were plenty of difficult items that needed to be dealt with, the countdown gave Kusin the opportunity to think them through carefully and come up with a plan to handle them.

The countdown period is also the time to identify the most important items on your "to do" list. It's the time to figure out the resources and the people you'll need to take care of those items. It's the time to clear the decks on the home front, so that you'll have as few distractions as possible for a given period of time, allowing you to devote your full energy and focus to the tasks at hand. And it's the time when you should make sure you're both mentally and physically ready to take on the challenges of the days ahead, challenges that are probably always more daunting than you think, particularly if you're coming in cold.

Do all those things right, and your chances of being successful in your first hundred days are greatly increased. But Dan Schulman adds one last caveat: "Having a strong countdown period isn't a guarantee. Now you actually have a bunch of stuff you have to do!"

CONCLUSION

TEN GUIDELINES FOR OPTIMIZING THE COUNTDOWN PERIOD

1. Effective planning will help you spend the scarce time available (about twelve hundred hours) in your first hundred days wisely.

2. Get set to learn. Perform an assessment of the company's strategy, competitive positioning, and financials using public information and available internal plans and documents.

3. Meet with the smartest observers you can find—employees, alumni, customers, suppliers, and analysts—to garner their insights.

4. Do not feel compelled to walk into your new role with a strategy already developed—it will be wrong, incomplete, and/or lack buy-in. Instead, integrate all the information into four or five issue areas or themes to discuss and focus on.

5. When you are a candidate for a top position, put together a draft hundred-day plan. Doing so well will help you win the job, and it will also begin to align expectations and allow you to hit the ground running. (See the Appendix for two such plans.)

6. Determine what "listening" questions you would like to ask key managers or employees and to whom you would like to ask them and in what time frame; keep the questions to five or six and plan to ask the same ones of everyone you meet with; doing so will build trust and accelerate the identification of key themes and issues.

7. Assess your own knowledge, skill, or experience gaps in terms of specialized training or functional expertise.

8. Use the countdown period to lay the groundwork for establishing strong relationships with your boss, board, and future colleagues; be open and receptive.

9. Prepare your family for the intense ride ahead. If you are relocating, seriously consider leaving the family at home for several weeks or even months; this will enable you to immerse yourself in your new role and minimize their disruption and angst.

10. Get in physical shape for the intense period ahead; do not defer or neglect your conditioning and fitness.

TWO

THE FIRST STEPS
ALIGNING EXPECTATIONS

Setting proper expectations is one of the most important things a new leader has to do to get off to the right start. It is also one of the most easily overlooked and mishandled.

Whether you are coming into a company from the outside or are being promoted from within, when you embark on a new leadership role you will develop expectations about all the things you are about to face: your priorities, the management team, the organizational culture, the quality of the company's products and services, its competitive positioning, its brand, its operating processes, and its decision-making style. These expectations will help shape your agenda, guide your thinking, and articulate your definition of success in your first hundred days.

You may not realize it, but you are not the only one with expectations. Everyone impacted by your arrival will also have a view, either explicit or subconscious, of what you should achieve in your early weeks and how you should go about doing it.

If these different perspectives do not align, you will be setting off on a path marked by misunderstanding, anxiety, tension, and all too often failure. You cannot achieve your goals if you are trying to navigate toward them with divergent maps. In an ideal world, you will have had a chance during your candidacy to make sure you have a shared understanding with your hiring manager or the board regarding the important issues facing the organization. "Make sure to find common ground even before you accept the position," advises 3M CEO Jim McNerney. "You will make much better progress in your early days on the job."

48

WELCOME TO YOUR NEW WORLD

Using the countdown period before your actual start date helps to develop a map of the territory and chart potential dangers. You will probably have developed an idea of the course you want to set and gained some sense of how you will navigate it. But remember this: Your map, however detailed, is based largely on secondhand insights and deductions up to this point in time. Like Christopher Columbus, Lewis and Clark, and other courageous men and women on a voyage of exploration, you don't really know what lands will emerge beyond the horizon and what the true nature of your discovery will turn out to be.

Now it's time to sail out into reality and see how well the map of your expectations matches the way things really are. That sounds simple enough, but there are bound to be gaps. You may not have had the time or the opportunity to lay the right foundation during your candidacy or countdown period, especially if you are entering a crisis situation. The people you talked to may not have been as forthcoming about their own agendas as they might ideally have been. And once you accept the new position, the wooing is generally replaced by a hot potato placed squarely in your hands. As a result, what you anticipate may be quite different from what you find when you actually get there. Many leadership transitions are made more turbulent than necessary because of misconstrued or misaligned expectations. We can't stress enough how crucial aligning expectations is to getting off to the right start. Making sure everyone agrees on the important issues and priorities is literally the foundation to building the first hundred days pyramid—and your future success.

But when you start, you may have a period of reassessment about your own expectations of success; about what you want to accomplish and how you want to do it; about how things work; about whether the right systems are in place, whether the financials make sense, and whether things are the way they were described in your research;

about the colleagues who can help you, who can hurt you, and how you distinguish between the two; and about your assumptions concerning which problems need immediate attention, how to fix them, and how long it will take.

That takes insight, a hefty dose of patience, and perhaps most important the humility to admit that you may not be as smart as you think you are. Tom Ryder, CEO of Reader's Digest, articulates a common refrain: "I walked in and thought I knew exactly what the problems were and what I was going to do. I turned out to be wrong."

MANAGING OTHER PEOPLE'S EXPECTATIONS OF YOU

Your reputation precedes you. The fear and anxiety people have about change is likely to focus on one aspect of your previous career and blow it out of proportion. In 1992 people at Sears dubbed incoming CEO and veteran New York retailer Arthur Martinez "the Ax from Saks"; people at The Home Depot worried that their new chief, General Electric veteran Bob Nardelli, would "GE-ize" their culture, taking out the joy and turning them into an army of orange-aproned automatons.

When you come from the outside, you can be sure that in the first meetings many will think, "I'm just as smart as she is, so what does she have that I don't?" And you can be guaranteed that *everyone* is thinking, "Is this new boss going to be good for me—or am I out of here?" It is a fact of life that people interpret the world through the lenses of their own preconceptions, expectations, and self-interest. While those lenses may change over time, the first lens is always going to sift for answers to straight-from-the-gut questions: Who is this person? Why did she get the job? What does this mean for me?

An internal promotion can also upset the apple cart, even if you are the clear heir apparent. You have to reearn your credibility from day one.

Not only will colleagues and employees be watching carefully;

your boss (or board of directors if you are the CEO) will want reassurance that he made the right choice. Your customers and suppliers will also be concerned about how you will affect the status quo; and depending on how visible and well known you are, if you are in a top position, the financial community will vote with their stock trades.

An example of the power of expectations is what happened to 3M stock. During much of 2000, 3M's stock floundered in the $80-to-$90 range, with trading volume averaging a lackluster one to two million shares a day. Then on December 5, 2000, the announcement came that Jim McNerney had been named 3M's new chairman and CEO. Thanks to McNerney's well-known reputation for performance, strategic prowess, and people leadership, and the visibility he garnered from being a finalist in the GE CEO selection process, his appointment hit the markets with a shock. The stock price skyrocketed to $119 on a trading volume of 14.5 million shares, soaring to a new fifty-two-week high of $122.94 on December 29.

It was an impressive—and doubtless much-appreciated—vote of confidence. But it's also both a symptom of the power of other people's expectations and a warning signal of why you need to manage them. When each of your speeches, actions, and decisions is scrutinized for its potential ramifications, you must not only be aware of the implications but also be alert to the messages you are sending as you take your first steps in this new world.

You have to work hard to set appropriate expectations for yourself and the people who work with you and link those expectations to the underlying reality of the business; the company's products, people, and processes; and the way they all affect the financial situation.

LET ME INTRODUCE MYSELF

Who, what, where, why, and how? are the five fundamental questions every journalist asks and every detective uses. They're also the questions behind every leadership transition, both in crisis situations and when the leader has moved up organically in an orderly succession. Therefore it should come as no surprise that these questions also form the backbone of how you introduce yourself when you start a new top job:

- Who am I?
- Where do I come from?
- Why am I here?
- What do I plan to accomplish?
- How do I hope to do it?

There are a variety of ways to answer these questions, whether in an introductory town hall meeting, a formal presentation to be broadcast around the world, or a new leader assimilation session with a smaller number of close associates, such as your department heads or, for senior executives, the top management team.

Asked to recount the highs and lows of his first hundred days as chief executive of Mattel, Bob Eckert recalls, "The highest moment was my first hour on the job, when I addressed seven hundred or so employees in our company cafeteria." Earlier that morning Eckert had gone through the process of getting his security badge: being marched unceremoniously to the security office, perched on a stool, and told to smile for a DMV-style photo. Now it was time to meet the other badge-holders. An article in *Harvard Business Review,* "Where Leadership Starts," eighteen months after his first day at Mattel, describes what happened:

> "The moment I was introduced, I took the cordless mike, walked off of the platform, and waded out into the audience, where I launched into the story of getting my badge," he recalled. "For five minutes I poked fun at the entire process: the stool, the camera, saying 'cheese,' the photo, the plastic badge. Though I didn't fully realize it at the time, the badge story offered an ideal symbol for the change that my arrival represented. Besides showing employees that I'd been humbled by a banal process, it also made the badge a focus of my newfound identity—my first step from 'food' guy to 'toy' guy."
>
> Then he [Eckert] briefly articulated his agenda to refocus the company. "My message was as simple as Mom and apple pie. I would concentrate on

three issues throughout my tenure: building brands, cutting costs and developing people. As I went on to explain my ideas for an employee-development program, people's eyes widened. I didn't know that this was the first time in many years that the CEO had talked about the importance of helping people build careers and rewarding them for a job well done."

Eckert then opened the floor to questions. "I could tell by the kind of questions I asked that their values were the same as mine. I knew right away that these were my kind of folks."

Eckert adds, "As the new guy, I realized that every first encounter with a Mattel employee had the potential to be fraught with tension, and I felt it was my responsibility to do everything possible to reduce it. Surprisingly, I found that in each situation, recognizing my own lack of knowledge about the company's people and culture—in effect, allowing the employees to be the 'boss' in certain situations—actually helped me lead."

JEFF IMMELT'S INTRODUCTION AT GE

Those five fundamental questions were also embedded in an effective introduction when in September 2001 Jeff Immelt became the seventh CEO in General Electric's history. After one of the most publicized leadership transitions ever, he presented himself as follows to GE employees at the Crotonville, New York, training complex:

> Our priorities, as I take over the company, really reflect my background and philosophies on leadership. I grew up in a GE household. My father worked for GE for about forty years in aircraft engines. I've worked for GE for about twenty years. I started my career in plastics, spending most of my early career in sales and marketing. I was in the appliance business in the late 1980s, running the service business. And I've run global P&Ls for the last ten years in GE Plastics and GE Medical Systems. I've been on the GE Capital board for the last five years.
>
> What it creates in me are a couple of passions. I believe in the customer. Every initiative in GE should start from the outside in and be

focused on the customer. I'm a growth person. I've touched every element of growth, from product development to customers, managing sales forces, globalization, business development . . . I've had the chance to work in two of GE's most global businesses, GE Plastics and GE Medical Systems. It's given me some real attitudes about globalization, some contacts and real beliefs in the future. I worked in GE's toughest business, GE Appliances, in our toughest time, during the compressor recall in the late 1980s. And I know the importance that even the tough businesses bring, that every person in GE is valued, and that it's very important to communicate, particularly in tough times.

I've learned context from my experience in Plastics and Medical. Experience in Plastics has made me very sensitive to the environment. And my experience in GE Medical really taught me that the world is about more than just making money, that the products we make do change people's lives. And lastly, I've had the chance to work with tremendous people throughout, and they've really helped shape my life.

I also have some attitudes about what a CEO does and what you bring to the job. I think of this as the first day of my career, not my last. And I'll always be measured by how fast I learn from all of you, not by what I know. I follow only three traditions: a commitment to performance, a commitment to integrity, and a commitment to change. I believe that the CEO is the chief competitive officer and that the will to win, the desire to win, comes from the top of the company and has to spread throughout the company.

In my case, the desire to win is built on founding great teams and having great disciplines. And you can look for that in the future. I think the CEO has to be a great communicator, not with fancy words but with simple words and with frequency of communication, with trust and honesty and consequence.

Lastly, like my predecessors before me, I know that people make the entire difference in this company. I'll never take our people for granted. And I believe the CEO has to get out and sell the company to the people each and every day. That's what I bring to the job.

After analyzing the state of the business and the individual divisions, Immelt laid the groundwork for delivering his vision of GE's future:

I understand where we are and where we need to go. I've spent the last eight months with Jack really listening to what's on people's minds. That's created for all of us in the new leadership team real imperatives for the future. I want to share those with you briefly. You're going to hear about them more and more as time goes on, but these are imperatives for a twenty-first-century GE.

Lastly, he concluded:

I want you to know as I take this job that I look forward to days like this, to challenging ideas and really expressing and discussing things in a very heated way about what you believe in and what I believe in the future of this company. But I also want you to know I start this job with two very strong and solid beliefs. One is a profound love for the company that's been part of my life from the day I was born, and the pride I feel in being a leader today, and an unbelievable belief in the people. I believe in this company. It's part of my blood. But I believe in every one of you as well. So I look forward to the future. I want you all to get back to work now so we can grow this company in the future.

JIM KILTS'S INTRODUCTION AT GILLETTE

Some new leaders make their introduction not through a large-scale employee speech but rather in a management meeting. This common approach is absolutely fine as long as you cover the essential five questions that people are waiting to have answered.

Jim Kilts, former CEO of Nabisco, was appointed Gillette's new chairman and CEO in February 2001. He held his first staff meeting within a few hours of arriving at Gillette's Boston headquarters on the morning of February 12. This was no mere meet-and-greet. Having had an unusually long and productive countdown period and having had prior experience starting as a new CEO, Kilts knew just how to present himself. After introductions around the operating committee he launched into a set of slides that both in substance and in form sent crystal-clear messages about who he was, his style, his management philosophy, and his expectations of each member of the team.

Kilts communicated in a direct way that his style was characterized by "what you see is what you get" and an action orientation. While he did not imply that he had the answers to the company's problems, he outlined the management process he was going to put into place to collectively find them. He articulated the behavior he expected of his team, including weekly staff meetings with required attendance, punctuality, active listening, striving for consensus, and proper preparation. Kilts discussed his management philosophy and linked it to why he came to Gillette: "It's all about building total brand value," something Gillette had enormous potential in, a belief that cost and quality are compatible, and a belief in keeping things simple and accountable. And he set his expectations for the team, which focused on keeping commitments, helping one another work out problems, and being leaders each and every one of them in their businesses and functional areas.

YOUR OWN INTRODUCTION

As you prepare your own introduction, be mindful that you will be laying the foundation for all your future exchanges and interactions. So while you find a way to cover the five key questions, remember several guidelines to make the very best first impression.

1. You Don't Have to Have All the Answers

No one expects you to know everything; in fact, people will be suspicious if you imply that you do. Avoid the temptation to think you have to be the savior and have immediate answers.

Given the magnetic pull that many leaders feel of having to have the solution to every problem, this point is worth reiterating, especially if the situation you are moving into is a sensitive one. When Jonathan F. Miller became chairman and CEO of America Online in August 2002, the media giant was struggling mightily to keep up with the rapidly evolving online market and technology it had helped ignite. Advertising had slumped, subscriber growth had stagnated, and employee morale was scraping bedrock in the wake of the ridiculed merger that created AOL Time Warner. Additional negative energy and pressure came from SEC investigations into AOL's accounting practices and the antipathy that other divisions of the media giant felt toward AOL. Miller was the third boss at America Online in less than a year.

In his first meeting with AOL's top managers, he was careful to avoid hyperbole and arrogance: "I didn't want to make the mistake of promising what I couldn't deliver or not knowing what I could deliver. It would have been foolish for me or anybody to come in and say, 'I know exactly what to do, here's how it will lay out, answers one, two, three, and four.' But I could offer an honest look at the issues and an honest process to get to the deliverables."

That kind of honesty is even more of a necessity when you come into a company from outside the industry. That's why Larry Johnston, who moved from GE Appliances to heading up the giant supermarket chain Albertson's would tell people, "Look, I don't know a thing about grocery stores or drugstores, except that we've shopped in them. But I'm a quick learner, and here's what I do know. I know we're in a very tough space. We're lucky to keep a couple of pennies from each dollar, and we've got category killers in our business that are going to be very formidable. There's going to be a global consolidation in this industry, and if we want to be one of the winners, here are the things we've got to do."

Johnston saw his lack of food and drug retailing experience as a plus. "I don't have any baggage," he says. "I'm going to look at things in a very objective manner and will not be afraid to make the tough decisions."

In fact, not only is it absolutely fine to admit that you don't have all the answers, it is usually even better if you invite other people to participate in coming up with them. As Paul Pressler blithely announced to four hundred employees on his first day as chief executive of Gap Inc., "I've got a gazillion ideas, many of which are really stupid. But what the hell—you'll let me know!"

2. Address Doubts and Fears

Whether you are a new CEO coming into a company or a manager coming into a new department, your arrival is bound to create anxiety. Being sensitive to this and having a process to address it will help you minimize the upheaval. Recognize that your reputation will be preceding you as you walk into the room. By the time of your arrival, you can be sure that you've been researched on the Web and that your former colleagues have been called. It's not just your individual reputation; if you are an outside hire, it extends to your previous company as well.

Some company reputations send tremors through the workforce, and it is wise to address the anxieties. Bob Nardelli's record of twenty-nine years at General Electric, where he had been one of the three finalists to succeed Jack Welch, rattled the informal culture of The Home Depot. "There was a lot of trepidation and anxiety that the new guy was going to try to turn The Home Depot into GE," Nardelli says. "I certainly wasn't going to forget what I learned at GE, but we needed to calm the waters. Quite honestly, the best way to do that was to be out in the field and walk in their shoes."

Nardelli set up a schedule designed to introduce him to as many Home Depot associates at as many levels as possible in a short time. In addition to the conventional meet-and-greet speech-and-a-handshake events, he made sure to spend a few hours at each store working the floor, manning the cash registers, checking off inventory in the receiving bays—to learn the processes at the most fundamental level. "I wasn't coming in as a reviewer, I was coming in as a dry sponge, willing to observe, absorb, and learn as much as I could and really humanize what could have been perceived as a very inanimate, inhuman object."

Many companies have a formal on-boarding process for new leaders, which is another way to address doubts and fears. Its purpose is to open the information pipeline so that the new manager and his new colleagues can exchange concerns and expectations. It's also another way for the new leader to describe his background, leadership style, and expectations.

Libby Sartain, senior vice president of human resources at Yahoo!, describes the essential elements of a new leader assimilation process:

- When a new leader is hired, convene a meeting with that person's new team members during the first week. With the leader in the room, give all the team members the chance to introduce themselves and say a little bit about who they are and what they do.
- Then, with the leader *out* of the room, have the team answer these questions:
  - What do we expect of this new person?
  - What do we want the new leader to know about us? What do we do well? Where do we need improvement?
  - What do we want to know about the new leader? What are our concerns about him or her?
  - What are the burning issues in our department?
  - What are the major obstacles the new leader will face?

- Put the answers on a flip chart—but make sure they're anonymous so that the leader won't later be able to connect the comments to any one specific team member.
- After a break, reconvene the team with the leader and go over the items on the flip chart. Give the new leader a chance to ask questions about the comments and explore the ways in which he or she can take quick action on some of the issues.
- This discussion is a great way for the entire team to discover with the leader some of the unspoken issues, misunderstandings, and disconnects. The anonymity of this exercise can bring to the surface more issues in one day than weeks of one-on-one meetings. Dirty laundry is aired. And in this open atmosphere, the team begins to gel. The new leader can now formulate an agenda for the first few months.

GE manages the on-boarding process for new managers in a similar way, according to Paula Madison, president of KNBC, the Los Angeles station that is regarded as one of the best run of all the company's owned and operated NBC stations. "When a new manager is appointed at GE, our human resources team takes charge and organizes an introduction meeting," Madison says, describing an agenda quite similar to the one cited above. "They have it down to a science, and it really works at speeding up the assimilation for a new leader, builds trust among the team, and deals with the natural anxieties that arise when a new boss comes in." As in the case at Yahoo! described above, the GE process is facilitated by HR and allows for the team to get their questions, concerns, and priorities surfaced in a safe environment. The effort can take literally weeks off of the process of personal introductions, aligning expectations and building the right foundation for a productive working relationship.

3. Neutralize Lingering Resentment

Inside promotions can lead to sensitive situations, especially if you're now overseeing your former colleagues. The way to build a new relationship, particularly if you're coming from inside, advises Henry Schacht, former chairman and two-time CEO of Lucent, is to ask a series of straightforward questions:

- What should I be thinking about that I wasn't thinking about when I was head of XYZ division?
- What should I know that I might not have known before?
- What's on your mind?
- What would you like the new CEO to be doing?

"You'd be astonished," says Schacht, of neutralizing lingering resentment with solicitous questions. "It's like peeling off a scab. The responses just flow."

4. Don't Disrespect Your Predecessor

Just because you're the new broom doesn't mean you should immediately start to sweep out all traces of old dust. Preserving a sense of connection and continuity to the past is vital. In a planned transition, your predecessor can be a valuable source of counsel, both to foster personal learning and to sustain a sense of continuity within the organization. Even in an unplanned transition, you will have a better chance of winning the hearts and minds of partisans of the previous regime if you demonstrate respect and consideration rather than implicitly or explicitly criticizing it.

This approach applies as much to a manager moving up to a superior's slot as to a new CEO taking over from the previous chief. It is especially true in entrepreneurial companies when someone comes in to succeed the company's founder.

Jeff Killeen had prior CEO/COO experience at Forbes and Barnes & Noble, both of which were "founder-intensive" companies, when he took over as CEO of GlobalSpec, the world's largest search engine and online information resource for engineers. He succeeded John Schneiter, one of the company's four founders, who was staying on as president. "There are some who look at an entrepreneurial situation and without even meeting a founder think a founder needs to be moved out," Killeen says. "But unless founders become unmanageable or otherwise destructive, I believe you're generally better served to build off their vision and make them feel like a million bucks than you are to get rid of them."

Killeen sought to make tangible the respect for the founders—and by implication the founders' support for the new CEO—by having an immediate personal interaction with all employees. "On my first day, starting at seven-thirty in the morning, John and the three other founders and I greeted everyone at the door, from company officers right down to sales people and production floor staff. We had a personal introduction and acknowledgment, a few sentences on what they did and why they liked the company.

"That afternoon we had an 'all-hands' meeting, only the second one in the company's history. I made sure to spend the first several minutes acknowledging the founders in depth. I said, 'If I can walk in as an outsider and see over the hill, it's because I am standing on the shoulders of some pretty big thinkers, and those thinkers are sitting in the front row.' Then, without laying out a specific vision or strategy, I shared my initial observations and asked John to join me at the podium for unlimited Q&A. When I didn't know the answer, I was conscious to say, 'I don't know. John, could you handle that?' My remarks started at three o'clock and were over before four, and we went to seven with informal Q&A, which was remarkable in a company where people all worked very hard, but most of whom liked to be home for dinner by six P.M."

In fact, how you treat your predecessor is so important and so easy to mishandle, we have determined that it is one of the top traps for new leaders and have therefore elaborated on the dynamic in Chapter 8.

DEFINING THE NEW REALITY

One of the first jobs of a leader is to define reality. As you gather more information—about the culture, the financial condition, the competitive situation, the day-to-day operating processes—your own picture of the reality will gradually clarify and become sharper. You will have a better sense of what the problems are and whom you can rely on to help fix them. How to get things done will become clearer. At the same time, your actions and decisions will help define the new reality for the colleagues and constituents you work with.

But is the new reality something they can wholeheartedly buy into? It is surprising how often the top people don't agree on where the company is, what its challenges are, and what its strengths and weaknesses legitimately are. The leader who starts to make decisions based on the premature assumption that her reality is the one that everybody else has may be in for a rude reality check.

That's why the process of defining the new reality should actually be a process of constructing a *shared* reality. If you don't do this, it becomes exceedingly difficult to get agreement on the most important things to do, how you're going to do them, who is responsible for what, and when those things will be accomplished. According to

Kevin Sharer, CEO of Amgen, "If you can't get a shared reality, political support, and alignment, you're in the ditch."

THE LEADER AS PRIME MINISTER

As a leader, you also have to be a politician and gather the votes—in this case, the support of your organization—behind your agenda. "People often forget in this job that you're not king," comments Sharer. "Maybe you're the prime minister. You've got to have a political constituency, you've got to have a support base."

As the designated heir apparent who then had a year between being named to become the next CEO and officially assuming the title, Sharer had plenty of time and opportunity to build a support base. It can be much more difficult—but equally crucial—for an outsider coming into a company with a strong culture.

That's why when Bob Nardelli succeeded the beloved cofounder of The Home Depot, Bernie Marcus, in December 2000, he set up a schedule similar to a candidate in the final weeks of a hard-fought presidential campaign: seven cities in seven days, with visits to seven stores at each stop. "There's a broad range of constituents—maybe even more than usual in this business—so I really needed to move from an unknown commodity to someone who was seen as approachable, willing to listen, to learn and then respond," he recalls.

BE A RECEIVER, NOT A BROADCASTER

As we said earlier, when you start a new job, you are in a temporary state of incompetence. You cannot have all the answers and shouldn't expect to. Your responsibility is to help produce the right answers. Your most important tool as you move into a new role is an open, questioning mind and manner. People at the very top levels don't get their positions because of what they know. They get them because of what they will be able to create, which in turn is largely based on the ability to learn and adapt.

"I don't care how long you've been in the company. You don't just show up and start giving orders and tell everybody how it's going to be," admonishes Kevin Sharer, who joined Amgen as president and chief operating officer in October 1992 and became its CEO in May 2000. "The most important thing I did was listen to the people who are on the top team to create an environment where you really, really listen."

"The first thing you ought to do if you're the new person in charge is *nothing*," says Schacht. "I have learned this over and over again. Resist the temptation to 'hit the ground running.' It is absolutely almost certain to be wrong." He stresses this is even true in a crisis situation. And he should know, having taken over Lucent Technologies (for the second time) in the midst of the company's implosion during the telecom equipment bust in October 2000.

"It's almost certain to be wrong for two reasons. One, you don't know as much as you think you know. No matter how much you think you know about what's going on, you probably aren't as smart about it as you think you are, even if you're the successor in an orderly transition. How many COOs are there who, when they're promoted to CEO, come back to you six months later and say, 'Oh my God, I didn't realize what it was really like.' So resist the temptation to prove to everybody how bright you are, how smart you are, and how in charge you are.

"Two, take the time to listen before you do anything else. You will set the tone; it will be very difficult to reset it. If you start off by imposing your views on people, you're not going to have what you most need when you most need it—namely, the commitment of the people you need to get the work done. Even if you're right and you end up in exactly the same place as you thought you were going to end up, the experience of stopping and doing nothing but being a very good listener for as long as you can stand it is the most important thing to do.

The whole act of talking to the top people is the first step toward gaining their commitment and understanding, which you must have if you're going to be successful. They don't get it the first time and you don't get it the first time. Until you get a consensus that everyone agrees on—these are the priorities, and here's who's going to work on them, and here's how our midcourse correction is going to be if we're not right, and here are the things we can't put off—take as long as you can stand to get that front end clear, committed, understood, communicated, massaged, and changed."

Schacht acknowledges that this is challenging due to the natural predisposition to act. "There's this adrenaline rush for new leaders that you might as well just let work its way out. But even during the adrenaline rush, the most important thing is to listen. Listen and listen and listen. Process the information you receive and integrate it with your own prior understanding and then cycle it. The process itself breeds commitment."

Ignoring the process, on the other hand, breeds antagonism. This is valid even if you are taking over a crisis situation. In such a case you still need to listen, even if you have to shoehorn the listening process into a number of days or even hours versus a number of weeks.

It is a tough balancing act between your past and your future. In the past, you had the right answers most of the time—that's what helped lead to this appointment. Now you have to ask questions rather than give answers and risk coming across as an arrogant know-it-all. In the past, you may have gotten used to a certain dynamic in which you were unquestionably the head of your group or division. Now you may have to serve and count on different constituents with whom you haven't worked before or to whom you related in a different organizational dynamic. In the past, systems were in place to let you surf the wave of adrenaline. Now, when the adrenaline is building up more irresistibly than ever before, you have to focus your energy on active listening.

If you don't, you make your job much harder and endanger your chances of success, as Lawrence Summers discovered.

MOVING INTO HARVARD YARD

"I didn't have a well-developed theory of what I was doing," recalls Lawrence Summers, who became president of Harvard University in July 2001. "I had a few theories, but in retrospect I don't think they were particularly sound or that they particularly caught the important aspects. I underappreciated the sense in which I was new."

But while Summers may not have appreciated the full extent of his newness for one of the oldest and proudest institutions in the world, he did have some well-defined views about how he was going to behave. Unfortunately, it turned out that some of his views and behavior caused serious friction. Impressively, however, Summers was able to achieve retrospective self-awareness of the impact of his words and actions.

"I had a strategy to make sure that nobody was going to think that this job was just a stepping stone for me and that my heart was still in Washington," where he had previously been Secretary of the Treasury. "I was going to be pervasive and present; everybody was going to feel that they had access to me.

"I also had a strategy that I was not going to allow myself to be locked into traditional institutional positions that were not mine and that I would find very hard to reverse two years later. There was a set of situations in which everybody said, 'Ratify this before you fully think about it.' I said no. Whenever I thought I didn't like the institutional position, I signaled it up front."

While these strategies were sound, Summers made some real mistakes. "One big thing I didn't get," he says, "was missing the realization that I didn't need to tell people 'it was a new day.' The fact that we had a forty-six-year-old economist with a reputation for being abrasive and blunt was already the message that it was a new day. And everybody was quaking plenty!

"People certainly said, 'Larry, you've got to go slower. Larry, you've got to go slower.' But they didn't make it credible to me that they were urging caution, not for caution's sake, but rather for the reason that *I'd be more effective on my agenda by being cautious*; it sounded as though they were urging caution because they basically liked the old agenda better.

"So whenever anybody I thought liked the old agenda better than mine told me to be cautious, I just said, 'Forget that. He's just trying to do it the way they used to do it.' I didn't get the dynamic of how strongly I was coming on in the negative sense of the word, because I didn't understand the imperative that existed merely from what had happened before I opened my mouth.

"Then I made two other mistakes. One was that I didn't fully appreciate the importance of simply providing traditional institutional reassurance. By asking and challenging everything, you create a lot of uncertainty, and that uncertainty can be debilitating to the ongoing functioning of the organization. I failed to appreciate that if you're going to be questioning everybody and challenging everybody, you have to do a lot of reassuring in return. I didn't say, 'Isn't Harvard great?' If I had said that, it would have been much more reassuring.

"For example, a student came to see me and said she was from the choir. I asked, 'Why is it important for the university to have a choir?' I was asking because I truly wanted to understand the reason. But the student took my question as a challenge to the existence of the choir. Unfortunately, I wasn't perceptive enough to figure out that if I just said, 'I think the choir is great, and I heard what a terrific concert you all gave. Sometimes people ask me why choirs are central to the university. What's the answer you'd give them?' If I had done that, I could have elicited all the information I was trying to get.

"I also didn't fully appreciate that if you ask ten questions and make ten suggestions, people may take them less seriously, even if they're all equally good. If you have only two issues or questions, people will take your two more seriously than they may take any of your ten. During my first hundred days in the Harvard presidency, I could have had things I identified as success and could have signaled that it was a new day without dissipating as much goodwill capital, if I had been smarter."

AN AGENDA FOR ACTIVE LISTENING—SIX KEY QUESTIONS

How do you figure out how much to listen, how much to say, and when to take action? The first thing to do is frame the situation, because the playbook and time frames are different depending on the environment you are walking into. An outsider coming into a crisis situation requires one playbook; an insider moving up in an orderly succession requires another. But both must glean their vital information the same way: through questioning and active listening.

Here's how Kevin Sharer did it in what was an organic and orderly succession process:

In December 1999 Amgen announced that Gordon Binder would retire as CEO at the annual shareholders meeting in May and that chief operating officer Kevin Sharer would succeed him. That day Sharer sent out a memo that laid out his immediate activity plan. "A key element of my plans for the next five months is to expand my listening by spending one-on-one time with and getting ideas from each of Amgen's over one hundred director-level-and-above staff. In fact, we will begin scheduling those meetings tomorrow. The discussions will be framed around the following questions:

- What are the five most important things about Amgen we should be sure to preserve and why?
- What are the top three things we need to change and why?
- What do you most hope I do?
- What are you most concerned I might do?
- What advice do you have for me?
- Anything else you would like to discuss or ask me?

Hopefully, these questions sound familiar. In fact, they are almost identical to those asked by Paul Pressler to the top fifty executives at Gap Inc. in his first hundred days, as we reviewed in Chapter 1. Pressler adapted and applied this strategy from Sharer after learning about it from us during the research for this book.

Having sent out the questions ahead of time and made it clear that he expected each of the Amgen executives to prepare their thoughts, Sharer sat quietly and listened for an average of an hour with each of the top hundred executives as they shared their views on these open-ended questions. "It goes against the grain to sit there pretty quietly for an hour and just listen," Sharer says. "But it's a really powerful technique, particularly when you're a guy like me who's often in broadcast mode. When I sit there like a shrink or something and just listen, I get a lot done."

Sharer analyzed and tabulated the results of the first hundred sessions and distributed them throughout the company the day before the annual shareholders meeting. The results became his guidelines, shaping his actions and decisions throughout his first year as chief executive.

This listening exercise was so powerful, in fact, that Sharer continues it to this day. "What I do now is I have continuous interviews with our vice presidents, two or three a week, where I just ask two things: 'How's it going?' and 'You got any advice for me?' It takes about forty-five minutes to listen to what they have to say. We have about fifty vice presidents, so I'm constantly refreshing what's going on."

LEARNING FROM AMGEN'S SHARER

The same strategy was used by two board directors of communications giant Motorola to gather input and ensure stability in the earliest days of the company's recent CEO transition. On September 19, 2003, chairman and CEO Christopher Galvin, grandson of Paul Galvin, founder of Motorola, announced his resignation from the company due to strategic differences with the company's board. The company announced that for the first time in its history, it would conduct a search for a new CEO and would consider both internal and external candidates. For a company as proud and traditional as Motorola, this decision created unprecedented anxiety among the employee and management ranks.

The board not only recognized this anxiety but took concrete actions to calm the waters while simultaneously achieving critical input into the company's requirements for its new leader. One week later, over the weekend of September 27–28, board directors John Pepper, who was leading the CEO search, and Sam Scott traveled to Schaumberg, Illinois, and had two-on-one meetings with the top ten managers of the company. The questions they asked of each executive were based on the same questions that Sharer and Pressler asked during their first hundred days:

- What are the three most important things about Motorola that we should be sure to preserve and why?
- What are the top three things we need to change and why?
- What skills and background do you believe are most essential for Motorola's new CEO?
- What advice do you have for the search committee?
- Do you have any suggestions as to specific potential candidates?

The results were just what the search committee sought to accomplish. The input helped form the basis of the situation analysis and key candidate selection criteria that the committee used to lead the CEO search, which resulted in the appointment of Edward J. Zander on December 16, 2003. Zander, whose background as a high-energy, recognizable, customer-focused sales and marketing oriented leader from a leading company in the high technology sector, was a precise fit with the feedback of the Motorola top management team.

LEARNING—EVEN IN A CRISIS

Even in a crisis situation, take as long as you need to find out exactly what you should be doing. Establish a clear understanding of what needs to be done right away, what can be put off, what can't, and who's responsible. You have to secure the commitment of your team and make sure that they have a consistent view of what needs to be done.

Schacht's advice is especially pertinent during a crisis. In troubled times you need as many brains as possible working on the issues, but those brains have to agree on what they are doing and why. "You have to have agreement on definition of duties," he says. "You've got to have roles and responsibilities and none of that is easily apparent, particularly in a crisis and particularly when you have to make changes." Listening and talking to people takes time, a precious commodity when everyone is breathing down your neck and demanding answers, direction, and a strategy for salvation. Nonetheless, Schacht declares, "This is not a luxury, it's critically important. It's the most important thing you can do."

When Schacht was called back to take the reins at Lucent in October 2000, the company was in dire straits. It was going to run out of money in thirty days. Under the circumstances, one might have expected Schacht to plunge into action; after all, as former CEO and chairman, he already knew most of the senior executives and the company needed to regain its equilibrium fast. Nonetheless, he stuck to his active listening process.

"You talk about a burning platform! We had two billion dollars a quarter flowing out of there, with bank lines of credit running out. That's not fun, and it was getting worse. So I wanted to know how much capacity we had in the tank. Did we need to be in crash-landing mode? Did we need parachutes?

"But I couldn't do anything about that. What I really had to do was get people to stop the two-billion-dollar loss, and the only way to do that was to figure out what was causing it. And even though I had a pretty good idea why, the only way to do that was to listen before I did anything.

"You've got to stop and listen. You can't have people running in six or seven different directions; you have to have a very clear direction and a very clear understanding of everyone's roles and responsibilities. That way, even if you make midcourse corrections, at least you're not wasting energy pulling against one another."

In his first few weeks, he made appointments to talk with the top 20 percent of management—fifty people in all—for an hour each. "I'd start at seven in the morning and finish at eight, nine, ten o'clock at night," he recalls. "I asked everyone the same question: 'What do I need to know?' Then I didn't say a word the whole time, except to encourage them to keep going.

"I didn't know anywhere near as much as I thought I would know and that I should have known. I learned so much in the first two weeks of this sort of nonstop listening process that filled in all the mosaic. I wasn't wrong. It was more understanding the details and the issues that were impinging on the organization's capacity to perform in a rapidly changing environment. Without that listening process, I don't know if we could have saved the company."

What sort of things were they telling him? "Everything, from the nits that were driving them nuts to the philosophy that they disagreed violently with to the things they thought we'd agreed to do and weren't doing. You just can't imagine." He listened and encouraged and listened some more. Then he called a meeting on November 10 for three hundred senior managers and executives and said, 'Here's what I've heard. Here's what I think we need to do.' "

EMBRACING PANDORA'S BOX

Questioning and actively listening to the responses might seem to open a Pandora's box of comments, complaints, and suggestions. Everyone always has their own view of what the issues are. But things typically boil down to a few major issues, and the one-on-one sessions not only let the issues bubble up but also distill them to their vital essence. Then you can act on them.

An added bonus: "People will tell you the places where you can quickly become a hero," says Dan Schulman, CEO of Virgin Mobile USA. "It's always nice to establish some quick successes, in the mind of both the board and the people working for you."

Most people, when presented with the opportunity to speak their minds in a confidential, no-holds-barred session, are delighted to comply. People genuinely like to be listened to and heard; it is motivating, almost life-giving. But what do you do if you encounter a tongue-tied colleague or two? "I start on a personal level—tell me about yourself," counsels Dan Kerpelman, president of the Health Imaging Group and senior vice president for Eastman Kodak Company. "By leading with the personal stuff, you get more knowledge per minute than when you ask narrow business-focused questions. In the process, the business substance comes out. And you can send an e-mail afterward if you need to know specific details."

Although the point of the listening sessions is for you to listen to other people's ideas, they're also a good opportunity for you to develop a rapport by inserting a few well-chosen comments to reassure people about the situation. Think of your words as a lifeline on the pitching deck of a boat in rough waters; they reassure people and help them regain their footing. Dan Stone walked into a challenging financial situation when he took the helm at Space Holdings (now Imaginova) in June 2002. As he talked with everyone in the company, he recalls, "I was being watched for whether I was going to jump out the window or cry. So when one of the executives pointed out that after only four hours I had filled fifteen pages of my notebook with issues, we shared a good laugh. The ability to have a sense of humor says a lot to people." So did the fact that he made a point of saying that he did not take this job lightly. He let everyone know that "I've had a successful career and came here also to be successful, so if they bought into the program and were willing to work for it, then we'll all live happily ever after."

Nor should you restrict your one-on-ones to company insiders. A leader is an ambassador, not just inside the company but outside to suppliers, customers, business partners, the financial community, and regulators. If you can squeeze in the time, it makes all the sense in the world to try to set up similar one-on-ones with these other crucial constituents.

And while you're at it, don't neglect your boss or, if you're the

CEO, the board of directors. Not only will you know what your direct reports are concerned about, but you'll also discover what most concerns your boss or board. Many CEOs underestimate the importance of understanding the board's spoken and unspoken interests and consequently fail to develop the broader relationships necessary for determining the best strategy and tactics for the company. We'll talk more about answering to "a higher authority" in Chapter 6.

Once again, it's a case of aligning expectations and establishing a rapport. And, points out Dan Schulman, CEO of Virgin Mobile USA, "it sets you up so well for the first weeks in the job. You can reestablish yourself if you get off on the wrong foot, but it's so much easier if you get off to a good start."

CRUCIAL CONVERSATIONS

The one-on-one listening sessions are sure to raise plenty of questions on your part, questions that should spark useful dialogues on fundamental issues about how things work and how you can make them work more effectively. We've come up with five strategic areas to stimulate your thinking about the right questions to ask:

1. The market
- What are the markets you serve?
- What are the issues facing the company in those and in new markets?
- What do you have to do to be successful?
- Who are the most innovative competitors?
- Why are they so successful in their core areas of strength?
- Are we setting the right goals?
- Are those goals consistent with the external environment?

2. The product
- How are we going to deliver a service to customers that people value and want to buy?
- What is our product's unique selling proposition?
- What is the pricing strategy?

3. The finances
- How do we fund our efforts?
- Where does the business create profits?

4. The people
- Do we have the right people to address the issues and implement the strategy?
- Who are the gatekeepers?
- Who are the people who really make things happen?

5. The processes
- How do people tend to work together?
- How do decisions get made and implemented?

Many of these topics are ones you've already examined during the countdown period. You may have thought that you knew the answers. But reality has an unnerving habit of sneaking up and derailing expectations. Don't take it personally; just don't be surprised.

That's what happened to Dave Peterschmidt. When Peterschmidt first discussed the possibility of becoming the CEO of Inktomi, the company was composed of nine scientists sitting over the See's Candy store on Shattuck Avenue in downtown Berkeley, California. "It had one of the dingiest elevators I'd ever seen, and we had to pass an office with punk rockers sporting more body piercings than I'd ever seen in my life. After leaving Sybase, where I was running six thousand people in a multinational organization, I wondered why I even showed up. But [cofounders] Eric Brewer and Paul Gautier were very articulate and passionate about what they were doing.

"They had started a basic search engine service business. I had never been on the Internet before I got there. But although I didn't know about search engines, I knew about scalability of software architecture. As I listened to them, it became apparent that they had created an architecture that could be huge."

Peterschmidt started that dialogue in May 1996 and decided to join the company on July 1. He devoted May and June to due diligence, examining the technology, the potential market, and whether there was enough money to keep the company afloat until it could deliver the product. Even so, his expectations of what he would find clashed with the reality—and once he defined the reality, it clashed with the expectations of the founders and investors.

"The first thing I missed was that the books were really messed up. Eric Brewer had appointed his cousin to be the acting CFO. His cousin was an attorney and was fairly qualified, but I couldn't make head or tail of the books. My reaction was, 'This is so bad that if I have to, I'll get Quicken and put it up on the computer and keep the books myself.'

"Then I missed understanding how unsophisticated our investors were. Eric didn't like venture capitalists, so the seed money came from people who knew nothing about technology. In software, it takes a minimum of eighteen months to produce a product. All the investors thought they were going to get twenty to thirty times their money in the first twelve months after investing. I figured out in the first week that the company was on shaky financial ground and I had to take quick action to stabilize it.

"Just as I was kicking myself for not having done better due diligence to understand the true cash position, the founders were struggling with the idea of how much they should receive for starting the company. So the company was running out of money at the same time that the greed factor was coming up. Those were the nights that I drove home and thought, 'How did I get myself here?' "

For the record, Peterschmidt overcame those initial hurdles, worked effectively with the cofounders, grew the company rapidly during the Internet boom, downsized it during the bust, and sold it off to Yahoo! for $235 million in early 2003.

CREATE THE CONDITIONS FOR CHANGE

The overall goal of aligning expectations is to create the conditions for positive change. According to Elspeth J. Murray and Peter R. Richardson, studies of corporate change have shown that what leads to success is not so much *what* people do as the fact that certain con-

ditions are established during the change process. In order to succeed, change efforts have to overcome organizational inertia and
achieve escape velocity. As always, there is no one silver bullet or simple recipe to bring about success. Leaders need to establish a set of
winning conditions that create the context for the successful execution of organizational change. Pace and sequencing are not as important as creating the right medium in which the transformation can
take effect.

Chief among those winning conditions are:

- Correct diagnosis of the change challenge—its nature, depth,
breadth, and the forces at play;

- Early establishment of a shared understanding of the change
challenge among the leadership team—a sense of vision, success
measures, and key programs and projects, and of the change process
itself;

- Multiple and ongoing opportunities to enrich this shared understanding through frequent progress reviews and action plan updates;

- A sense of urgency, emphasizing speed when building an
awareness and understanding of the need for change, and an insis-
tence on early tangible deliverables;

- A limited and focused agenda for change, identifying two,
three, or four major priorities, at a maximum, and driving them hard
and fast;

- A human flywheel of commitment, engaging the early adopters
very rapidly and bringing along the "fence-sitters" in a timely manner;

- Identifying the sources of resistance and dealing with them
ruthlessly, eliminating the "drag" in the process that can prevent the
buildup of momentum and waste a leader's valuable time.

In other words, assess your expectations, measure them against
reality, and then find the common ground that will create the conditions that nurture success. With your expectations now properly set
and aligned, let's step up to the next layer of the first hundred days
pyramid. Chapter 3 will bring to life what any great business leader

knows: No one can do it alone. How—and how well—you shape your management team will have a major effect on getting off to the right start and building the momentum for enduring success.

# CONCLUSION

TEN GUIDELINES FOR ALIGNING EXPECTATIONS

1. Ask the board or hiring manager, "What is the underlying objective of this appointment?" Make sure to find common ground about key goals.

2. When you introduce yourself to the management team for the first time, prepare to answer these questions: Who am I? What's my background? Why did I join? What do I hope to accomplish? How do I hope to work together?

3. Recognize that in that first meeting and other early gatherings, most employees will be listening through the lens of their own self-interest: "Is the new boss going to be good or bad for me?"

4. Use your early management team meetings to do more than meet and greet; this is the moment to establish what you expect of them, to communicate your management philosophy, and to set the tone for weeks to follow.

5. You do not have to have all the answers, on day one or throughout the first hundred days. Ask a lot of questions, too. When you are posed with a good question, make sure to pause, and when you don't have the answer, promise to get back to them, and then do so.

6. Be a receiver as much as a broadcaster—listen and learn. People genuinely like to be listened to and heard.

7. Even if you are taking over in a crisis, take whatever time you can to listen, question, and consider before pronouncing.

8. Create an agenda for active listening. Engage in one-on-one meetings to pose key questions on the market, the company, the product, the financials, the people, and the management process. All of this will accelerate your diagnosis and help you solidify relationships with key constituents.

9. Don't necessarily restrict your one-on-one meetings to company insiders. When possible and appropriate, reach out for customers, suppliers, analysts, and alumni for their views.

10. Synthesize your learning and provide feedback to the organization and those with whom you've met, whether through memos, presentations, intranets, videos, and the like. By giving feedback to the organization, you help create a new shared reality and improve your chances for broad-based buy-in. This is the beginning (which is the subject of Chapter 1) of the process to develop your strategic agenda.

THREE

NO ONE CAN DO IT ALONE

SHAPING YOUR MANAGEMENT TEAM

"Our most important assets walk out of the building every night."

No one would dispute that the most talented and high-performing people make companies both powerful and defensible. Creativity, innovation, product development, technology, customer service, efficiency, execution, and of course, culture—all of these competitive issues and potential advantages are people-related. "Any idiot can identify the problem," says Robert Tillman, retired chairman and chief executive of Lowe's, the gigantic home improvement retailer. "It takes intelligent, capable people to come up with the solution."

There's a lot of truth in the familiar saying "None of us is as smart as all of us." The problems and challenges businesses face are too complex and interdependent to be solved by any one person or any one discipline, especially in the time frame that today's business environment demands. But you don't just need a team, you need a good team. Your management team is one of your most crucial resources since, as management expert Warren Bennis says, behind every great leader is a great group. A great group bonds into an effective partnership of talented people from a variety of backgrounds and disciplines who concentrate their complementary strengths for a common purpose. In this way, they become an organization's ultimate competitive weapon. Jim Collins perhaps put it most memorably when in *Good to Great* he implored, "First who, then what."

"A business isn't run by one person. It's run by teams," points out Allen Questrom, CEO of JCPenney. "My job is to set the objectives and to get people to understand and execute them."

Establishing a strong team is the best first step a manager can take toward executing vision and strategy, and taking steps to do so in your first hundred days is an essential objective of getting off to the right start in your new leadership position. An effective team is the greatest source of leverage for implementing your agenda. As such, your team should become an extension of your personal leadership, a force that projects your vision, values, objectives, and requirements. And that's why before you even think about introducing a strategic agenda, you need to assess whether you have the people who can hone it, own it, and implement it.

TEAM BUILDING STARTS WITH YOU

The team you construct will magnify your management methods and your message. Who you are and how well you recognize the strengths and weaknesses in your skills will directly affect how effective your team is. In fact, everything about your team is a reflection of you— for better or for worse.

As astonishing number of managers surround themselves with people of similar backgrounds. But Jeff Immelt explains that he looks for team members who can complement, rather than supplement, his strengths and weaknesses.

"There's a notion that picking my own team means I want people like me. But when I look at GE's businesses, I want to create complementary strengths. You get the best of everybody by making sure you're not getting repetition. I look at the office of the CEO, CFO, and senior HR leader as a triumvirate. If, say, the CEO is a broad thinker, then you probably want a CFO who's a hardass. The fact is, I'm probably as good an organization-staffing person as Bill Conaty

[GE senior vice president of human resources]. But I don't have time for that, and Bill is the best handler of talent that I've ever seen. His job is to do those things I don't have time for."

A new manager can help define his true strengths for a new role by giving himself a 360-degree evaluation that examines needs, expectations, strengths, and shortcomings. Everyone has several—and only several—areas of naturally endowed strengths and weaknesses, such as logical problem solving, word memory, numerical facility, spatial relationships, hand-eye coordination, or musical pitch. By asking yourself, "What has been the pattern of my professional feedback over the years? What do my closest family members, friends, and trusted colleagues say about my most natural—or 'genetically encoded'— strengths? What are my weak points and skill gaps? What sorts of things do I routinely avoid or procrastinate on?" Write down your answers in a sort of personal balance sheet. And make a determination about whether the key gaps are skills that you are likely to develop or it makes more sense to find someone else who is better at them.

Let's face it, no one, regardless of how experienced or talented, is equally adept at every aspect of a job. In any case, as Immelt points out, even if you are above average across the board, no leader has the time to concentrate on every aspect of the job, especially in the earliest days of a new position. Think about where your personal involvement will yield the most leverage and where someone else might do an even better job.

ASSESSING YOUR POTENTIAL TEAM

Each new manager, whether promoted from the inside or recruited from the outside, inherits a legacy of an existing team: their ambitions and aspirations, their hidden agendas, their possible mistrust and questionable loyalty, as well as the history of relations among them and between each of them and the rest of the organization. Sorting out these dynamics early on is never easy, but it is essential.

Your first challenge is to gain a sense of each of the team mem bers and the overall team dynamics. Beyond assessing each person's competence and credibility, you need to evaluate the personal contribution and impact each person makes both on the team and on the rest of the organization by asking yourself the following questions about each team member:

- Is she a positive influence on the people she works with?
- Is her concern for self-interest more than balanced by a concern for the collective good of the organization?
- Does she nourish her peers and subordinates or exploit them?
- Do her actions uphold your standards and values, or does she merely pay lip service to them?
- Is she a good role model for the kind of leadership the organization needs?

As you begin assessing the team, keep in mind the environment in which people have gotten used to operating and how it may have shaped their past decisions and actions. It is not infrequently the case that managers who were less effective in an earlier regime may blossom under new leadership simply due to a new management or decision-making style. Lou Gerstner recognized this when he took over IBM in 1993. In his very first management meeting, he made it clear that his personnel assessments would begin that day. Prior mistakes and prior triumphs were fine, but for Gerstner what counted, what would be evaluated, rewarded, and punished, would begin that very day. And while many of the old IBM team didn't survive the new regime, some of the leading players in IBM's transformation were members of the management team that others wouldn't have expected.

Conduct one-on-one meetings with each team member to gain their observations and insights about the business and to discuss their aspirations and goals and how these connect to your own road map. This is the time for both of you to share explicit expectations of each other going forward and to identify the most capable employees and those most committed to your new leadership.

If time is tight, as in the case of a turnaround, you can save a little time by focusing on gaining the buy-in of key influencers. Not all of those key influencers may be a part of your immediate management team; there may be other people within the organization who act as gatekeepers or sounding boards or who perform other roles that affect the way the team operates. Ask others who the key influencers are within the company; patterns will emerge after as few as five conversations. Then concentrate your efforts on them for maximum gain on your own time and energy.

These one-on-one meetings are also an opportune time to establish whether you share the same values. "It's like, if you were going into battle, who would you want on your right hand and who do you want on your left hand," says Lowe's Tillman. "You want somebody you know is as equally committed to getting the job done and has the tenacity and willingness to do it." When Tillman speaks about all the people he has personally hired over the years, he identifies a common attribute that has always won for him: a fear of failure. "They absolutely will not fail."

Do not automatically rule out people who disagree with your views. Someone who pushes back may be a creative thinker. His willingness to challenge the status quo—even if he comes across as more of a devil's advocate—can be a valuable asset to the group, forcing it to question assumptions and circumvent conventional wisdom. The person who initially comes across as a bit of a rabble-rouser might see her role as getting things stirred up early but then strongly supporting a decision once it's made.

When he became CEO of GlobalSpec, Jeff Killeen held a series of individual meetings with his managers at which he asked them the following questions:

- How do you define this business? Is GlobalSpec a technology company, some kind of Internet company, or a media company, and what do you mean by these things?
- Who do we compete against? How does the landscape of our competition suggest an underlying strategy of actions and responses on our part?

- What are the drivers and metrics of this business? Which ones are you most worried about? Where do we have to focus most to really move our sales needle? In what ways are our customers most underserved?

- How large do you think this company can really be in three years? How do you think we can get there? What do we have to do differently?

"My motivation in asking these questions was to find out how engaged these guys were. Were they superficially engaged with the business as 'just a job,' or were they fundamentally knowledgeable about both the day-to-day details and the strategic issues? How deep were they into the metrics, and how aspirationally had they thought about the business? We had some wonderful conversations, and that too contributed to my getting off to a quick start."

Gary Kusin, who became CEO of Kinko's in 2001, believes that a new leader should always talk to the people in place about the business to see how they think in the context of the issues that come up. "If you talk with someone about their business and they aren't in control and can't grasp their numbers, they probably shouldn't be around," Kusin says.

"I remember my first meeting with our international people. I looked around to see if there was a *Candid Camera* team in the room, because it was a pathetic joke. That group had lost ten million dollars the year before, and business was cratering. Yet not one of the five VPs had traveled internationally in the prior six months. I had a meeting one afternoon to try to understand what was going on. I've never done anything like this in my life, but at the end of the meeting I fired them all. I said, 'Guys, you're not doing anything, so I'm sorry to say it, but you don't get to stay here.' I replaced them with one person, who turned the international business around in ninety days."

"I throw questions at people," agrees Dan Kerpelman, president of Kodak's Health Imaging Group. "If someone is responsible for the P&L, I'll ask for numbers. If someone is responsible for a technical program, I'll ask for voice-of-customer verification and how the program fits customer needs. It's not a test but a calibration on an individual's savvy."

Larry Johnston asked for presentations on projects, such as new promotional strategies, new merchandising approaches, and new human resources tactics, when he became the CEO of Albertson's, the $35 billion supermarket retailer. "Then I'd spend time in the stores to see whether the strategy was connecting down on the retail floor."

When Ed Breen took over at Tyco International, he had a strong feeling that he would have to replace the corporate team. But he didn't want to—nor could he afford to—dismiss the operating managers wholesale. To evaluate them, he held operations reviews: "You spend a full day going through things, pounding questions at a team for eight to ten hours, and you learn really quickly who knows what's what and who's behind."

Breen also immediately implemented what he calls the "Jack Welch calendar," scheduling regular and consistent meetings to go over the broader topics of leadership and strategy as well as operations. And he instituted an hour-long teleconference staff meeting with all his direct reports every Monday morning. "Everyone hears what's going on, you know what the big-impact items are, and it's an easy follow-up system for the next Monday's meeting. People really value it. They feel more involved and get to know what everyone else is doing. And it's a great way to spread best practices."

It's also a great way to spotlight who's on top of things and who isn't and, depending on your reaction, sends a strong message to the rest of the team about your standards and expectations of professional behavior.

Having round-table discussions with a subordinate's subordinates (commonly known as skip-level meetings) offers another kind of opportunity to hone your antennae and test your assumptions. "When you're in a room of people and you start to ask questions, you can size the team up and you can really size up their leader, especially if that leader is not present," says Johnston. "I'll never forget the first skip-level meeting we had. The executive vice president came into the room and sat down next to me. I looked at him and said, 'This is a skip-level meeting.' 'What's that?' he asked. I said, 'That means you're not supposed to be here.' "

Outsiders, such as financial analysts or customers, are another good source of data. When Kerpelman met with customers as part of the get-acquainted process after becoming the new president of Kodak's Health Imaging Group, he found that talking with customers revealed as much about his direct reports—who was responsive, who was strategic, and who approached issues from the customers' perspective—as it did about the state of the business.

DOES THE TEAM HAVE WHAT IT TAKES?

Beyond evaluating individuals, you also need to assess the capability of the team as a whole: Does it work well as a unit? Which configuration comes closest to putting the right people in the right places? Which people put into which positions will maximize your leadership capacity? Does the team have what it takes to serve the company in the future?

The composition of the team has to be able to match the company's constantly changing challenges. It has to enable you to do your best job for the organization. It should also reflect the values and standards that you want to prevail throughout the enterprise.

When Steve Bennett became the CEO of Intuit (the tax preparation and personal finance company made famous by Quicken, Turbo-Tax, and QuickBooks) on January 24, 2000, he was planning to listen and learn: "When I came here, I said, 'I don't want to make any moves for at least ninety days.' " But he quickly determined that the company, given its assets and opportunities, should be performing at a much higher level. "The fact of the matter is that the things that had to be done were so clear and compelling that I went ahead and reorganized the company the fifth week I was here. I didn't want to do that, but as I went out and traveled all around and met with the staff and the employees and saw how we were running things, I just couldn't wait." The major conclusion he reached was determining that he did not have a strong enough management team to achieve his aspirations.

"My theory about the management team is very situation specific," Bennett professes. "Intuit was a company of under a billion dollars when I got here, with people who had never had much experience in billion-dollar companies. They were great, but they didn't have the skill set, the leadership, or the experience that we needed to reach our goal of three billion dollars."

RAMBO IN PINSTRIPES?

While many believe that new leaders typically come in and clean house, the fact is that a clean sweep seldom happens right off the bat. First, it's not realistic: the right new people may not be available. Second, starting with a clean slate comes with its own set of difficulties, primarily that there will be a drawn-out transition before any traction is gained.

Last and most important, it ignores the opportunities created by establishing new expectations and instituting your new management style. The change in leadership and operating environment can cause people whose careers were previously unremarkable to blossom.

Lucent chairman Henry Schacht believes in watchful waiting, and with good reason:

"People have enormous capacity if you give them half a chance," Schacht says. "Don't change anything until there's a reason to change it. Presume that the people there have the capacity until they prove otherwise. My favorite story about this is that when Lucent was formed in 1995, the conventional wisdom was that we didn't have any talent. That company went from four dollars a share to eighty-five dollars a share, from being the dummy of the world to being the fourth largest company in the universe [in market capitalization]—and we didn't change a single person. Now, if there's a clearly incompetent person there—say ninety percent of your colleagues think your CFO is a jerk—then that's not going to work. But if you're going to gain commitment, chopping heads is about the worst way to do it."

Most experienced managers have learned to make quick evaluations. But they have also learned to let reality validate their gut instinct. "I can often get a sense within five minutes whether someone can make it in a new environment," says Jim McNerney, who held seven major leadership roles throughout his General Electric career before becoming the chief executive at 3M. (That's seven first-hundred-day experiences before his first hundred days as CEO of 3M.) "But my take is that over the short and medium term, everybody deserves a shot, especially in a place like 3M where you've got a lot of good people. You will ultimately have choices on who fits better where."

Every manager has his or her own approach to making judgments about their legacy teams. One popular approach is to classify people into three categories: keepers, goners, and watchers. "Keepers" are clearly major assets; you may want to inform them of their status even before their formal roles are decided, so as to reduce their anxiety and minimize the risk of losing them. "Goners" are the major liabilities who subtract from the overall leadership and team capacity. Removing them quickly not only sends a clear message about your standards but often unleashes frustrated energy in the organization. Finally, "watchers" are people who could become major assets if they could address one or two deficiencies within a reasonable time, say twelve to eighteen months; it's worth telling them why they are on probation and what they have to work on and by when. Meanwhile, they represent a net addition to the overall capacity of the team.

That's how Dan Stone evaluated the management team he inherited when he became CEO of Space Holdings (now Imaginova), the company that owns leading space-related properties, Space.com as well as newspaper *Space News* and software publisher Starry Night.

"At the end of the first few weeks," Stone comments, "I classified people in buckets. There were those people who got the program and had the ability to work with it, those who got the program but had a question mark next to their names about whether they had the right attitude, and those who either didn't get the program or were bad apples. Category one people are the easy keepers, category three people ultimately have to go, and those in category two require management. In retrospect, I think my reads were pretty accurate. The category threes are symbolic. People aren't stupid. They see people undercutting the overall mission, being lazy, or having a bad attitude. You can't just lop off the category threes on day one. But I had to manage the perception that if Dan is saying he'll make changes, why is 'that guy' still here?"

While it's not difficult to identify the keepers and the goners, watchers occupy a huge gray zone—which can suck up a lot of your energy. George Tamke, former chairman of Kinko's and prior to that president of $13 billion industrial giant Emerson, tries to waste as little time as possible before deciding whether to invest further time in a potential keeper or cut his losses.

"You can make B-players into A-players if you work with them, but it's very hard to take C-players and make them into A-players," Tamke believes. "You've just got to recognize that as quickly as you can, have the conversations with them in a very fair, open, and honest way, and give them a chance to improve but recognize that the responsibility rests with them. If they can't get to where they need to get with your help and support, then you've got to move on in a fair way."

SENDING STRONG SIGNALS

As important as making the tough people choices surely is, the decision about when and how to communicate those choices is equally important in the first hundred days of your leadership tenure, when all eyes are on you. Should you do it sooner rather than later? Should you leave people to interpret the signals and figure out the message themselves? Should you have explicit, face-to-face conversations with the people affected?

Leadership changes present new managers with an opportunity to reexamine the status quo and obtain new insights into the old ways of doing business, and it's natural to want to hit the ground running. Furthermore, since the existing management team expects to play musical chairs, many new leaders want to take advantage of a period when there's a higher tolerance for change.

But unless the company is in a crisis, most experienced managers caution against making personnel moves right off the bat. *Think quickly but act thoughtfully* should be the watchwords, says Lew Platt, former chairman and CEO of Hewlett-Packard:

"There's a tendency when it comes to people decisions to make some of them too quickly. Most of them are made in the first hundred days, and if you think about it, a hundred days isn't very long to get to know someone and their personal capacity and what they can contribute to the organization. Just because someone doesn't see eye to eye with you doesn't mean they're not the best person for the job. Often you need someone to disagree with you. But those things take a long time to assess. When you come to a new job as an insider and you've worked with these people, you've come to an accommodation and you see their value. But when a new CEO comes in and cleans house, as many do, they lose a lot of very good talent."

Kodak's Kerpelman agrees. "One of my golden rules is 'Love everybody and make no snap judgments.' Give people the benefit of the doubt. Never take as gospel other people's potentially critical comments. Judge people on their own merits and actions."

Ed Zander also followed this advice when he became chairman and CEO of Motorola in January 2004. While it was clear to most everyone involved with the company—the board, the management team, the investment community, and the customers—that the communications giant needed a major adrenaline jolt in how it did business, Zander determined that he should be cautious about making any management changes in the first hundred days. He says, "In my first three weeks, I got lots of opinions and reviews about the management team. But rather than be rash and take some of them out, I decided that many of them just needed to be 'watered' and tested—given a chance to show what they could do in the new environment. And I'm glad I did. Some have changed my mind and are absolutely thriving. Others aren't going to make the cut, and we'll take the appropriate action. But it took me about three and a half months to really get calibrated on the team."

On the other hand, if you parachute into a crisis situation, you don't have the luxury of longtime love. Says McNerney, "If the business is broken and the management team doesn't have credibility, you've got to make changes on day one." *Credibility,* the intangible magic that gives you the organizational permission to take leadership action, is the key word in McNerney's comment. Not only do your prior track record and reputation affect your credibility when you take over a new leadership position; so too do your early decisions on key hires and fires, both from within the company and also externally, in the financial community and in the market for executive and management talent. When Ed Breen recruited David Fitzpatrick to Tyco International in September 2002, for example, the news that the highly regarded CFO of industrial giant United Technologies was coming on board shot the stock up 15 percent and caused investment research firm Morningstar to upgrade its outlook on the company.

Fortunately, in the case of 3M, McNerney was able to determine that things were not too broken when he arrived in Minneapolis in December 2000. He and the top eighteen executives of the company developed a new business plan and new expectations about what it meant to execute with excellence. As for the team that he inherited, McNerney says, "Over the short- and medium-term haul, I wanted to give everybody a shot." He went through a process with his team with the attitude that "unless you absolutely have to, don't make any moves with people during the first hundred days. First fix the business, and then get on with the people stuff later." And before too long he did reshape his management team. "You know, now three years later, seventy percent of the people who report to me are different today than when I took over the company."

Whatever changes you make and however you make them, everyone will be watching your actions and reading all sorts of meaning into even subtle shifts of roles or resource allocation. Who is in favor? Who is down and on the way out? Left unclear, these signals will encourage political jockeying, rev up the rumor mill, and shunt a lot of otherwise productive energy off in an endless guessing game. Consequently, it's crucial to clarify your expectations and objectives—and to make absolutely certain that your people decisions exemplify them right from the start.

"Bringing people in says so much about you as a leader," says Stone. "That's probably more important than anything. You've got to be really, really thoughtful."

Whom you choose and the process you use to make those choices send substantive signals about your standards, expectations, and management style. The signals are especially strong when you look outside the company for candidates. If you're an outsider yourself and tend to hire primarily from the network you established in previous positions, people will get a message of "Well, if you didn't work with the new leader before, then you're not in the inner circle and won't stand a chance." On the other hand, if the person you hire from the outside is so demonstrably more experienced or stronger than his or her predecessor that a new set of standards will pertain in the future, you send a different message.

That was exactly the message Dan Stone wanted to transmit with the first person he hired, a new division head for Space Holdings. "He is a type A personality, a can-do guy," Stone shares. "People would come into my office and say, 'He is great. Where did you find him?' I would say, 'He is great, but that's not so unusual. Everyone who walks in the door is going to be like that. This should be your expectation going forward.' "

Thinking long and hard before making your first hiring decisions maximizes their chances of success. Leaders in startup and early-stage growth companies are often faced with the conundrum of whether to conserve their resources and stick with the managers who brought the company to its present position or to overhire to acquire heavy hitters who can bring the company to the next level and, in the process, attract more top-notch managers like themselves.

Firings are an opportunity to send a signal that's often stronger than those sent by hiring. Sometimes the question is about attitude more than ability.

Dave Peterschmidt said that at Sybase "I got rid of the people who were going to try to undermine me in a really negative way. They didn't buy into the program, would never get on board, and would be destructive. I'm not talking about people who had healthy disagreements, open debate, and strong points of view. I'm talking about those who would knife you in the back, sell you down the river, try to destroy what you're trying to do. You can't kid yourself that those guys are somehow going to come around. You've got to make the cuts fast, you've got to be decisive, and you've got to move on. There was one particular guy who so did not embody what I thought the values of the company ought to be that if I didn't move to fire him, my credibility would have been shot. I would have been seen as a hypocrite, and rightly so."

Dan Stone also made sure that everyone got the message by laying the groundwork for a dramatic change: "The thing that made the biggest statement was firing two people, one of whom everyone really liked. He was a really nice guy and so was positive for the culture, but he was unwilling or unable to step up to a more aggressive agenda despite several attempts to get him on the right track. I had held a meeting at the end of the year, a year-end wrap-up where I went over what we said we'd do and what we had accomplished. Then I said, 'Frankly, everyone who is with this company is here for an important reason. Every job is critical—we have no excess. The flip side is that if you're not doing what you're supposed to be doing, the company is suffering, and it's not fair for one person in this room to negatively impact others' livelihoods. So everyone has to leave this room and make sure they're working at a hundred and ten percent.'

"When I let those two people go a few days later," Stone concludes, "the cause and effect was very clear. The meeting provided the context that helped everyone understand why they had to leave and why they were replaced with people who were much better equipped to meet the challenges ahead."

YOU NEED A "REVOLUTIONARY YOU CAN TRUST"

While it can make sense to bring in outsiders who can help change the culture and create a sense of urgency, experienced managers house the company's intellectual capital—the memory of the company, years of experience, and significant relationships with customers and other outside constituents—and they are certain to have deep understanding about who really does what from within the trenches, and how well they do it.

How do you balance the two?

Tom Ryder, CEO of Reader's Digest, believes that "if you're going to change an organization, the right mix is to keep most of the people in place but to introduce into positions of prominence people who will help stir the thinking process, who are in effect burrs under the saddle. Based on just an instinct, I thought I would need to change thirty to forty percent of the top people. Somewhere in this range allows you to create enough turmoil in the organization to facilitate change but leaves enough existing management in place to provide continuity and the institutional learning you need. More than that, and you begin to encroach on the organization's belief in itself and you kill off everybody."

During his countdown period before taking the job, Ryder identified four positions that were crucial to jump-start change: the heads of HR, reengineering, marketing, and editorial. He even knew the people he wanted to attract to fill those positions. Ryder was willing to wait to bring most of them in—and, in fact, he took a year to check them all off his list—with one exception.

"I told Jim Preston [retired chairman and chief executive of Avon Products and the Reader's Digest board director who led the CEO search] that I wanted to bring only one person, and I couldn't do without him—Gary Rich, the head of HR. It was a requirement of my taking the job. If you're going to create a revolution, you need a revolutionary you can trust. And I knew I had that in Gary," Ryder stresses.

Leadership can be a tough and lonely position, even in the best of times, but it's especially isolated when you want to make changes. You can't and shouldn't try to do it all yourself.

You need someone trustworthy with whom you can brainstorm, discuss sensitive personnel decisions, test the waters, and gather opinions in situations when people might not be completely honest and forthcoming with the CEO. You need someone discreet whom you can turn to during the "what do I do now?" moments that hit everyone at some point. Call it partner or confidant, the position can be second in importance only to you.

When Gary Kusin thinks over the factors that played a significant role in the success of reorganizing Kinko's, he immediately names Dan Connors, executive vice president and chief administration officer, whom Kusin had worked with at his previous organization.

"The first factor for me was having Dan Connors on hand as a confidant and strategy guy," Kusin confides. "I knew revamping our strategy was one of the most critical things we were doing, but I also knew there was no way I could be as involved in that process and still touch all the bases with the field.

"You have to win the hearts and minds of the electorate, and you can't do that when you're sitting in a conference room with a consulting firm. So you have to have a trusted person who knows your shorthand, who you know can manage that process. We were literally running parallel paths."

As an outsider coming into a financially constrained early-stage situation, Dan Stone didn't have the luxury of bringing in a partner— and certainly not a consulting firm. He had to place a bet on an inside confidant, and he had to do it quickly.

"I didn't have the time to make decisions based solely on personal observations from being on the job," says Stone. "I needed the benefit of corporate history and an insider to calibrate my observations with the historical realities of what happened before and some of the organizational dynamics. I ended up relying heavily on the Finance VP. His integrity was implicit in his responsibilities but more fundamentally was one of his personal strengths, and I came to learn that his instincts were generally correct. In return, in order for him to be a valuable sounding board, I needed to be able to trust him implicitly as a confidant."

Some managers prefer a brain trust rather than one designated person. The size of the brain trust is important: too few, and you may not get enough input from enough areas of expertise; too many, and the circle loses its cohesiveness and risks breaching confidentiality. Dan Kerpelman refers to his inner circle as "an internal board of directors." He explains, "It's composed of the HR director, the CFO, and the COO. We meet on a weekly basis. That created a broader pool of brains to think about things. We bounce ideas around and it's a good way to get validation or pushback on almost every facet of the business, including people and their abilities."

SHAPING THE TEAM IN A CRISIS

In a real crisis situation, you may not want to place your trust in—or publicly endorse—any of the existing management. It may not be possible to bring in the people you want as quickly as you want. And in those cases where the previous management may have committed malfeasance, it's most practical as well as diplomatic to look for counsel from an outside firm whose corporate reputation automatically confers probity on the individual consultants.

That was the course of action that Ed Breen chose at Tyco. The magnitude of the crisis of management was revealed on his first day as chairman and chief executive, when he tried to convene a senior staff meeting and discovered, as he recalled, that "there was nobody to have a meeting with." Some executives had quit following the departure of the former CEO, L. Dennis Kozlowski, who resigned just before he was indicted on charges of sales tax evasion and, with his chief financial officer, looting $600 million from the company. Others were literally not around.

"Coming into these situations, you are going to make a lot of management changes," Breen says. "We replaced the full board of directors and most, if not all, of the corporate management team. The sooner you move, the better. I asked [former CFO] Mark Swartz to leave after my first week. I got rid of everybody else within ninety days.

"But you can't hire people that quickly. I couldn't walk down the hall and have a conversation with the legal department. There was no legal department here in New York. Investor relations was me. In those situations, you need to bring in a lot of outside help, and they become part of your team until you bring in your own. They kind of became our crisis-management team." Specifically, Breen brought in Wharton leadership guru Michael Useem to take charge of corporate governance, legal ace David Boies to serve as counsel, and crisis-management specialists Linda Robinson and Walter Montgomery to operate as communications and media relations experts, and he relied on a team from our firm, Spencer Stuart (specialists in executive search and board director recruitment), to identify the right candidates for the new board of directors and top management team and to coordinate the hiring process.

THE POWER OF THE PREDECESSOR

No lesson about creating a management team could be complete without a discussion of how to think about and relate to the predecessor. Whether that person is still around or has left the company, his presence is everywhere, manifested by the health of the company or division and exemplified by the people who were responsible for maintaining it. It can create serious problems for incoming leaders, but it can also work to their advantage.

The predecessor conundrum applies to any manager at any level. In most cases, if your predecessor is still at the company, he'll be in another job. While he's available for advice, he's usually focused on his own new responsibilities and quickly loses touch with the nuances of your area.

The exceptions are outgoing founders and CEOs.

One school of thought holds that to establish a new CEO's leadership, there has to be a clean break with the past. When the founder or CEO leaves, he should really leave—get out of the building and off the board. "It's dangerous to have the former CEO walking the halls, hearing what you're doing and disapproving of it," says Richard Cline, president and cofounder of Voce Communications. "It's also hard to pick up the bush and shake it if the guy who planted it is still around."

THE WINE COUNTRY ISN'T ALWAYS WHAT IT'S CRACKED UP TO BE

Lew Platt followed this advice when turning over the Hewlett-Packard CEO post to Carly Fiorina in 1999. Ironically, he sank into this very quagmire when, shortly thereafter, he became the CEO of Sonoma County, California–based Kendall-Jackson Wine Estates.

"How successful was I at Kendall-Jackson?" Platt asks. "Not very. It had to do with the founder, who owned all the stock and had a different idea every morning as to what I should be doing. I was absolutely unable to set an agenda. While Jess Jackson wanted someone running the business, he didn't really want someone *running* the business. Therefore every initiative that I started, he found some way to interrupt. Everybody told me that this would be the case before I took the job. Jess and I are good friends, and I have incredible respect for what he's done—he's built an amazing company from scratch. But everyone I talked to said that he's impossible to work for, that it was going to be a disaster. What didn't I hear? I heard, but I thought, *He's never worked with a guy like Lew Platt before*. So much for that! My answer to someone going to work where the founder is still active:

Don't do it. Honestly. There are plenty of other jobs around—you don't have to take that particular one."

One person who didn't follow this advice was Barbara Banke; she became CEO of Kendall-Jackson after Platt left in 2001.

YOUR PREDECESSOR AS ROCK STAR

Others hold that if you, as the new CEO, push out the founder or exile the previous CEO, you excise the company's DNA, to the company's and your own detriment. Our view is that in most cases reaching out to and embracing the predecessor is the better approach. That way you can sustain a sense of continuity within the organization, instill a sense of connectivity, and learn the critical unwritten information that the previous CEO has amassed over the years.

That's especially important when you're succeeding a legendary leader who has built up tremendous loyalty. Having your predecessor confer his or her official blessing on you can help transfer that loyalty—or at least prevent it from turning into resentment.

For that very reason Gary Kusin deliberately reached out to Paul Orfalea, the founder of Kinko's, as soon as Kusin became CEO. Even though Orfalea hadn't been CEO there for years, there were still plenty of acolytes throughout the company who wanted reassurance that the outsider would honor the Kinko's legacy. That's exactly what Kusin did.

"I went to dinner with Paul," Kusin says, "sought out his thoughts about what the company needed, and bounced all of my ideas off him, so I could work that side of the equation. At my first kick-off meeting, when we invited our top two thousand people, I invited Paul to come speak. Even though he was out of the company by then, I wanted to be sure the company knew that I respected him, that I would always honor what he had done for the company, that he had his name on the door and that this meant something to me.

"Well, that son-of-a-gun walked out on the stage, and the place went bonkers. It was like a rock star had come out. They jumped on their chairs, they were screaming, yelling, all that. He came out and, right in the middle of the stage, planted a kiss on me. That was a pretty big deal. That told the company that he had given me his blessing."

At the same time, Kusin turned to George Tamke, the interim CEO who had led the search for Kusin and become nonexecutive chairman when Kusin came on board. Even though Kusin brought in Connors as an outside confidant, Tamke quickly turned into an inside one.

"Every single Friday night or Saturday morning—and I don't believe I missed a week until we sold the company—I sent George a three- to six-page, single-spaced update of what I was doing, what I was thinking about, what had been going on in the company. We then spent one to two hours late Saturday afternoon going over it. He thought about what I said, and he offered his advice. Sometimes he was able to say, 'That happened to me once, and here's what I thought about it.' Or 'Have you thought about this?' In doing that, we developed a relationship that enabled us to play off each other. It's a relationship that I never would have guessed would have blossomed the way it did. George has his faults, of course, and I have mine, but we figured out how to get the best out of both of us to move this company forward."

Even when you forge a positive give-and-take relationship with your predecessor, it still needs to be understood that only one person can be CEO at a time. Assuming the power of the position, making the decisions that the previous person used to do without making them feel unappreciated or sidelined is a tricky balancing act, but one well worth the effort.

FORGING THE TEAM

You can gather together the highest-quality ingredients, but that doesn't guarantee a delicious cake. Similarly, as a leader, it is not just the individual talents you assemble, but how you forge them together that makes the difference in creating an efficient, tight-knit team. Gap Inc. CEO Paul Pressler noted the top items on his team's to-do list: "How to get the team to work together, what processes to put in place to make sure they operate as a team before I shove an agenda on the table, and how to make people feel that they're part of that process."

Bear in mind that the early meetings you have with your team after you take on your position will set the tone for those that follow. The messages sent by how you structure the agenda, who is invited, when the meeting takes place, how forceful you are in guiding the discussion, and whether decisions actually get made and how they will directly influence future attendance, punctuality, meeting preparation, and whether people are "present" or are keying their BlackBerries under the conference table.

The early meetings should model the kind of team process you want to instill for the future. For example, you may want to articulate and clarify the objectives and desired outcomes of the meeting and of each topic being discussed. Pick important but unaddressed issues that have to be resolved, and encourage a frank and open conversation about them. As a new leader, you may want to run a "check-in" exercise at the beginning of the meeting to provide a transition from the emotional and physical state people were in before the meeting to where they are now. And at the end of the session ask for feedback about what went well and what needs to be improved about the meeting.

"GETTING TO KNOW YOU" AT MATTEL

Bob Eckert designed his first meeting with the executive team at Mattel as a kickoff event. Prior to accepting the CEO position, he investigated the management team. The board of directors had already cleaned out the executive suite, replacing not only Jill Barad, the former CEO, but most of the management team as well, so Eckert didn't have much history to go on. But through conference calls and public meetings, he got a sense of how people handled themselves and what was important to them. Based on this, plus additional input from the board, he called a two-day off-site meeting for senior management within his first month on the job.

"The purpose of this meeting was to draft the company's vision, strategy, and values," Eckert points out. "It's important for people to know where the company is going, especially in a situation like ours where only ten percent of the workforce operates at the headquarters in El Segundo, California. I can run into people in hallways and do a lot of lunches, but that doesn't really work when you consider the breadth of our responsibilities. So I've felt it helpful to have a simple road map so the employees can understand where we're going and how we're going to get there. Before we began the meeting, I called a friend who is a professor at the University of California at Davis and asked him to suggest an icebreaker to get it started. He suggested that I walk into the meeting and say, 'I've heard some things about you and you've heard some things about me. Let's clear the air. You can ask any question about me and I'll answer it. I'll go out and have a cup of coffee while you write down the questions, and to make it easier, we'll do it anonymously.'

"I thought we would be finished in half an hour. My little icebreaker lasted for four hours, with such pointed questions as 'I've heard you are an in-the-trenches manager who listens to the lower levels. Does that mean you'll go around us and make decisions without involving us?' I discovered that I had completely underestimated not only their wariness but also their ability to read between the lines. I also realized that they had done as much homework on me as I had done on Mattel, which told me I was walking into a sharp team of managers. It was a pivotal meeting. I was able to get a lot of things off the table that would have caused anxiety. It didn't take me long to see where the holes in the management team were. And we had our sheet of paper written in two days and we still use it today."

GALVANIZING A LEGACY TEAM AT 3M

At 3M Jim McNerney inherited a team that had overseen the slump in the business that had led to the company's hiring the first outside CEO in its history. Many people assumed that McNerney would bring in a group of people from GE, where he had most recently been CEO of the aircraft engines unit. He surprised them all by deciding to play the game with the hand he was dealt. In interview after interview, he reiterated the same message: "I'm trying to reset the performance standards here," he said. "I think the story at 3M is rejuvenation of a talented group of people rather than replacement of a mediocre group of people. This is taking a very good company and making it better."

Because of McNerney's success in revitalizing 3M's growth, its profitability, and perhaps most important, its hallmark innovation—which earned him recognition as one of *BusinessWeek's* Managers of the Year in 2004—we feel that his thoughts on how a new leader should galvanize a legacy team carry extra weight.

"You've got to find a leverage point for leadership early and get after it," McNerney says. "Because you've got to create a team, and you don't do that by running around shaking hands. You just have to figure out a way to assert yourself, but not do it arbitrarily; not from on high, but to make your impact felt with the team quickly. You can gain tremendous leverage from that if you do it successfully. You certainly get much more energy from the organization, and you get quick respect if you do it right. If you grandstand, you get negative leverage.

"I tried to confront the team with the reality that things were very different from what we all thought it would be. It was no one's fault that it was different, but it was really dramatically different. Quite frankly, we didn't have a plan that responded to the reality. So I tried to energize the group around the fact that we'd had a sea change in everything that we had assumed in every market, and what we had to do was together figure out a way to respond and to redo our strategic plan in the next few months.

"The book on taking over a new job says, 'Go out and meet customers, go meet suppliers, go shake hands at the factory, etc.' But the fact was that my first hundred days here were spent in a foxhole with the top eighteen guys. It's not that I didn't meet customers or do those other things—I did them—but there was just a lot more time together.

"I'm not a guy who sits off in his office alone and dreams up great thoughts. I need to draw from the team, they need to draw from me, and we need to figure out a way to go forward together. This was a team I had inherited. The way I handled that was to say, 'Hey, guys, the existing plan isn't a horrible plan, right? But, the world has changed, and we've got to change our plan and change it fast.' I didn't spend any time at all on the quality of the existing plan. I spent my time saying that reality has changed, so let's go."

As a leader, you need to lead by example, demonstrate engagement and personal involvement, and show that you have skin in the game. How did McNerney do that? "I tried to maximize the amount of input that I was putting into the process as one of the team members, as opposed to just sitting around reviewing stuff. My strategy was very much to lead by example. I said things like 'Here's how I want you to act. I want three or four ideas from all of you on how to fix our telecom business, and by the way, here are a couple of mine.' I tried to find examples where I could use analogies from prior business experiences to bring in ideas that way. With this approach, there was a constructive, always-moving-forward element to the discussion, with no looking back. So the headset was, we had to figure this out, we had to go forward, and it didn't matter who had put together the plan before."

SAN FRANCISCO IS NOT BURBANK

When you are a new leader coming in from the outside, be prepared to adjust your expectations about the team—and maybe even your modus operandi—as you see how well they operate together. Paul Pressler was accustomed to a certain type of group dynamics at his previous job at Disney, where all his colleagues knew one another's strengths and weaknesses and knew how to challenge one another and spark creative and productive thoughts. Pressler made the mistake of expecting to find the same at Gap Inc. when he took over.

"I was massively naïve," Pressler admits. "I came into an organization where the prior leader had such a different management style. The company was more decentralized, and there was a lack of appreciation that the headquarters functions could create value for the company. There was a strong culture of complete separation of the corporate functions—marketing, finance, IT, legal, HR, and so on— and the operating divisions.

"The executives I inherited didn't have a common purpose; nor did they act as an executive leadership team. We had to learn how to work together, to have a shared purpose and understanding, so that any crafting of strategy wasn't just my idea but rather something we did together. I realized that we needed to take a step back and figure out *why* we needed to be a team and *how* to be one, rather than move ahead with my agenda of 'here are ten things we need to fix tomorrow.' "

How specifically did Pressler put this concept into action? "We held regular off-site meetings with an outside facilitator starting about a month after I joined the company," Pressler says. "We talked about the strengths and weaknesses of the company and the competition and the challenges facing us. I gave them feedback from all the interviews I had done with our top fifty managers, and they validated it. It was at that point that I shared my observations about some fundamental needs of the business, what I called our enabling backbones. These are the core or mechanical pieces of the business that needed to be addressed or fixed before we could even think about growth, such as being a consumer-centric company; improving our supply chain; having the ability to "micro-merchandise"—that is, get the right product to the right customer set; improving our technology as a strategic weapon; and managing talent.

"Eventually, we moved to biweekly tactical meetings about day-today issues of what was going on in the organization. So there were two tiers of meetings: the tactical meetings and the full-day sessions about trying to build a process. But it was a real balance between getting my agenda moving forward and getting them to work like a team." Two years into Pressler's tenure, insiders say that Gap Inc. feels like a different company, much more team oriented and collaborative.

FILLING THE BIGGEST PAIR OF SHOES

Jeff Immelt had to deal with a different set of expectations when he became the CEO of General Electric: the expectations of his colleagues. Was he going to follow Jack Welch's famously brusque style, or was he going to work with them in a different way?

"Transitions such as mine," Immelt says, "where you become the boss of your peers, mean that you're going to have to run the company for a period of time like a partnership. At the end of a meeting, Jack might say, 'That's a completely stupid idea. Now what do you guys think?' I decided not to do things that way, since the people on the team could go out and get just about any CEO position they wanted elsewhere. When you get bumped upstairs, there is a real risk of losing good people if you don't treat them right. During my transition I was much more concerned about losing a good person than keeping an average performer. Working for Jack, we all felt like workhorses pulling the sleigh together for the greater good of the company. I was horse number seven and was fine with that. But when I became CEO if I then turned around and treated Dave Calhoun [CEO of GE Aircraft Engines] like horse number seven on the sleigh, his next call was going to be to Spencer Stuart!"

As you take over your new leadership assignment and forge your team, you need to be sensitive to how each individual will be motivated. Great leaders tailor their management styles to the recipient rather than approaching the top team from a one-size-fits-all perspective.

NEW TEAM, NEW ATTITUDE

As they looked back over their first year, many of the CEOs we interviewed calculated that more than half of the original management teams they inherited were no longer there. As the composition of the team begins to change and as the new team starts to notch up wins inside and outside the company, it will start to develop its own expectations of individual members and of the group as a whole.

One year after taking over at Tyco, Ed Breen reflected, "There's nothing like changing leaders to change the attitude and create a new culture. In the first six months we hired sixty to seventy key new executives. The whole direct report team at the corporate level is brand-new, and every single board member is brand-new. There is nobody on this floor, except one woman at the front desk, who was here when I arrived.

"When people saw the whole board change," he continued, "as we started to bring in a new CFO and new general counsel, they began to realize, 'These guys are serious. They're going to do the right things, they will improve their governance, they're looking to change things. Tyco's looking to assemble one heckuva good team.' "

NO ONE *CAN* DO IT ALONE

Whether you are coming in as CEO to rescue a fallen icon, or are the internal successor carefully groomed by your predecessor, or are a manager moving to take charge of a new department, the most important lesson to remember is that *no one can do it alone*. Even entrepreneurs, who were born to be individualistic and to go against the tide, need to heed this lesson. In our research, we have found that the ability to forge a great management team is the single most common trait among those rare and special entrepreneurs who make the transition from startup manager to enduring great business leader. Take inspiration from Michael Dell, whose partner is Kevin Rollins; Howard Schultz, whose complement is Orin Smith; and Bill Gates, who has flourished in both his Microsoft and philanthropic work thanks to teaming with Steve Ballmer. After all, it is not enough just to have the most resources or even the best. The difference between moderate success and enduring great performance is how you exercise your leadership to shape your management team in your early days, then motivate and develop the team over time.

ONCLUSION

TEN GUIDELINES FOR SHAPING YOUR MANAGEMENT TEAM

1. Establishing a strong team is the best first step a manager can take toward executing vision and implementing his or her strategic agenda. Simply stated by guru Jim Collins, "First who, then what."

2. Avoid surrounding yourself with people of similar backgrounds. Focus on building a team of people with similar values and passions but *complementary* skills.

3. Recognize that everyone is endowed with certain aptitudes and areas of natural strengths and weaknesses. Create a team in which everyone is playing to their greatest strength such that the whole is far greater than the sum of the parts.

4. Determine whether you have a strong enough management team to reach your aspirations. Gain a sense of each member of the team individually and how they contribute to the overall team dynamics. The composition of the team should match the company's challenges, enable you to do your best job, and also reflect the values and standards that you want to prevail throughout the enterprise.

5. To assess legacy managers, talk to them about their business and dive deep via operational reviews and Socratic questioning. If they are not in control and don't have command over their numbers, it may require a change.

6. Unless the company is in utter crisis, try to avoid making critical personnel moves immediately. "Think quickly, but act thoughtfully" to avoid the natural inclination to make key people decisions too quickly. Recognize that people have enormous capacity if you give them a chance, set clear expectations, and hold them accountable.

7. Call it partner or confidant, you need someone trustworthy, discreet, and possessed of superior judgment with whom to brainstorm, discuss sensitive personnel decisions, test waters, and gather opinions, especially in situations when people might not otherwise be completely honest and forthcoming.

8. Your early team meetings will set the tone for the meetings to follow; they should model the kind of team process you want to instill. The messages sent by your words, energy, and conduct will set the example for how topics are raised, worked on, and addressed. Articulate the objectives and desired outcomes, select important but unaddressed issues that have to be resolved, and encourage a frank and open conversation about them.

9. Recognize the power of your predecessor, whose presence is everywhere, whether or not that person is still in the company. While it may be tempting to push out or vilify him or her for the challenges you've inherited, doing so will likely create unnecessary ill will. Acknowledging and in some cases embracing your predecessor can sustain a sense of continuity within the organization and instill a sense of connectivity with employees' shared past.

10. As you forge your team, seek awareness of how each individual is motivated. Great leaders tailor their management styles to the recipient rather than approaching the top team from a one-size-fits-all perspective.

FOUR

CRAFTING YOUR STRATEGIC AGENDA

When you get a spare moment, you may want to thank FDR. You will certainly want to thank Lou Gerstner.

For years new leaders and all those around them—employees, boards, shareholders, the media—have assumed that job number one in a new position is to deliver *The Strategy*. Whether you're a new CEO, a new team leader, or the president of the United States, the pressure to descend from the mountain and deliver the tablets of truth can be overwhelming. When confronting this pressure, FDR responded very simply; he calmly put his forefinger to his lips, smiled, and said, "Shhh."

Lou Gerstner used words rather than a gesture to keep the forces at bay, and the result was his famously misinterpreted comment that the last thing IBM needed was a vision. More on this telling episode a little later.

Not too many new leaders can get away with FDR's approach for shutting down questions. But these precedents, especially the Gerstner case, have recently worked their way into how many new leaders think about transitions, giving them the much-needed permission not to be the messiah, at least not on day one. Many CEOs now cite the Gerstner example to help them resist the pressure to deliver a fully baked strategic plan in the first hundred days. And employees and boards are coming to respect this view. At the same time, people want—and have a legitimate right—to know what you as a new leader plan to do and how.

Finding the right balance between creating a compelling picture of where you plan to lead the organization and not becoming prematurely locked into a plan of action is one of the most important ways to make the most of your first hundred days. Think not about developing your strategic *plan* but about crafting your strategic agenda.

"A journey begins with a single step," but when determining the strategy and priorities for the organization, what is the right first step?

THE TIMELESS LESSONS OF LOU GERSTNER'S RIGHT START AT IBM

While the story of Lou Gerstner and IBM has been told many times, its lessons are valuable and timeless.

IBM in 1990 had its most profitable year ever. Three years later, as the personal computer era had fundamentally changed the computer industry, Big Blue lost nearly $16 billion, and the company that helped invent the PC was slated for breakup—or worse, extinction. Although IBM was Gerstner's first technology company, he had plenty of experience running large and/or troubled businesses at RJR Nabisco and American Express. Gerstner started at IBM on April 1, 1993, and he held his first major public discussion in July about what he planned to do to revive the company.

At the first press conference, he made his memorable statement: "There's been a lot of speculation as to when I'm going to deliver a vision of IBM, and what I'd like to say to all of you is that the last thing IBM needs right now is a vision."

People were so startled at Gerstner's dismissing the need for a strategic vision that few heard what he thought was more important at that time: a clear agenda laying out the key priorities and operating principles for the company.

"What IBM needs right now is a series of very tough-minded, market-driven, highly effective strategies for each of its businesses, strategies that deliver performance in the marketplace and shareholder value. And that's what we're working on." What Gerstner delivered was a sound assessment of the critical needs and priorities, which is exactly what all new leaders should be focused on in their early days.

"Now," Gerstner continued, "the number-one priority is to restore the company to profitability. If you're going to have a vision for a company, the first frame of that vision better be that you're making money and that the company has got its economics correct. And so we are committed to make this company profitable, and that's what today's actions are about.

"The second priority for the company is to win the battle in the customers' premises. And we're going to do a lot of things in that regard, and again, they're not visions—they're people making things happen to serve customers.

"Third, in the marketplace, we are moving to be much more aggressive in the client/server arena. Now, we do more client/server solutions than anybody else in the world, but we have been sort of typecast as the 'mainframe company.' Well, we are going to do even more in client/server.

"Fourth, we are going to continue to be, in fact, the only full-service provider in the industry, but what our customers are telling us is they need IBM to be a full-solutions company. And we're going to do more and more of that and build the skills to get it done.

"And lastly, we're doing a lot of things that I would just call 'customer responsiveness'—just being more attentive to the customer, faster cycle time, faster delivery time, and a higher quality of service."

Gerstner was castigated for his "lack-of-vision thing." But Gerstner pointed out that fixing IBM was all about execution. He didn't want his employees pinning false hopes onto a magical silver bullet that would produce a turnaround to put the company out of its misery. He wanted to promote urgency in the here and now of day-to-day operations.

In crafting his strategic agenda, Gerstner:

• Took the time to diagnose the company's problems, always starting with a customer perspective, coming up with a series of steps that, if properly executed, would lead to a resolution;

- Limited the number of those steps so that they could be remembered easily and understood by everyone across the organization;
- Prioritized them so that his team knew where to allocate the resources of each of their departments; and
- Painted the priorities in broad themes, providing enough structure to set direction while allowing sufficient freedom to tailor to individual situations.

One of the key talents of any leader is the ability to identify the truly critical issues and establish a short list of top priorities to keep people focused. It is important to make the complex simple. We don't mean simplistic, but easy to comprehend and take action on. Gerstner's agenda deftly achieved this objective.

BUILDING OFF THE *RIGHT* FOUNDATION

A well-grounded view of what your organization stands for, its reason for being, is the foundation on which to build your strategic agenda. When an agenda is not built on such a foundation, it can point the organization in a dangerous direction, losing sight of what it really stands for. Sometimes the skewed agenda results from one leader's view of the business landscape.

When Jill Barad culminated her seventeen-year rise up the ranks at Mattel to become CEO on January 1, 1997, she created a vision to position it as a diversified family consumer products company. Her expanded definition of what the company stood for made it "on strategy" to pursue a disastrous acquisition of interactive software player The Learning Company for $3.6 billion in December 1998. This large sum was invested into a totally new business at just the wrong time—when the Internet was moving into the mainstream, minimizing the demand for shrink-wrapped edutainment. Equally troubling was the fact that it took the management team's eye off the ball of its core toy brands. Mattel soon foundered and put the money-losing

Learning Company up for sale. The acquisition debacle did more than just create an ill-conceived strategic agenda. When coupled with Barad's notorious management style of stifling dissent (more about this in Chapter 8), it was the straw that broke the camel's back and led to her forced departure in February 2000.

Barad's successor, Bob Eckert, called these events "a strategic error" and reemphasized Mattel's identity as a toy maker. In his first extensive press interview after becoming CEO, Eckert said, "The theme I'm going to repeat over and over is that Mattel represents the world's premier toy brands today and tomorrow. This tells you what we are. This is what we're going to do for the next fifteen years."

Corporate focus can also get off kilter from the tenor of the times. "My predecessor, Ed Pratt, did a really good job with our company," recalls William Steere, who headed pharmaceutical giant Pfizer from 1991 through 2000. He noted that Pratt was influenced by the idea of diversification, the operating fad at the time. It was the time of the big conglomerates whose rationale was that if one of your businesses failed or had trouble, then the others would fill in the slack.

"Pfizer diversified into businesses that you could say were related, although it was a reach. And it became clear to me, as I came up through the company, that if anything happened to our pharmaceutical business, nothing would save us. All these other peripheral businesses were interesting and at times profitable, but in the end it was always the pharmaceutical business that carried the rest of this diversification."

Diversification wasn't the only fad Steere fought. "When I became chairman [in 1992], the first thing people said was, 'You've got to buy a generic pharmaceutical company. You've got to get into generics.' But my assessment was that we are a research-based pharmaceutical company. Generics are not our business. They're scavengers. They live off patent expirations. Intellectual property is the lifeblood of our company."

Steere's strategic agenda therefore oversaw a reemphasis on Pfizer's core competency as a pharmaceutical company, clearing away a lot of the distractions that might have prevented Pfizer from becoming the preeminent company in its industry. "I couldn't believe that the analysts were essentially downgrading us for a lack of vision because we were not in the generic business. But they eventually came around and said we did the right thing."

An identity crisis knocks a company's compass off kilter. It clouds its people's ability to make clear decisions, to choose which route to take, and to allocate the proper resources. How can you hire the right people if you don't know what you're hiring them to do? How do you know which projects and products to support if you don't know how they will ultimately fit into the whole?

Almost every leader will say that their lodestar is defining their business focus, which comes down to what you can do to build long-term value. "If anything, what the last few years have taught us is that building long-term value is critical for any company," says Dave Peterschmidt. "If the company is going to be in there for the long haul, it has to understand the core value it brings to the market and the reason for its existence in a crowded marketplace. Then you can do an assessment to get the company tracking toward long-term values."

Think of that assessment as conducting a reality check of the operating environment. If you want to get the company tracking toward long-term value, consider what conditions pertain that will help or hinder you. The answers will shape your short-term agenda.

MICHAEL ESKEW AND THE FOUNDATION OF UPS'S STRATEGIC AGENDA

Giant UPS was performing well when thirty-year veteran Michael Eskew became CEO in a well-planned succession in January 2002. Within three weeks of becoming CEO, Eskew assembled the senior management of the company for a three-day off-site session, at which they charted the critical challenges facing the company.

The foundation for UPS's long-term agenda was an organic outgrowth of sharpening existing strategy rather than making revolutionary changes. Eskew had two important advantages that allowed him the relative luxury of developing a long-term agenda in his first hundred days. First was the fact that he was a long-tenured inside successor who had been a participant in the shaping of UPS's strategy up to that point in time. Second, while competition from FedEx and other companies was ferocious and the global economy challenging, the power and financial strength of UPS meant that it had no sense of crisis, reinforcing Eskew's view that an increased concentration on how to do what they did well even better was the right direction in which to head.

With an eye toward UPS's hundredth anniversary in 2007, they created the Centennial Plan, a description of the services the company would need to provide, the people it would need to attract, the issues it expected to face, and the strategies for addressing them.

"We spent a lot of time thinking about where we wanted to go," Eskew recalls. "Two thousand and seven gave us a focus. The Centennial Plan wasn't so much about numbers of packages shipped, transactions processed, bits and bytes, or the bottom line, as about our capabilities in terms of people and customers and solutions and the way we execute. It boiled down into four imperatives:

- Creating a *winning team* comprising passionate people who work seamlessly with spirit and commitment to UPS's long-term vision;
- Sharpening *customer focus* by establishing an environment to deliver unique distribution solutions, customer by customer, package by package, rather than having a one-size-fits-all approach; to act like a small company even though the company has massive scale and scope throughout the world;
- *Adding value* for customers beyond the delivery of the package by seamlessly synchronizing the movement of goods, information, and funds to allow customers to take their businesses wherever they want to go;
- Maintaining *enterprise excellence* by continuing to perform with consistency, reliability, and perfect execution in all of the company's operations and functions.

THE SHORT-TERM AGENDA

Most new leaders don't have the relative luxury afforded to Michael Eskew. So as your agenda coalesces, the critical questions are how to balance long-term planning with near-term demands, and when to turn a directional agenda into a more formalized strategic plan. When talking about their strategic agenda during our research, most leaders understandably thought differently about their short-term agenda and their long-term one. In contrast to the direction-setting role of your long-term view, your short-term agenda is all about allocating your time, setting priorities, and letting the organization know exactly what you want to do right away, "on Monday morning."

Short-term agendas have to be solidly rooted in the current reality. Assessing and understanding your organization's competitive positioning, capabilities, resources, and culture as they exist today is an essential first step. As we discussed in Chapter 1 on the countdown period, this comes first from effective listening. But it also comes from carefully assessing the management team. To take control of organizational fires before they burn unchecked, you need to move beyond assumptions and determine if your employees really do have the proper mind-set to accept the changes you believe are required, if they are capable of performing as you intend, and if they have access to the resources required to successfully implement the change.

Some new leaders feel compelled to make promises without being certain that they can deliver on them. Wanting to be liked and accepted, they let good intentions cloud their business judgment. This is a more perilous proposition since there are so many larger factors and forces that you can't anticipate, let alone control. And the price for breaking a promise is your credibility. So make sure your short-term agenda is based on a foundation principle of underpromising and overdelivering.

GET A SENSE OF WHERE YOU ARE

Gillette's Jim Kilts, who has had multiple successful first hundred days to refine his agenda-setting approach, sums up how to think about the short-term agenda and how it feeds into long-term planning.

"Get the company assessment done and get a sense of where you are," he says. "That points to what has to be done immediately—getting the bleeding stopped, and any urgent people changes made. That should occur in the first four months. Then go through the more detailed strategic planning, where you develop a governing statement for each business and fine-tune resource decisions against the business. At Gillette, I felt comfortable only about a year after I walked in that we knew exactly what we would need to do over the next five years.

"A leader must take action immediately to fix obvious problems. But developing an insightful strategic plan will take three to five months. There is too much information and too steep a learning curve to try to implement solid strategy in the first thirty to sixty days."

But he certainly knew just what to do in the earliest days as he prepared for the longer-term planning ahead.

When Kilts took over Gillette in February 2001, the once-high-flying manufacturer of Mach3 razors, Duracell batteries, and Oral-B toothbrushes had missed its earnings for fourteen consecutive quarters. Two-thirds of Gillette's products were losing market share, and neither sales nor earnings had grown in five years. Brought in to stop the downward spiral, Kilts, a veteran of more than a dozen turnarounds at Kraft and Nabisco, realized that the first step was to instill a sense of accountability in the company's culture.

He started his campaign on his very first day. At a meeting with all fifteen of his division and staff chiefs, he asked, "How many of you think our costs are too high?" Fifteen people in the room immediately raised their hand. Then Kilts asked, "How many of you think costs are too high in your department?" Not a single arm went up.

Kilts announced a two-hour open-door session afterward for

anyone who wanted to discuss costs. "Almost all of them came and lobbied the fact that their group wasn't over cost, but they were happy to point out their peers who were. Manufacturing told me the sales guys' costs were too high, the sales guys told me the marketing guys were over cost, and so on."

According to Kilts, that's a common response among managers of companies in trouble: Everybody knows there's a problem, but nobody thinks it's his or her problem. "People always like to say, 'Management made me do it,' " says Kilts. "Well, we are all management. Now if there's a problem, it's everybody's problem."

Intuit's CEO Steve Bennett agrees that you have to separate short-term and long-term agendas. "It really depends on the complexity of your business. Intuit is a portfolio of six different businesses. Who's going to be smart enough to figure all that out in a hundred days? At the same time, some things," which found their way into Bennett's short-term agenda, "became readily apparent to me. And frankly, I talked about some of them during my interview process. Take our consumer strategy. We were losing money in online insurance, mortgage insurance, and Quicken.com, and somehow we thought we'd make up for it all in volume? I said in my interview that I thought the consumer strategy was dead on arrival.

"Obviously, I wanted to move pretty quickly on that, but I did not come in here with any profound changes in strategic direction in the first hundred days. The company had been performing fairly well (other than the consumer business). There was no burning platform. The issue was execution and resource allocation and focusing on businesses we could win. It would have been silly for me to come in and say, 'Oh, I'm going to do strategy.' They would have said, 'Who are you? What do you know?' "

YOU HAVE MORE TIME THAN YOU THINK

Most likely you have more time than you think to develop your strategic agenda. While people expect a fresh perspective from a new leader, a new style, and probably a new energy level, most do not expect a wholesale new direction, at least early on.

There's a lot to be said for effective listening and for not sharing plans prematurely. Not only does it tamp down the amount of potential distraction within the organization, it also nips public scrutiny and second-guessing in the bud. The last thing a new leader needs, especially in a crisis situation, is to have the media and industry pundits questioning, analyzing, and deconstructing your plans even more than they already will be doing. Big pronouncements, especially early in your tenure, make big impressions that can come back to haunt you. "If you're going to make big calls, you'd better be right," counsels Steve Bennett. "Because if you come in early and you make big calls and you're wrong, the whole organization is going to lose a lot of confidence in you."

Vision for vision's sake is counterproductive. Determining a course for the organization is a process that usually requires more time than most people foresee. It should be iterative, building off your strategic agenda, sharpening and clarifying the path based on experimentation and feedback.

FOCUS ON A FEW THEMES

The great English lyricist W. S. Gilbert quipped, "If everybody's somebody, then nobody is anybody." Put in the context of running an organization, if everything is a priority, then nothing is a priority. At times there seem to be two hundred critical things to do—and even when you pare the list down to ten, you still feel overwhelmed. But when things get overly complicated, it's easy to get lost—and to lose others.

Focus only on the things you can get your mind around at any one time. Self-awareness and simplicity are the best guides to help you get your bearings and navigate the maelstrom. "My bandwidth is five bullet points wide," says Jon Miller, CEO of AOL.

It is not just your own bandwidth that has limits. Your team cannot absorb and adapt to too many changes at once, either. When people

122 THOMAS J. NEFF & JAMES M. CITRIN

are deluged with long complex lists of priorities and action plans, their eyes glaze over and inaction reigns. But when they are given a couple of concrete priorities wrapped around a clear and simple theme, they can move ahead with purpose, leaving room for individual imagination and experience to fill in the details.

"You can't have twenty-five things on your list. It doesn't work," says Richard Notebaert, who became CEO of Qwest Communications in June 2002, at a time when Qwest was plagued with dismal financials, a sinking stock price, and a Securities and Exchange Commission investigation into its accounting practices.

"You've got to triage. You constantly have three or four or five things that you pound home and repeat, repeat, repeat, 'Look, we can't win if we don't do this.' First, fix the balance sheet. Next, get that flywheel of revenue going. Take care of legal and regulatory issues. Then, as you start to get the big things done, you can get more granular. For example, why do we have broadband in only forty locations instead of sixty-three? How are we benchmarking against other companies?"

Kevin Sharer, CEO of Amgen, established five themes intended to support accelerated growth: (1) Invest in R&D at an industry-leading percentage of sales, (2) Aggressively build and advance the new product pipeline, (3) Invest aggressively to support new product launches, (4) Attract and retain the best people, and (5) Balance near-term earnings with investment for long-term growth.

A small number of themes actually liberates rather than hamstrings an organization. A good theme is specific enough to provide focus but general enough for different parts of the organization to be able to adapt and interpret. For example, one of Ed Zander's themes at Motorola is to manage "from the outside in." This straightforward statement can find dozens of different manifestations across a large organization, from the way the sales force interacts with customers (listening more versus pushing existing product), to the way product-development engineers work with customer service (establishing an information flow to provide feedback loops), to the way human resources builds performance appraisal systems (monitoring and rewarding desired new behaviors). To provide a numerical illustration of this effect, one CEO claims that an effective agenda meets the rule of "3 and 300": three simple but compelling themes can legitimize and sustain up to three hundred separate but consistent organizational initiatives.

When creating your own short-term agenda, you should take the following issues into account. The short-term agenda should:

- Link to your business assessment, so that people understand the rationale;
- Identify the core initiatives you intend to launch and explain why they are important;
- Address short-term issues while not detracting from the long-term direction for the organization;
- Be built as a joint effort with your team; and
- Incorporate an explicit plan to address cultural issues and barriers to change.

Moving quickly to articulate a few simple themes satisfies an organization's hunger for a sense of what the new order might entail. It provides both a direction and an overall context, so that people know where they are going and what resources they need for the journey, what is important and what can fall by the wayside.

JUST SAY "A.G."

When A. G. Lafley took over at Procter & Gamble after his predecessor, Durk Jager, was pressured to resign, he was not expected to bring dramatic change. He was simply asked to restore the company's equilibrium, which was significantly off kilter after Jager had tried to implement too many changes too quickly. "I had to come up with something quickly to get people focused," recalls the twenty-five-year P&G veteran. "I didn't want everyone sitting around worrying that our stock price had dropped in half."

He announced his priorities within days of taking the job. (Benefiting from one of the major advantages of internal succession, Lafley had been able to think about how to fix P&G before he was in the top position.) In his judgment, P&G needed not a radical makeover but to do what it did well, only more so. Stop trying to develop the "next big thing," Lafley told his troops, and focus on selling the company's *major* brands.

Lafley refocused the company on its top ten brands, the best-sellers that each generated over $1 billion in sales and combined to make up more than half of P&G's total revenues. "It's a basic strategy that worked for me in the navy," says Lafley, who, as a supply officer, ran a department store for servicemen. "I learned that even when you've got a complex business, there's a core, and the core is what generates most of the cash, most of the profits. The trick was to find the few things that were really going to sell, and to sell as many of them as you could."

The plan was shocking in its simplicity. Everyone down the chain of command could understand it. Selling more Tide is less complicated than trying to invent the new Tide. More important, P&G already knew how to do it—and to do it very well. Furthermore, the strategy of focusing on the core brands spotlighted corollary actions: shutting down skunk-works projects that were distracting focus and absorbing resources, pulling the plug on failed product launches of secondary brands, and selling off units that no longer fit the major-brands strategy. Together these measures cut P&G's out-of-control costs by some $2 billion.

The imperatives aren't any different at a nonprofit organization. John Read was familiar with Outward Bound as a member of the national board and as a participant in its wilderness courses. He boiled his strategic agenda down to two items.

"The most important item in my judgment was that the core wilderness programming of Outward Bound was in a crisis. The open enrollment programs of the wilderness schools had been in a nine-year decline. Each school on its own had wrestled separately with how to solve that problem, and each new director and marketing committee of the local boards had come up with their own solutions, which served to proliferate different messages of who we are and what we do. It was terribly confused.

"The decision making of Outward Bound is so process-laden and complex for an organization of our size that it was at times as if we were standing in the middle of a burning building and creating committees to discuss fire prevention instead of picking up the ax and hose to fight the fire. It may be specific to nonprofits, but I find an extraordinary level of talent, intelligence, and capability on our board, and disconcerting the extent to which competent businessmen and -women seem to check their business sense at the door when they enter the boardroom. And in a decentralized membership organization such as ours, this is a job with limited authority. So it's a job where you marshal the data, hold the mirror up, use a bully pulpit to articulate what needs to be done, and provide the supporting data to prove the point.

"From my first day I directed my comments to the national board and to the boards of the local schools, and I used my first hundred days to say that the situation was unacceptable and that we had to change. The nature of the change that we needed to make in programming and decision-making processes required each local school to think about merging its programs together and then act. (Much of this was accomplished through successive drafts of a vision paper that Read wrote.) The trick was to merge the schools from where they are, rather than superimpose the point of view of the national board. The response from the boards was, 'Gee, we've never heard that before, but you may be right.'

"My second priority was to focus and downsize the national office consonant with our ability to raise money and support ourselves. The reputation of the national office was low among the Outward Bound schools, and it was my view that this office needed to focus on doing a few things well and living within its means, for example to say what we would do, and to do what we said. Within a few months—no surprise to anyone—there was a thirty percent reduction in the staff here."

SMOOTH OPERATORS

Short-term agenda, long-term agenda—the time frame doesn't much matter if the organization is not operating smoothly enough. "One of the biggest contributions a leader can make, although it's often underrated, is defining the operating mechanisms—the meetings, the information flows, and the decision-making processes used to conduct day-to-day business," says Dan Kerpelman, president of Kodak's Health Imaging Group. Sometimes you need to be directive.

Jeff Killeen not only defined the need for new operating practices at GlobalSpec, he initiated a process to standardize further the overall set of business procedures and to create the platform for rapid growth for the early-stage company. The catalyst was a staff meeting held on his second day on the job. "At several points in that first meeting, I thought I was at a university or in a research lab," he recalls. "The discussion was largely open-ended. Every idea seemed to be surfaced, the agenda was loosely structured, and the conversation focused more on the things we could test and learn from (which is great in the right context) than on hardcore decisions such as sales, strategy, and cash flow. The tendency to have point-counterpoint debates on everything and agreeing to continue analyzing issues and opportunities was an understandably engineering and scientific approach to creating and running a business.

"But at the end, I said, 'Here's the way we are going to run the meeting next Tuesday. We'll discuss our financial performance versus plan, our sales results, and the big 'move-the-needle' projects for the business. We all must understand that we have to pick up our pace dramatically.' I shared a story about Defense Secretary Colin Powell in which he said that decisions can—and must—be made with between forty and seventy percent of the data in hand. Almost no one ever gets the luxury of being able to make decisions based on a hundred percent of the information. We simply needed to move faster and be confident enough in ourselves to make big decisions based on prior experience and judgment. We're a smart but relatively inexperienced management team. Everyone has to know the key elements of our integrated business model and support the actions that will turn us profitable and simultaneously grow sales at a hundred percent annual rate. We began to run our staff meetings with *that agenda* starting immediately."

Jim Kilts saw that firsthand when he took over at Gillette. "When I came in, given the results, I expected a below-standard quality of people. Then when I got to know the organization, I realized we had some of the best people I had ever seen in consumer products. They were handicapped because we were doing the wrong things and encouraging them to do the wrong things."

As a result, Kilts introduced a series of basic operating disciplines. He established communication processes so that there would be no surprises and so that follow-up action could be taken quickly. Weekly staff meetings involving all of Kilts's direct reports were instituted during his first week on the job. He asked for weekly e-mail reports from the heads of commercial operations in the regions across the world, the heads of the global business management units representing the products, and all his functional group heads.

Kilts also started quarterly one-on-one meetings with each of his reports to review the completed quarter prior to a quarterly two-day off-site meeting with all of them. Part of the review included each executive grading his or her own performance on previously agreed-to topics, then comparing it with Kilts's review of their performance. Many executives felt that setting quarterly priorities, which Gillette had not done before, was one of the most important practices Kilts instituted to lead the business back into growth and profitability.

The weekly staff meetings were so vital to managing Kilts's short-term agenda and laying the groundwork for the long-term agenda that he put together a presentation explaining the rationale behind them, the requirements demanded of them, and the etiquette expected to prevail. Notice how well thought through his seemingly mundane items were. As you read Kilts's notes following, imagine how the new management process felt to the Gillette executive team after a couple of years of drifting. The feedback was something in the order of "We *finally* have someone who's willing to take charge."

KILTS'S WEEKLY STAFF MEETINGS

- Why weekly?
  - Want firsthand update on the business
  - Business conditions warrant it
  - Assure alignment
  - Share what's going on so you can do your job and gain full executive communication

- Attendance required; on time; no substitution without prior Jim Kilts approval
- Weekly, Monday, 10:00 A.M. to noon; can be extended as needed
- Agenda
  - Suggested items and requested time needed to Chuck Cramb (CFO) by Wednesday preceding meeting . . . indicate if significant action/decision desired at meeting
  - Agenda reviewed by Jim Kilts and issued by Thursday

- Confidentiality
  - No gossip
  - Reinforce with your assistants and others

- Decision process
  - Consensus—all views heard
  - Final decision by Jim Kilts as needed

- Behavior
  - Pay attention; no sidebar conversations or secondary tasks . . . really listen
  - Stick to subject
  - Openness
  - Pre-work: preparation when needed
  - Jokes, fun—OK

- Once-around-the-table process
  - Limited to three minutes each—no borrowing
  - Items requiring more time to be on agenda

People like to be led. Following Jim Kilts's example of setting clear, concrete direction and management processes is something that can be modeled by any manager.

SETTLING DOWN THE TYCO CRISIS

When Ed Breen walked into troubled conglomerate Tyco International, he realized that one of the most pervasive problems was a lack of operational discipline. "I had a feeling there wasn't much infrastructure, but the extent surprised me when I arrived. Four key presidents of operating businesses came to see me during my first week and said they hadn't had a meeting together in a year."

The former second in command at Motorola with a reputation as a quick-thinking, skilled operator, Breen promptly instituted an hourlong staff meeting every Monday morning with all of his direct reports. "It's a systematic meeting. Everyone hears what's going on, you know what the big-impact items are, and it creates an easy follow-up system for the next Monday's meeting. They really value it. They feel more involved and get to know what everyone else is doing. And it's a great way to spread best practices.

"I came in with a strong premise up front that we were going to run a disciplined operating company. I delivered that message strongly. You've got to understand, this had been an acquisition machine, and I was saying, 'There will be no acquisitions for at least two years. We're going to run an organic operating machine, and we're going to put in disciplines to drive that.' I put a core process in place that had us run as an operating company, and a calendar that showed how we would reap the benefits over the next few years."

Even internal successors can use the opportunity offered by tweaking operations to send a signal about change. Alan Lacy had been the CFO of Sears from 1998 to 1999, becoming president of services in 1999 and finally CEO in December 2000. Even as an internal successor, he wanted to make a fresh start.

"I felt I needed to take full advantage of my knowledge of the company, but I needed to approach the job as if I'd never worked here a day. People who worked for me knew how I think about things and how I approach the job, but I had never had the need nor opportunity to articulate that to a broad group of people.

"I needed to level-set the organization. The vice president group—about a hundred people—had historically gotten together once a quarter. I increased that up to a monthly meeting.

"And I did a couple of things where people went, 'Oh, he's really serious about what he's talking about.' For a period of time, whatever you're saying just sounds like nice words. People shake their heads and say, 'We'll see.' We'd had a bunch of false starts previously, so the word was, 'He's saying that this month and may say something else next month.' Until the pieces of the puzzle start falling together and hanging together, people don't believe that you're serious."

LOOK FOR QUICK WINS

Streamlining the operating process yields immediate benefits. Similarly, the sale of a nonperforming division or hiring a crucial member of your team also sends a signal that progress is being made. Look for these quick wins and leverage them. "If you can find a few things that were serious flaws in the organization and fix them quickly, you can establish your credibility as a leader very fast," says Lew Platt, former CEO of Hewlett-Packard.

Reflecting back to 1992, when Platt was the successful internal candidate for the HP CEO position, he had the advantage of having already done his own evaluation on the company. "When you're a senior employee, you should have your own thoughts about what's right and what's wrong and what you'd change if you were in the top seat. The real advantage to me was time. I stepped into the job knowing what needed to be changed and didn't have to spend several months doing a diagnostic."

But an outside point of view also spotlights bad habits that have become so ingrained as to be invisible or considered immutable. Platt briefly served as chief executive of Kendall-Jackson Wine Estates after leaving HP and spotted a fixable flaw almost immediately: "Every expenditure over twenty-five dollars had to be approved by Jess [Jackson, the winery's founder]. I put in place a standard expense approval system. That was a simple but symbolically important change. People still talk about it, about recovering their dignity and being given the authority to go along with what they were being held responsible for."

Plan your promises, and promise only what you can deliver. Once those goals are part of the public record, keep an inventory of evidence that supports your claim to have accomplished them. Without blowing your own horn, it can be helpful in those early months to call attention to the early successes that align with what you have already identified as priorities for the company's success and growth.

Not all early actions may be happy ones, but they are worth emphasizing if they help the organization move in the direction you want. An example is the September issue of Bob Eckert's company-wide intranet column "What's On My Mind?" written five months after he arrived at Mattel.

In the previous month's column, he discussed the strategic plan to refocus Mattel as the world's premier toy brand and discussed the need to bolster and build its core brands. In the September issue, he announced a series of difficult decisions that were part of a financial realignment to help reposition the company for profitable growth: selling The Learning Company, reducing the workforce by 10 percent, and slashing the cash dividend.

"These actions are consistent with the strategies that I've previously communicated to you," Eckert wrote. "For those of you who saw my last Employee Update, you'll recall that I reviewed a chart showing that since 1997, our gross margins have declined while SG&A and interest expense have increased. As a result, our profits and cash flow have declined.

"The actions announced today are designed to jump-start our plans to return profit margins to historically high levels and position

Mattel for profitable growth. These are tough decisions because they involve real people. I do not take them lightly, nor do I expect you to. But they will help put the past behind us and build a stronger future."

XPECT PUSHBACK

Effective communication opens up new opportunities by systematically revealing the assumptions behind the logic of your initiatives. By involving key stakeholders early in the process, exchanging mutual concerns, identifying areas of agreement and difference in outlooks, and negotiating joint solutions, you increase everyone's commitment to making the change successful. During this process of mutual questioning, objectivity is crucial to gain new insights and information, build on agreements, and constructively resolve differences.

Because there *will be* differences of opinion. Pushback is a natural response to change, whether change is real or only anticipated.

As you involve more and more people in the change process, you may feel as if you're treading water. This feeling comes from having to introduce and convince each new wave of people as your changes percolate down through the organization. During your first year there will never be a time when your strategic agenda isn't being criticized, questioned, and debated. Be patient, and remember that the new converts will need the same time that you and others did to get it.

Sometimes, though, you might get a pleasant surprise, a realization that your ideas have taken root and are beginning to flourish. That's what happened to Dave Peterschmidt when he tried to institute standard operating procedures at his Internet startup.

"At Inktomi, the management team was composed of academic scientists and engineers who had never had to build commercial code and didn't understand mission-critical, twenty-four-seven reliability and the ability to respond when a bug was discovered. I went to co-founder Paul Gautier, who was handling day-to-day operations, and said, 'Paul, you may think I'm nuts, but I want to bring in a firm that will help us set up specific engineering processes to make sure that when we build a product, when it gets released into the market, it will be a high-quality product.'

"I was anxious because I thought that Paul would feel, 'Here comes the guy from bureaucracy bringing us bureaucracy.' To my amazement, Paul said, 'That's a great idea. We're tired of sleeping in our cubicles and not knowing how long it takes to do something.' "

"People like to be led," concludes GlobalSpec's Jeff Killeen. "If they feel they're not being led, they get frustrated. They like milestones and scorecards. People like to rally around something, particularly in a young company, and feel that they're all there for a good reason. If you channel things right, you can get this rush of energy, morale, and uplift and can fashion it into something cohesive and concrete. A newly arrived CEO has a unique opportunity to seize the moment and transform frustration into positive energy."

TAKE YOUR BEST SHOT

A well-defined strategic agenda can be used both to direct and to mobilize people, ensuring that their attention will stay focused on the core initiatives that will have the greatest impact on the organization's performance.

Done right, your agenda evolves into your strategic plan, which can in turn be used in multiple ways with multiple constituents, ranging from the numerous presentations you will give to employees and your management team, to industry conferences and interviews with the media and the financial community. For some, it will be a road map; for others, it will be a reassurance. In some cases, it will serve as the starting gun to galvanize people into action. In other cases, it will buy you the time to make necessary changes in the organization— and in your agenda. But for all concerned, a well-done process of developing the strategic agenda will help prioritize in the short term, support the long term, and give people a sense that they are part of a coherent direction. This then minimizes the angst and uncertainty that can paralyze organizational decision making and action taking.

You will need time because you're invariably going to make mistakes. "Anyone coming into a new situation is faced with the fact that they feel that they have to do the most at a point when they know the least," notes AOL's Jon Miller. "You may have previous experience, and you may be smart and have insight into how things work, but you know the least about the actual company you're engaged in. And at the same time, you have to set things in motion and see what transpires. You have to take your best shot—and the company may live or die by your calls."

"It's been a little bit contentious," says Steve Reinemund of the agenda he instituted at PepsiCo. "I've gained *and lost* credibility on a daily basis."

Don't be a perfectionist. Not everyone has to be convinced of the advantages of your agenda. Achieving the buy-in of key influencers will provide the leverage you need. You don't even have to make the right decisions nearly all the time. The key is to *make decisions* and create an environment where you can see how things work out and make course corrections as necessary. Confront your own fallibility and keep moving forward. Success is as much about taking action and recognizing your mistakes and addressing them quickly as about striving for the ideal. Here's what Jon Miller says to people: "I try to be right seventy percent of the time first off—that comes with experience and understanding—and I try to fix seventy percent of the mistakes I make. If you do the math, this gives you a ninety percent success rate." (Mathematician's note: Miller's 90 percent success rate is calculated by multiplying the 30 percent mistake rate the first time by the 30 percent mistake rate the second time and subtracting that from a 100 percent success rate.) "This is about three times the batting average of a Hall of Famer, in baseball at least. One of the worst things you can do," adds Miller, "is not admit mistakes you've made."

THE TEST OF TIME

One measure of any strategic agenda is its ability to withstand the test of time, such as the plan Gary Kusin introduced and implemented several months after he became the CEO of Kinko's in August 2001.

"One of the things that Gary made very, very clear to everybody was that major change was in the wind," recalls Kinko's chairman, George Tamke, who was also senior partner of the private equity firm Clayton, Dubilier & Rice, which controlled the company at the time (since sold to FedEx). "You couldn't pin him down to say A, B, C, D, and E were going to happen, but he let everybody know very early in the game that major change was going to happen and it was going to be helpful to the organization, so just get ready for it and don't be afraid of it. Meanwhile he required open and honest feedback from people as he made his sojourns into the field, so he really got an understanding of what they thought and why. Then, on the basis of what he heard and with some help from some very smart outsiders, he would articulate exactly what the game plan was going to be in the not-too-distant future.

"That's what turned the strategic agenda into the strategic plan that got presented to the board about a hundred fifty days after he started. I use the term *plan* a little bit loosely," Tamke editorializes, "because that strategic plan was kind of heavy on tactical things that we were going to get done in the next year and a bit lighter on the strategic direction, with more of the blanks yet to be filled in. But they did get filled in during the course of the next year, through updates that Gary did with the organization."

Kusin recalls announcing his agenda to a meeting of seventy-five district marketing managers, twenty-four market directors, and the top field leadership, at the company headquarters in Dallas. "I stood in front of everyone and said, 'Guys, everyone is going to give blood in this process. Let me tell you what blood you're going to give.'

"I told them that I wanted them to think about our strategy going forward. Up to that point, every Kinko's store considered every other Kinko's store a competitor. They vied against them for work, they bid against them for work. I said, 'You have to think about being part of a team. As a team, we have too many [copying] machines, so we're going to be stripping out machines. And we've got way too much head count, we're not getting the productivity we need.'

"We spent two days going over this. [Executive vice president and chief administrative officer] Dan Connors dug in real deep detail about how the strategy was built and focused on extracting best practices at Kinko's. This was not some quant jock sitting in a room; we were literally going out into the field to find what our best stores did, then mandating that everyone run their business the way the great Kinko's stores ran their business. So I was able to present it as an entrepreneurial package.

"At the end of the two days, I gave them a speech about accountability and alignment. I laid out my leadership principles, and those were the first two—neither of which had ever been in a Kinko's vocabulary. I marched through why I thought this was the right thing to do, and at the end I said, 'What you guys need to do is think about what I'm saying and decide whether or not I'm smoking something. You may think this is doomed to failure. But you need to decide. I'm going to give all of you thirty days to decide. Anyone in this room who decides they want to vote with their feet, I'll personally ensure that you get another job. When you find a company you like, I'll call them and tell them how great you are. But on the thirty-first day, anyone in this room who is not a hundred percent aligned with what I'm saying, I will personally find you and weed you out.'

"The room got very quiet," Kusin recalls. "But that was what it took. Two people voted with their feet, and I helped them get jobs. But you know what? Now we have all sorts of alignment and accountability all over the company. People now take ownership for what they do."

Strategic agenda now firmly in hand, with the short-term priorities linked into and supporting the long-term goals and direction, you are now well positioned to step up to the next layer of the first hundred days pyramid. One of the most subtle and challenging aspects of getting off to the right start in a new leadership position is the subject of the next chapter: how you start to transform the organizational culture.

ONCLUSION

TEN GUIDELINES FOR CRAFTING YOUR STRATEGIC AGENDA

1. You have more time than you think. You don't have to deliver a fully baked strategic plan on day one . . . or even in the first hundred days. Find the right balance between creating a compelling picture of where you want the organization to go and not becoming prematurely locked into a plan.

2. In developing your agenda, diagnose the company's (or department's) problems starting with the customer perspective and continuing with a grounded view of what the company stands for.

3. Strictly limit the number of themes and priorities so that they can be easily remembered by the organization.

4. When crafting your short-term agenda, always endeavor to underpromise and overdeliver.

5. Build the strategic agenda in a joint effort with your team versus in a silo.

6. Incorporate an explicit plan to address cultural issues and barriers to change.

7. Define the operating mechanism/process—the meetings, documents, and report formats to conduct the day-to-day business.

8. Secure some early wins; look for obvious flaws in the organization and fix them quickly to establish your credibility as a leader.

9. Expect pushback on your agenda, but rather than resist, coalesce that input in a positive way to maximize buy-in.

10. Don't be a perfectionist; your strategic agenda is by definition a work in progress. Use it to help you and the organization make decisions, see how they work, and make adjustments as necessary.

FIVE

CULTURE IS
THE GAME

STARTING TO TRANSFORM THE
CORPORATE CULTURE

Before his IBM days, Lou Gerstner considered culture just one element in an organization's makeup, no more intrinsic to success than any other aspect of good management. But the decade he spent morphing IBM from industry dinosaur to dynamic leader convinced him otherwise.

"Culture isn't just one aspect of the game—it *is* the game," Gerstner says. "In the end, an organization is nothing more than the collective capacity of its people to create value. Vision, strategy, marketing, financial management—any management system, in fact—can set you on the right path and can carry you for a while. But no enterprise—whether in business, government, education, health care, or *any* area of human endeavor—will succeed over the long haul if those elements aren't part of its DNA."

Chris Lofgren, chief executive of Schneider National, the large transportation and logistics company, believes that "culture is a foundation upon which you build your long-term strategy. If you build a strategy that isn't consistent with the culture, it isn't going to work."

One of the imperatives for any new leader is both understanding the organization's culture and determining whether change is needed. Most managers, however, receive little or no training in how to define an organization's culture, let alone how to change it.

THE SERENE LIFE OF NOT-FOR-PROFIT?

Many business executives burned out on the grind and politics of corporate life fantasize about a more serene existence on the not-for-profit front. The notion is that it would be fulfilling to "give back to society" by finding a leadership position in a mission-driven enterprise. The perceived icing on the cake is the opportunity to establish a better balance of job satisfaction and lifestyle, even if it means trading off compensation.

The logic also goes that applying for-profit management disciplines to a not-for-profit culture would bring accelerated transformation to an organization, hence even greater satisfaction. So it was not at all surprising that two-time corporate CEO Norman Blake would jump at the opportunity to become chief executive of the U.S. Olympic Committee when he had the chance in early 2000. His experience, however, should serve as a cautionary tale for business executives attacking a not-for-profit culture or trying to change any organization's culture.

Blake's experience running and turning around Promus Hotels and insurance giant USF&G, both multibillion-dollar corporations, gave him the edge over five other finalists. His mandate was to shepherd the USOC through a restructuring approved by the organization's 113-member board of directors. Blake's reputation as a hard-driving, up-front turnaround expert was considered exactly what was needed to institute in the USOC many of the management disciplines common to efficiently managed corporations. The rationale behind Blake's selection is not atypical—bringing in a change agent to lead a cultural transformation.

The key lesson is to take care not to try to do too much too soon without fully diagnosing where the power lies. This is true anytime but especially in the exaggerated case when a corporate leader is being asked to change a not-for-profit.

The USOC CEO was a newly established position. Its holder is responsible for the operations of the organization while sharing responsibility for overall decision making with the executive board. "The role was a complete change for me, and it was on the premise of bringing about change that I entered," says Blake. In evaluating what turned out to be a very short and frustrating tenure at the USOC, he confesses in retrospect, "It was one of the more disappointing experiences of my life."

He did many things right in his early days and weeks. But what he failed to do was appreciate and effectively deal with the culture. To set the stage, Blake had a tight time line. "I came on board in January [2000]. Anything I wanted to do in resetting the organization had to be done by June or July, because the two months before the Games [held in Sydney, Australia, the following September] is all about preparation for the Games. I had only a four-month window, which I understood going in."

But what he didn't fully understand was the deep-seated and Byzantine culture of the organization. Much as Winston Churchill once described the Soviet Union as "a riddle wrapped in a mystery inside an enigma," so the USOC was a labyrinth of some forty committees, boards, and councils, many staffed by volunteers and former Olympic athletes. "There were committees for just about everything, and literally every operating aspect of the organization was run through the committees," Blake recalls. "Although the staff had all the responsibility, they had no authority. I had to go through these committees and gain their approval on how the staff operated on a day-to-day basis."

Blake had already given notice of his intentions to reduce bureaucracy and increase accountability in an introductory letter sent out on his first day. "Going into any new working situation, you have to have a game plan to make sure to touch base with all the important constituencies. I write a first-day letter to the folks to communicate what they can expect of me and what I expect of them. In the case of the USOC, the staff had been so subordinated to the interest of the volunteers, so disenfranchised from the services of the athletes, that they were very demoralized and there was no direction or sense of mission for the organization. The letter spoke about that."

While the staff reaction to Blake's letter was, he recalls, "overwhelmingly positive," the Athletes Advisory Council felt threatened. The situation promptly intensified with a bold management decision that Blake determined was necessary. The next day he fired an eighth of the staff and cut committees and task forces from forty to four. The organization's gossip mill dubbed him Norman Bates, after the deranged killer in the movie *Psycho*.

Even to the survivors of Blake's staff reduction, his full-steam-ahead approach made many within the USOC administration feel disenfranchised. It is important to remember that Blake was following an action plan for which he was hired and mandated by the board. Despite this, his failure to marshal support among the athletes, their parents, and their coaches chafed deeply. Feelings erupted six weeks later, at a mid-March meeting to approve Blake's overall plan for restructuring the USOC.

The steering committee had already approved the plan, but now it ran up against the Athletes Advisory Council. "It became clear to the Athletes Council that I was proposing a complete dislocation of their interests in terms of running the day-to-day operations," Blake recalls. "We went to vote on the plan, and they voted it down in a straw vote. I said, 'If you don't like the plan, you'd better get a different CEO. It's your choice. This is what needs to be done, you hired me to chart this path and granted me the authority. I'm willing to listen to why it's not a good idea. But unless we have some meritorious reason for changing it after the steering committee already approved it, then we have an issue as to whether we can do what you brought me in for.

"That was it," Blake says. "That was the turning point. Late that night I told my wife, Karen, 'This is a short-term job.' " He stayed on through the Sydney Games and the Para-Olympics that immediately followed, then resigned and returned home.

It is tempting to lay the blame on Blake for pushing too hard too soon. It's similarly alluring to point a finger at the board for failing to support him in following the plan they hired him to create, or at a culture clash between the operating disciplines of a for-profit organization and a not-for-profit one. But despite the board mandate coming into office and the authority of the steering committee's approval of his plan, Blake failed to appreciate the true balance of power and the deep cultural influence of the Athletes Advisory Council. He felt that he had his ducks in order, with a board mandate and plan approval to carry out the change that he—and many others—believed was essential. In a corporate setting this may have been relatively straightforward, given the generally clear scorecards of financial and organizational performance. Then again, it may very well have been just as difficult and ultimately unsuccessful. Why? Because whether it's a powerful group of employees, retirees, restive shareholders, or even customers, a failure to assess the culture and the readiness for change among different interest groups can be lethal.

"YOU'VE GOT COPIES"

To illustrate that these lessons are just as applicable to transforming a corporate culture, let's examine the case of another organization that also had a history of a delicate balance of power between headquarters and the field. Kinko's was not just a company to most people, but a way of life for many franchisees, who were known as partners. It was their company. But when the Kinko's board of directors rolled up the 127 individual partners into one central organization in 1996, the board decided that the best person to weld together a new culture would be someone with a strong command-and-control background. "They went to the number-one command-and-control company in America, Wal-Mart, and they took the CEO of their most crisply run division, Sam's Wholesale Club," recalls Gary Kusin, CEO of Kinko's. "This was a guy who by every aspect of his résumé and everything else should have been just what the doctor ordered. The problem was, they needed just the reverse of a command-and-control guy."

When Kusin later joined Kinko's, part of his cultural assessment was to study the history of change—and attempted change—at the company. With antennae up, he was able to accurately determine where prior efforts had run asunder. "One of the major blunders of that earlier change program was trying to change the culture without changing the people; those 127 partners were allowed to remain in the company in management roles," he says. "So if I owned Kinko's Dallas, after the roll-up I got to be the district manager for Kinko's Dallas.

"What naturally happened then was that when they tried to centralize or hand down some new way of doing business, all these district managers and field operations leaders were able to say, 'Well, I tried that in 1988 and it didn't work. We're not going to be doing that here.' Or when people from the central organization traveled the field and told them what to do, they'd say, 'Sure, no problem,' to their face but then tell their organizations to get back to doing it the way they wanted when they left.

"It's my firm belief," Kusin adds, "that the board made the wrong assessment of the culture and the implications for the right leadership. They literally spec'd not just the wrong spec, but a hundred eighty degrees off spec. There was no way in the world that you would ever get that organization to take to the new command-and-control dynamics." This was especially true with those same people remaining in control positions when they were brought into a fundamentally different approach. "It just wasn't going to happen," Kusin concludes. He correctly diagnosed that if the board indeed wanted cultural change, he would need to make structural and people changes while at the same time establishing a concerted program to address the cultural legacies of the organization.

HOW TO ASSESS A CULTURE

The words that most companies use to describe their cultures usually sound comforting: *customer focus, excellence, teamwork, shareholder value, entrepreneurial, innovative, responsible corporate behavior, passion, integrity.* But of course, these kinds of words don't necessarily translate into real behavior in real companies. How people actually go about their work, how decisions are made, who gets promoted, how employees interact with one another, what motivates them—these are the things that really count. What makes things especially tricky, especially for an outsider, is that as with real cultures of any type— from corporations to schools, towns, and even nations—most of the really important rules are not written down.

The place to start assessing a culture is to listen, really listen, to how employees describe a place. We believe that within most generalizations there lies an inner core of truth. Just as certain distinguishing characteristics are common and generally true about certain countries—"Germans are regimented and well organized," or "Italians are passionate and creative," or "Chinese are entrepreneurial and ambitious"—so too with company labels. These unofficial but generally accepted monikers often accurately define a company's personality and modus operandi. *General Electric is all about general managers being on top of and delivering the numbers. Microsoft lives for writing killer software by the smartest engineers who will go to extraordinary lengths to win. Dell is analytical and measures, systematizes, and optimizes everything. You can't rise to the top of MTV if you are not a creative. At Amgen, it's all about the scientists in R&D. The core of Merrill Lynch is its army of retail brokers. You succeed at Cisco Systems by being associated with customer success stories. True Brown UPSers start as package delivery drivers.*

Paul Pressler refers to Gap Inc. as "a merchant-centric culture." Gillette, before present CEO Jim Kilts started shaking it up, was a product-driven organization; so fascinated was it with its own inventions that analysts said it lost sight of whether they satisfied the needs of people who might buy them. After inventing and literally creating new markets from the walkie-talkie to the cell phone over its seventy-five-year history, Motorola too developed an engineering-driven, "build it and they will come" culture.

One of the important points regarding assessing the culture is to think through the implications of trying to change it. When Merrill Lynch appointed Stanley O'Neal as CEO, his lack of history on the retail brokerage side of the business was an important signal that the firm was ripe for change. Amid a chaotic financial services industry environment buffeted by the bursting of the tech bubble, the shutdown of the IPO market, the recession, and 9/11, O'Neal's relative outsider status from the cultural and historical core of the operation freed him up to lead an aggressive and ultimately highly successful restructuring. He unapologetically cut billions in costs, shaped the management team to his preferences, streamlined decision making, and ultimately repositioned the firm to come out of the recession a leaner, meaner fighting machine.

HOW THINGS WORK AROUND HERE

New leaders have to tune their antennae to the covert signals and the invisible knowledge networks that are the nervous system of an organization. These unwritten protocols—as well as the people who maintain them—and the unspoken taboos and conventions are wrapped up in the question everyone asks: "How do things really work around here?"

Even if you're an insider, different ways of "how things work around here" may await you at your new level, poised to trip you up. "Here" might be a different psychological location. There could be someone who serves as an unofficial gatekeeper for information about the organization, or a different "go to" person who can get things done, or someone who's regarded as a backstabber.

For outsiders, coming into a different culture is akin to landing at Charles de Gaulle Airport after studying high school French (and vowing to speak only French while on your trip). You'll hopefully know enough to get through baggage claim and customs and maybe even buy an espresso. But the subtleties of how to buy a phone card, take the RER into Paris, and get into the right restaurant may elude you. "How things work around here" becomes a constant test of whether you really get it.

LEARNING THE LAY OF THE LAND

Most new leaders instinctively know they must be on the lookout for the cultural norms that define a company's accepted behavior. It is difficult, however, to delve deeply enough into how the organization really works or how different people will react to different actions. This is especially true in the early days of a new assignment when there are many other seemingly more urgent pressures.

How do you learn the lay of the land?

First, during the countdown period, conduct a cultural assessment, drawing on all your sources and other preparation. For example, Jim Kilts realized that the culture at Gillette needed to be changed even before he walked in the door. From his external competitive review, detailed financial analysis, board interviews, and meetings with company executives, he saw that the company was underperforming. "When I asked the HR chief to take me through an overview of how we were rating our people," he says, "I was told that seventy-three percent were rated as 'exceeds expectations.' I asked him how we could be exceeding expectations when we hadn't grown the business for the past five years on either the top or the bottom line."

The numbers indicated to Kilts that employees' performance evaluation wasn't connected to results. "We were working on effort instead of results," he diagnosed. More recently Gillette rated 70 percent of its employees as "meets expectations." Only 20 percent exceeded them.

Follow Kilts's example of doing your homework and getting external and internal input. Solicit views and opinions from people who know the organization. The universe of constituents you tapped to evaluate the health of the business—the members of the board, the management team and employees, customers, suppliers and strategic partners, members of the financial and regulatory communities, and the media—is also a good source to get a sense of its culture. As you learn more, keep trying to sharpen and improve your questions; remember the best questions lead to the best answers.

- What is the essence of what the company stands for?
- How is it really different from its competitors?
- What do the people who are most successful share in common?
- What are the common traits among those who have failed?
- Who are the five most respected people in the organization and why?
- What are the characteristics of the organization's failures or missed opportunities?

Ask these kinds of questions and their logical follow-ups to the smartest people you can find, and important patterns will quickly develop.

 ORDS ARE POWERFUL CLUES

Compare too the words used to describe a company and those that might best describe your own personality and work style. Gillette, for example, under Kilts's predecessor, had a reputation of being "gentle" and "paternalistic," as described by *Fortune*. Kilts himself, however, is usually described as anything but. The adjectives that current and former colleagues most frequently use are *disciplined, demanding,* and *intense*. This verbiage alone portends a potential culture clash. But at least if a cultural gap is identified, it can be bridged or even closed over time.

You can learn a lot about a place by paying attention to its words. The way people in an organization speak to others inside and those outside says a lot about how it sees itself. At McKinsey, it's about problem solving and client impact. At Capital One, it's about modeling credit risk. At Cisco Systems, it's customer wins and "Show me the money," according to Gary Bridge, leader of the company's Global Internet Business Solutions Group. "They use that expression here every five minutes," Bridge says. "What that means is, 'I heard what you said, I sort of like what you said, but I don't really believe you.' I'm being heavy-handed, but when they say, 'Show me the money,' that's it."

Bridge came to Cisco from IBM, whose language contained so many code words and acronyms that Gerstner recalled his early days when he would sit through meetings and frequently have no idea what a presenter was referring to. He'd stop the speaker and "ask for a plain-English translation." Gerstner compiled a lexicon of *IBMisms*. Many of them have since become part of standard American business-speak: "boil the ocean," "level-set," "take it offline," "hard stop," and "pushback," to name a few.

Words aren't the only indicators of an organization's culture. Superficial though it may sound, clothes also send some of the most obvious signals. For example, when Jim McNerney became CEO of 3M, starched shirts still prevailed at the top, while most of the employees dressed in workplace casual. For McNerney, the formal attire was a clue of the disconnection between management and the rest of the organization.

YOUR INNER ANTHROPOLOGIST

Take on the role of a sleuth uncovering clues, or perhaps more accurately, an anthropologist examining and describing a different society or tribe. Look for clues in the company's cafeteria and hallways. How do people dress? How do they communicate? Do they look happy? Notice the office architecture and the kind of furniture and artwork that fill the offices. Does it create an informal and upbeat physical environment? Do the offices have lots of windows and open spaces that encourage easy interaction among employees, or do they have walled hallways and closed doors that portend a more rigid structure or hierarchy?

Dan Kerpelman, president of Kodak's Health Imaging Group, had been a top executive at GE Healthcare. He made sure to be sensitive and address cultural issues when he spoke with colleagues after he joined the company. "There were a lot of questions about my style and expectations," he says. "People in Health Imaging wanted to prove that they had as much knowledge, passion, and skill for the industry as the next company. I therefore spent a lot of time pointing out the positive things about Kodak Health Imaging, which I said ultimately led me to vote with my feet and come there. I felt that was the strongest statement I could make about my confidence in the company."

Kerpelman recognized the need to do things differently early on, but he made sure to institute his changes within the parameters of Kodak's "respectful" culture. "I spent a lot of time nurturing the culture of this business," he explains. "It wasn't about the GE culture or my personal culture or that everything about Kodak Health Imaging needed to be changed. It was taking the best of what was in place, feeling out the gaps, and bringing in what I learned from prior jobs, along with some intuition and opinions."

Fitting in well enough to the Kodak culture was an important requirement for ultimately transforming it, Kerpelman realized, so he did something smart and highly recommended: he used a coach. His coach was a long-serving top company executive, Michael Morley, Kodak's now recently retired chief administrative officer, who also oversaw human resources. Kerpelman says that "Mike was a real consigliere to top management." Morley had assumed the coaching role with all new senior executives. "I found I had monthly one-on-one meetings prescheduled with him and quickly came to appreciate the value of his advice in how to deal with personalities and cultural artifacts and protocols. I could ask him, 'Mike, I have a sticky issue. What's the proper way to marshal it through the Kodak corporate culture without stepping on too many toes?'"

Kerpelman also relied on other GE alumni at Kodak to decipher Kodak jargon: "Someone would explain something in Kodak-ese about the 'GOLD' process and someone from GE would say, 'Session C,' and it was 'Okay, I got it.'" The translation went the other way, too. "Sometimes I would try to explain a concept and use GE terms. I would go to a former GE-er and say, 'I need to say this. Would you translate it for me?' "

Even though it's crucial for a new leader to show that he or she fits into the culture and "gets" it, the paradox is that you don't want to settle in too comfortably if the culture needs modification. But of course, changing a culture is never as simple as ordering it to be so, especially if the organization is very proud of its traditions. And what organization isn't?

THE EXPEDITION OF OUTWARD BOUND

When Outward Bound USA hired John Read to become president in 2002, it had already gone through several top leadership turnovers. Read's predecessor lasted a mere four months.

The former CEO of Heavy Duty Holdings, a global supplier of components to the North American heavy truck market, Read was also a veteran of numerous Outward Bound courses and chaired one of the independent Outward Bound schools. Read generally knew what to expect, and he knew he would have to prove that he "got" it.

"This culture is powerful," Read says. "It grows from the inside out and has the ability to spit out leaders who don't fit into it. It's comparable to the culture of a manufacturing plant." Although in some ways Outward Bound is exactly the opposite of a manufacturing plant ("No one was waiting for me to issue directives"), in other ways it was very much the same. "They were waiting to see what I did and whether I 'got it,' or whether, as my last two predecessors had done, I would fail to insinuate myself into the organization and its priorities as the organization saw them."

Read recognized the critical point that even if the organization had the wrong priorities, he had to be accepted and fit into the culture before he could start transforming it. "I think I was right in very quickly making some visible changes to the national office to bring spending and staffing into alignment with its means," he says. "There were a couple of people here who had been in place for a long time and needed a change. Their departure reinforced the message that changes in Outward Bound were needed and would start here.

"Decentralized organizations like ours generally don't react well to directives," Read adds. "It's more of a cat-herding exercise than command and control. I went to business school to learn how to keep the club in the closet until needed. In this job, there's no club and no closet that I can locate, so it's more a matter of organizing the data to make visible what the problems are, so the people who have the authority have no recourse but to face up to the real issues. In this kind of culture, expressing the facts with data succinctly can drive action.

"Coming into an organization having been a customer or having had some other relationship can be an effective way of determining whether you've got something to offer and are a good fit. My predecessor had great experience with other relevant organizations but no experience with Outward Bound."

One of the strategies Read pursued for fitting into the culture—which would then provide him with the ability to change it—was establishing and consistently communicating a linkage between his new role and the impact that Outward Bound had made upon him. "I was fortunate to have had an Outward Bound course that changed my life," he says, "and my own experience gives me a genuine enthusiasm for the impact we have on young people." This theme provides a framework to work with the organization. Read adds, "I want our commitment to change young lives to express itself in fifty different ways in the work we're trying to do here. And I think that if we are successful, we can hold the attention not just of the trustees but of the instructors and staff as well." His personal experience with the program provides not only additional opportunity to demonstrate that he "gets it" but something else as well: "By taking a course every year, I get to recharge my batteries and check the alignment between what we're trying to do here and what we do in the field."

Read was also conscious of how he and other leaders in Outward Bound were perceived, which varied with different audiences. Outward Bound has expanded well beyond its early wilderness orientation. "When I came into the job, the national board viewed me as a 'wilderness guy,' and they were generally right in that wilderness is what I knew. I had a lot to learn about Outward Bound urban centers and our school reform program. But a school executive director would look at me and say, 'You're not a wilderness guy, you're a suit.'

"My response became, 'Bruce [one of directors of schools], I may not be a wilderness guy, but if an instructor looks way, way up, she can barely make you out, and you're as much a suit to her as I am to you.' He still chuckles about that, and we both know it's right. It establishes a rapport to know that in manufacturing parlance the differences between a foreman and a plant manager are like the differences between a plant manager and corporate. Equally in my business experience, if one wants to understand how customers are feeling, go visit your purchasing department and listen to them yowl and hoot about suppliers. Nonprofits have customers and are themselves customers of other organizations. But they may not think in these terms, let alone as customers and suppliers within an internal workflow. Being able to translate my own work experience into language and terms that relate to the mission-organization relationship here has helped to establish common ground.

"I'm beginning to learn how to turn the complex processes of Outward Bound back on themselves to get change done," Read says. His approach to organizational change sounds suspiciously like the philosophy of an Outward Bound course: Bring disparate groups together; let them discover how much they have in common; then, over several months and with good information, have the group chart their own courses. Offer plenty of support from headquarters, but let the group lead the effort itself. "We're a lot further along in making change by having it be 'of' the system," Read says. "And the school boards would say that they're leading the change, not the national board."

DEVELOPING PEOPLE AT THE HOME OF BARBIE

Bob Eckert took a different course of action at Mattel. While his predecessor had presided over splashy acquisitions and new businesses—and a plummeting stock price—Eckert looked to Mattel's past to fix the present and burnish its future. "Mattel evolved from a small, family-run company to a successful *Fortune* 500, number-one-in-our-category company, to a company that had gotten off track for a few years," he says. "I saw my job as an opportunity to influence the culture, to go back to the old days and even more.

"Literally on my first hour on the job, I talked about developing people. Mattel has not been seen as a people-developing machine; it's not GE. We really didn't have Human Resources 101 well defined at Mattel, and we've been working hard to do that. I spend a lot of my time on management education, which didn't really exist when I got here. In my first year, we built a human resources strategic plan that we're still executing that talks about the sort of people we want to attract, hire, retain, and develop. We've put our top hundred fifty people through an executive leadership seminar, we have entry-level programs, e-learning initiatives, and a classroom in a building right next to headquarters, where we do formal teaching. We do management development from soup to nuts. Ten years from now, if we're successful, folks will say, 'Look at the kind of people who come out of this place.'

"We also needed to focus on creativity. We developed a skunkworks to train creative people on how to be more creative. It cost only a few thousand dollars, and the class project turned out to be a new product that's been very successful."

FIGHTING TO CHANGE A LEGACY CULTURE

The issue of trying to transform a culture, especially a deeply embedded one from many years of the corporate equivalent of geological layering, extends well beyond your first hundred days. Sometimes it takes years. The critical point for the early days in a new role is to be highly sensitized to the issue, make an effective cultural assessment, and plant the seeds for the long-term change you are committed to achieving.

Arthur Martinez confronted an intractable legacy culture at Sears when he became chief executive of Sears Merchandise Group in 1992 and once again when he became chairman and CEO of Sears, Roebuck & Co. in 1995; he remained CEO until 2000. "I was described as the first outside hire since General Robert E. Wood," he says. (Wood left rival Montgomery Ward, where he had been vice president, in 1924 and soon became president and, eventually, chairman, a position he held until 1959.)

When Martinez came to Sears from Saks Fifth Avenue, where he had been vice chairman, Sears's retail business was in a tailspin, the catalog business was hemorrhaging money, and the company as a whole had posted more than five straight years of disappointing financial performance. "There was no question that there was a burning platform," Martinez recalls. "The fact that there was a burning platform by itself should have given permission to invite massive cultural change. But we were suffering from a classic insider syndrome, where the only reference point was what we had done five years ago," Martinez explains. He set out to change that.

How well did he succeed?

"Oh, boy." Martinez sighs when asked about the results of his efforts to change Sears's culture. "I thought at the time I was doing better than I actually was. In retrospect I would give myself a C-plus grade on meaningfully impacting the culture of the company. It remains one of the most profound challenges that legacy companies like Sears have to face.

"The positive energy that came of out my early days made some people—and me—think that we had that culture issue fixed. The unfortunate fact, though, was that there was deep-seated resistance to change—a feeling of 'This guy will be gone in three years and I've had my job for twenty, so why should I change? With three hundred thousand employees, the problem is inevitably in the middle. It was relatively easy to get the top management in line—if not, I could fire them—but I couldn't do that far into the organization. I couldn't personally determine, for example, who in the tax or logistics department was obstructing progress."

Martinez started with a bang, closing 125 retail stores and laying off 35,000 employees out of a then-payroll of 325,000—and in the process earning the nickname "the Ax from Saks." But a combination of inertia and resistance hobbled his efforts: "It became harder as we went along, especially as our momentum slowed down, because people started to revert to old behavior patterns. Rather than the new culture taking hold and accelerating momentum, after four years it started to slow down, and I realized we hadn't changed all that much. We had calmed the surface, but underneath there was massive reluctance to profound organizational change."

Alan Lacy, Sears's former CFO who succeeded Martinez in 2000, points out that a hundred-year-old legacy can also have its good points: "We had a culture that wanted to do the right thing and people who wanted to do a good job for their customers. But we inherited a culture that had become comfortable in losing competitive advantage and that tolerated things not working far more than anyone should. Yet ironically, it also didn't feel as if it had the ability to change.

"Because we had such an illogically designed structure, no one had any accountability or authority. As we transition to a new structure, accountability is very clear. The metrics are clear. The expectation that people will improve their performance is there. And in fact, the teamwork environment is much better, and it's a much more customer-driven culture than before.

"I thought I got good traction from the beginning, and it continued to build. We have made wholesale changes to the business; we have one-third fewer salaried management than we did eighteen months ago. We had gotten used to running the business with an average group of people. Coupled with good talent management, that meant we could quickly force-rank our employees and figure out who was in the bottom third, and largely speaking, we got rid of the bottom third pretty quickly.

"When you go through that degree of structural change," Lacy adds, "in hindsight it turned out to be more of an opportunity for cultural change than I thought. We disoriented people so much that we couldn't go back; things were so different that people lost most of their reference points, so they couldn't regress to the old ways because there was nothing remaining to regress to. In fact, we could accelerate the pace of change and make the change stick better."

CHANGE LEADERS SOMETIMES TAKE ARROWS IN THE BACK

Why has Lacy been able to make progress while Martinez found it more difficult to get traction? Gary Kusin made a comment referring to his predecessor at the top of Kinko's that could just as easily apply to the situation at Sears or any other company with a strong cultural legacy and the exalted memory of a founder. "There are situations where you have such a strong founder and culture that the first outside leader kills himself trying to break all the molds," Kusin says. "He may do all the right things and still lose. I believe you can make a really good argument that in our case the first guy in here was doomed, no matter who it was. And there are those situations where you never want to be the first guy in; you would rather be the second guy in."

Still, whether first in or second, being a change leader is a perilous proposition. "New change agents don't make it through the entire process most of the time," says Robert Tillman, former CEO of retail giant Lowe's. "They normally get assassinated because they build up so much ill will among other people within the corporation that they subsequently are ostracized."

The bottom line is that in order to minimize your risk, you need to really familiarize yourself with the subtleties and idiosyncrasies of the culture, understand the power bases, recognize that a mandate from above may not automatically ensure a mandate from below, and not try to change the world in your first hundred days. Patience is often an essential virtue when it comes to cultural transformation at a large scale.

At Schneider National the culture change was done at a deliberate pace, carefully orchestrated by a management team that sought to change itself as a way to change the organization. CEO Chris Lofgren explains, "From the company's roots and even into the early nineties, we were a very strong operational company. Our predominant product was the truckload product. Over time we have broadened our service offering. Part of our challenge was that there was an almost exclusive practice of promotion from within. As a result, we didn't have all the leaders or the diversity of perspective we would need five years from now. To accomplish the growth trajectory we put forth, we couldn't develop the necessary human capital quickly enough; so we would need to attract them from the outside and retain them. It's critical to the health of any high-growth organization to do this in a balanced way. Balance is paramount when bringing talent from the outside, because there are a lot of capable people in the organization. So it's more of a rounding out than a wholesale change."

Lofgren himself epitomizes that rounding out of the company's culture. He came to Schneider as an outsider in 1994; today he is its CEO.

AN INVITATION TO CHANGE

As Lou Gerstner says, "Changing the attitude and behavior of hundreds of thousands of people is very, very hard to accomplish. You can't simply give a couple of speeches or write a new credo for the company and declare that the new culture has taken hold. You can't mandate it, can't engineer it.

"What you *can* do is create the conditions for transformation. You can provide incentives. You can define the marketplace realities and goals. But at some point you have to trust. In fact, in the end, management doesn't change culture. Management invites the work-force itself to change the culture."

There are many ways to word that invitation to make it even more compelling.

Adopt New Measures of Success.

One of the most effective ways to get people to change their behavior is to change their measures of success. This step can be done in the relatively early days of a new leadership position. To instill a perfor-mance culture at Gillette, for example, Jim Kilts instituted a review system that was linked directly to the P&L and market share and backed it up with a robust incentive program. These are not general objectives. Instead, managers are told, "Here's your budget target, and here's your market share target. They're metrics that can be measured. So if you're hitting your numbers, you win, and if you win, you'll get paid more in bonus than in the past. And if you don't win, you're going to get significantly less," Kilts explains.

Choosing the measures, defining the relevant market, and estab-lishing performance metrics is more easily done in some businesses than others. In consumer products, such as Gillette's razors and Du-racell batteries, the markets are well defined and carefully measured by firms such as A. C. Nielsen and IRI. In other businesses, however, the lines are not as clear.

At Gap Inc., for example, Paul Pressler realized in his early days that the management team needed a common set of metrics to create more shared accountability for overall corporate performance and shareholder value. Existing metrics focused on performance within each brand, without creating a strong link to corporate financial goals. This approach reflected the company's historically decentralized ap-proach to managing the business. As a result, the management team was accustomed to maximizing performance within its respective divi-sions, but was less focused on ensuring that what was good for a par-ticular brand was also good for the company as a whole. While this decentralized approach had worked well for the company throughout most of its history, it had unintentionally created too much internal competition and ineffective use of corporate resources and capital. It also contributed to the Gap, Banana Republic, and Old Navy brands converging their designs and going after the same customer segments. To change behavior, Pressler implemented a new compensation structure for his executive leadership team that incorporated incentives for corporate performance as well as divisional results. "I got a lot of resistance initially," Pressler recalls. "People asked, 'How am I to be held accountable for something I don't control?'" Pressler's response: "You do. We're a team, sharing responsibility and accountability for what's best for our brands and for our company. We will set our agenda and determine our priorities together." The result: "We still had to learn how to work effectively as a team, but this helped us begin to change our thinking and our actions."

Institute New Operating Processes.

You can also encourage and reinforce the new behaviors by making changes in the operating process, such as instituting regular staff meetings with clear-cut agendas. As described in Chapter 3, Ed Breen set up what he calls the "Jack Welch calendar" at Tyco: consistent operating meetings with all the lines of business, a leadership development process, and a strategy process. "You spend eight to ten hours with a team, pounding questions at them, and you learn really quickly who knows what and who's behind," he says.

This is in addition to the hour-long staff meeting every Monday morning with all the direct reports to discuss what's going on, spotlight items of major importance, and follow up on the previous week's to-do list. "The team has come to really value it," says Breen. "They feel more involved and get to know what everyone else is doing. And it's a great way to spread best practices."

Choose a New Management Team.

Making changes in your management team is another way to begin changing the culture. This requires a delicate touch. Many leaders coming from the outside bring a trusted confidant who can leverage and amplify the change strategy. Jim Kilts, for example, routinely rides with a three-person posse composed of longtime associates Peter Klein, who became senior vice president of strategy and business development; John Manfredi, senior vice president of corporate affairs; and Joe Schena, vice president of planning. Gary Kusin refused to take on the top job at Kinko's unless he could bring along Dan Connors as strategy chief.

It is, however, all too easy to create resentment if you bring in a personal SWAT team. When Jim McNerney left GE to become CEO of 3M, fears that 3M would become "3E" were somewhat alleviated because he did not arrive with an army of GE executives in tow.

Set New Expectations.

You can also invite the management team itself to make the necessary changes. When Bill Schleyer became CEO of Adelphia Communications, the troubled cable company had to change its culture. It was in bankruptcy, and criminal charges had been filed against the former CEO. Almost exactly on the date that would mark his first hundred days on the job, Schleyer threw a metaphorical bucket of cold water on the senior management at Adelphia to get them to take notice of the new order. "We had our first meeting of forty members of senior management in April 2000, to roll out our strategy. Under the previous CEO, Adelphia made all decisions at the top. In fact, managers were given incentives not to make decisions and were reprimanded when they did. I said, 'From now on you will be held accountable for results against the aggressive targets we've set. If you can't operate in that environment, you need to get out of the room right now.' That's a strong statement: This is the behavior we need, and if you can't handle it, you need to leave. But we can't be as patient as we normally would like to be. Urgency is one of our core values now. We have to achieve industry-level performance in short order. If we emerge from bankruptcy and aren't operating at industry level in terms of performance and profit margins, we'll be vulnerable."

Identify Change Leaders.

You can search out the people who want to change and make them your microphone to broadcast the new philosophy. When Gary Bridge arrived at Cisco Systems to lead the company's highly regarded Global Internet Business Solutions Group, he found "a couple of raging wars going on. People wouldn't share resources and were spending as much time knocking each other down as they were building up their own case. The team had taken control of the part of their lives they could control, and they'd gone back into their silos." So he assessed which of the top leaders shared his vision and would have the credibility of the broader organization to become leaders by example and spokespeople for the new approach. This worked, according to Bridge, because "if you went below the top management level, there was this really skilled group of people that hungered for something new. I also spent a tremendous amount of time on getting the team out of their proverbial caves into common spaces, establishing a common vocabulary so they could learn to listen to each other. I made sure that I didn't arbitrarily join sides but that all of my decisions were very fact-based, and I always explained why I did what I did." And these messages were similarly expressed by the other leaders of the division. "Team building was number one and getting people in proper assignments with the proper metrics. Number two, I was consistently told that Cisco is a place that lives on stories of your customer successes. It's a customer-obsessed company. And this is one of its hallmark strengths."

Lead by Example.
Critical to all aspects of leadership and to cultural change in particular is modeling the behavior you want others to emulate. "If employees don't see the key changes in what you say and do and in your behaviors and mannerisms, it's hard to change the culture," says Tyco's Ed Breen. "The culture reverts to what it was. If you're coming into a situation where you need to change culture or reinvigorate it or, in my case, create one, you'd better be demonstrating it real quickly."

 AKE YOUR FIRST MOVES COUNT

Another requirement of successfully starting to create cultural change in the first hundred days is to recognize that your first moves are important signals as to how you would like things "to work around here" going forward.

One of Gary Bridge's first moves was focused on modifying the operating process at Cisco. He changed the hours of operation to break his group's San Jose, California–centric view of the world. "It's absolutely imperative that I not just say that we're going to behave globally but that we *behave* globally," he says. "Before I got here, senior staff meetings were held at four P.M. because it was most convenient. I said, 'Do you realize that you're asking somebody in Europe to be up at midnight or one o'clock, depending on whether it's Daylight Savings Time, to talk about really critical things like personnel decisions and promotions?'

"I started holding meetings on a rotating basis. Seven A.M. is the new time in San Jose to have a meeting, because it's already ten A.M. on the East Coast and they're almost finished with their day in Europe. This single move was viewed by the Europeans as a huge vote of confidence, that they were important and that we cared what they did."

Making a change in people's daily work schedules is significant enough, but there are even bolder ways to make your first moves count—such as attacking one of the core cultural foundations of the organization.

REIGNITING INNOVATION AT 3M

One of Jim McNerney's significant early moves at 3M involved altering the McKnight's Principles, based on the ideas of 3M's longest-serving president, William L. McKnight,* who was as revered at 3M as Thomas Watson Sr. was at IBM. McKnight had flattened the organization and made sure that management knew to get out of the

* William McKnight was 3M's fourth president, from 1929 to 1949, and chairman of the board from 1949 to 1966.

way of innovative entrepreneurial spirit. "Mistakes will be made," he said, "but if the man is essentially right himself, the mistakes he makes are not so serious in the long run as the mistakes management makes if it is dictatorial."

One of McNight's Principles was the "30%/4" rule: 30 percent of 3M's sales each year must result from products introduced in the past four years. It was a tough decision, but McNerney felt that the "30%/4" rule had become something of a hollow metric. "To make that number, some managers were resorting to rather dubious 'innovations,' such as pink Post-it Notes rather than yellow. It became a game. What could you do to get a new SKU created? We had a lot of products, a lot of SKUs, but no growth. People were declaring victory at the end of the year from having met that metric, but the company wasn't benefiting.

"We had to refocus commercialization activity to result in business growth, not just a proliferation of things that sat in our warehouse. I was most nervous about it because "30%/4" was at the core of 3M's mythology. The top hundred executives spent a lot of time talking about it. Now we focus more on incremental business growth than on the number of new products. That seems like a subtle distinction, but it leads to dramatically different investment results. You tend to invest in bigger things, things that are going to go after new businesses rather than things that just create extensions and flankers for stuff you've already got. It's a dramatic change in the way we invest."

Another McKnight's Principle was the "15%" rule, which allowed technical people to devote 15 percent of their time to projects of their own choosing, without needing the approval of management. It too was changed; "15%" supported the environment of "Systematic Innovation," which had spawned some of 3M's most serendipitous and successful inventions, such as Scotchguard, the result of a 3M scientist who spilled chemicals on her tennis shoe, and Post-it Notes, the brainchild of a researcher who wanted a better way to mark the pages of his church hymnal and couldn't find an alternative use for a "permanently temporary" adhesive. Stories about these and scores of other innovations were part of 3M's cultural mythology.

McNerney's example underscores the leader's opportunity to act as a catalyst for cultural change, especially in the early days when people are most open to change. What made his actions so effective were that besides assessing and communicating the need for cultural change, and talking about it with a broad group of managers, he implemented concrete changes within long-established organizational and cultural structures that allowed people to change in the desired ways.

In the early days of McNerney's tenure, some employees worried that 3M's famously idiosyncratic devotion to innovation would be stamped out. McNerney was acutely aware of the fear that he would impose the very dictatorial management that McKnight had warned against. "I think we're world class at the front end of the [innovation] process. If I dampen our enthusiasm for that, I've really screwed it up." But he is equally aware of how the past can hobble the present and cripple the future. "The mythology here is 'Against all odds, I ended up with Post-it Notes.' Mythology supports a lot of important and good behavior," he says. "But when it becomes apocryphal, it becomes dysfunctional. You want to get people onto a more reality-based way of looking at the world."

What was McNerney's own assessment of 3M and its culture? "We don't have a broken business equation here. We just need to learn to do things faster. . . . I'm not trying to change the engine," he says, comparing himself to an auto mechanic. "I'm trying to put in a new chassis, a new clutch, and a new turbo, but it's still going to be a car when I'm done. It's not going to be a boat."

Two years into McNerney's tenure, 3M became leaner (some 6,500 of its 75,000 workers were laid off) but still recognizably 3M. McNerney says, "I did change the rhythm of the company. We spend more time talking about results, and we have more meetings that focus on delivering what you say you're going to deliver. It's pretty simple stuff. And I established that very fast."

DEFINE WHICH ASPECTS OF THE CULTURE TO CHANGE

In the spring of 1994 Lou Gerstner convened his first senior management meeting at IBM with the goal of creating cultural change. He wanted to motivate the group to focus its talents and efforts outside the company, not on one another. In a presentation to the 420 top managers, Gerstner decided to use a graphic depiction of the behavioral changes that would be necessary to achieve this goal and create the results that would be necessary to survive:

IBM'S REQUIRED BEHAVIORAL CHANGE:

From	To
Product out (I tell you)	Customer in (in the shoes of the customer)
Do it my way	Do it the customers' way (provide real service)
Manage to morale	Manage to success
Decisions based on anecdotes & myths	Decisions based on facts & data
Relationship-driven	Performance-driven & measured
Conformity (politically correct)	Diversity of ideas and opinions
Attack the people	Attack the process (ask why, *not* who)
Looking good is equal to or more important than doing good	Accountability (always move the rocks)
United States (Armonk) dominance	Global sharing
Rule-driven	Principle-driven
Value me (the silo)	Value us (the whole)
Analysis paralysis (100+%)	Make decisions and move forward with urgency
Not invented here	Learning organization
Fund everything	Prioritize

LEVITY, AOL, AND HAVING YOUR CAR TOWED IN NEW YORK CITY

Even when most people in the organization welcome change, there are bound to be areas of resistance embedded within the culture. It is essential to deal with it both sympathetically and dispassionately. Another tactic to deploy, if you are so bold, is humor.

That's how Jon Miller approached the thorny problem of rebuilding the badly burned bridges between America Online and the other divisions of Time Warner when he became CEO of AOL in August 2002. Not only did Warner Bros., Time Inc., HBO, Turner Broadcasting, and Time Warner Cable feel betrayed by the broken promises of the AOL merger, they had developed palpable anger over the dismissive and dictatorial style that Miller's predecessors had used in dealing with their executives.

One of Miller's first tasks when he started was to meet with the top executives of the other Time Warner divisions. Before he could even start to talk about how their businesses and AOL could work together, he had to find a way to begin to repair the damage. He described walking into conference rooms in New York and Los Angeles and being "greeted" by fellow executives with fire in their eyes.

Miller quickly figured out how to start these meetings on a less antagonistic note. He explains: "I asked, 'Have you ever had your car towed in New York City? They tow it to a huge garage on the West Side of Manhattan. You go there, and you're in a bad mood like everyone else waiting there to get their car back. You're waiting in a long line, and when you finally get to the clerk, you're ready to take his head off. But there's a sign in the window: *The people here did not tow your car. They are here to help you get your car back. If you cooperate, you will get your car back sooner.* Then I said, 'I did not tow your car. I am here to help you get your car back. If you cooperate, you will get your car back sooner.' "

With the pressure released, Miller was then able to start talking about moving forward: "I talked about how we were here to add value to what they did and they were here to add value to what we did. It was not an 'I win, you lose' situation. And that would be the framework in which we would engage and how we would conduct ourselves as a business."

TIMING IS EVERYTHING

Creating the conditions for a cultural transformation takes all the tools at your disposal. You can't, for example, command an internally focused culture to magically metamorphose into one that canonizes its customers. You have to nudge, suggest, cajole, and ultimately convince people that the new environment you're proposing really is the best one for the business and, perhaps more important, for themselves. That takes time—and a good sense of timing.

Some leaders look back on their first hundred days and say, "If I could do it again, I wouldn't hesitate so long to make those key people changes or that strategic move." Others were glad they exercised restraint. In most cases the timing is dependent on the situation.

"I think all bets are off [in terms of patience] if the business is badly broken," Jim McNerney says. "If the business is broken, the management team doesn't have credibility, so you've got to make changes from day one. If the business isn't broken, as was the case with 3M, the issue is optimizing an already decent business model. You've got time. And if you move too quickly, all you'll accomplish is that you'll have to redo it eighteen months later.

"It depends on the situation," he concludes. "If it's a disaster, you will always regret not moving quicker. If it isn't, you tend to regret moving too quickly."

"There's a balance between listening and learning, and when to stop learning and take action," Dan Kerpelman recalls of his early weeks at Kodak. "But it wasn't like throwing a switch based on a schedule. When you had the knowledge and confidence to make a decision, whether it was week one or month one, you made the decision.

I had such an opportunity within my first couple of days at Kodak. I went to Monthly Operating Review, a sacred operating mechanism on managing the P&L, thought it was inefficiently run, and immediately made a decision to change the meeting and the mechanism. Instead of the thirty-six-page book that was being used, I developed and issued a three-page template. After all, I believe that if you can't say it in three pages, we're into a level of detail that's beyond clarity. And I cut the time in half."

If you have a company in crisis, you have the burning platform to help bring about change, and in such cases dramatic decisions are often more acceptable. This remains true even in the most rigid of cultures. In fact, Lou Gerstner claims that his greatest ally in breaking free from the past was IBM's own precipitous collapse. But he also knew that the task of shaking people out of their stupor and getting them "to think and act collaboratively, as hungry, curious self-starters," would take at least five years—and even then, he confesses, he underestimated the time required.

At the other end of the spectrum, if you have an organization that's generally working pretty well, you want to protect the part that's working by going a little slow, as McNerney did.

These are the two extremes. If your organization is neither in crisis nor working smoothly but somewhere in the middle, you will inevitably wonder which way to lean: Do you take action while you have the permission, or do you dampen your response, to exercise patience? If there's no crisis calling for change, should you create one?

Steve Bennett thinks the answer is yes. When he became the head of Intuit, the company had a long track record of good performance, so no urgent need for change was apparent. But both Bennett and the board of directors felt that the company's performance was nowhere near its potential. Bennett looked for a way to galvanize everyone into action without "crying wolf."

"When I started," he explains, "I said, 'My job is to deliver for all three stakeholders—employees, customers, and shareholders—and delivering both in the short term and the long term.' I went to the employees and asked questions: How are we doing? What do you feel good about? What do you not feel good about? And our employees back then, as they continue to do today, overwhelmed me with insight, feedback, and perspective.

"Then I went and saw customers too and asked them the same questions. I made the voice of our employees and the voice of our customers the platform for change. Their voice and their desire to get better is what created a burning platform for us to change."

PACE YOURSELF

Just remember that too much change can break the culture—or more likely destroy the change-maker. You have to pace yourself and continually assess the tolerance of the organization. "I haven't fully come to a comfortable synthesis of doing what I want to do and figuring out how to work with more effectiveness in a hugely democratic culture," confesses Harvard University president Lawrence Summers. "My footing has not been perfect. Occasionally I'll get too far out ahead of democracy, and then I'll have to do more democracy than I would have done if I had just moved a little more slowly. If I'd moved more delicately and democratically, I could have gotten to where I was going faster. I now know that I set myself back by being too impatient."

Taking on and leading cultural change is one of a new leader's most important and challenging tasks, but it is also one of the most delicate. Now that you know how to plant the proper seeds in the first hundred days, it's time to turn your attention to the next layer in the pyramid, building a productive working relationship with your board or your boss.

ONCLUSION

TEN GUIDELINES FOR STARTING TO TRANSFORM THE CULTURE

1. As a new leader, work to understand the culture of the organization, diagnose how great a change is required, and take the right steps to start making the transformation.

2. Recognize that many new leaders fail because they cannot make headway against an intransigent culture, pushing too hard in the wrong ways, resulting in the proverbial "body rejecting the organ."

3. The way to start assessing a culture is to listen and observe. How do people really describe the place? Words are powerful clues—within most generalizations there lies an inner core of truth. Look for physical evidence—how people dress, how they communicate, how happy they look, and the kind of furniture and artwork that fill the offices.

4. Next, identify how "things work around here." Hunt for the knowledge networks, key influencers, decision-making protocols, and unwritten and unspoken conventions that are the nervous system of any organization.

5. Be sensitive to the fact that even having a change mandate from your board or boss may not be enough. Understand where other sources of power lie, and make sure you gain the support from that power source.

6. With a truly obstinate culture, you may need to make structural and people changes, but do so with the bought-in support of the key power center and also establish a concerted program to address the cultural legacies of the organization.

7. Create the conditions for cultural transformation: Adopt new measures of success; institute new operating processes; choose a new management team; set new expectations; identify change leaders; and lead by example.

8. Make your first moves count. In your early days, when people are most open to change, you can have a magnified impact by implementing carefully considered, concrete changes to long-established organizational and cultural structures.

9. Experiment with ways to convince employees to pledge their hearts and minds to change. Be aware of what is working and what is not and refine your approach.

10. Remember that too much change can break the culture—or more likely the change-maker. Pace yourself, continually assess the tolerance of the organization, get feedback, and adapt along the way.

SIX

ANSWERING TO A HIGHER AUTHORITY

ESTABLISHING A PRODUCTIVE WORKING RELATIONSHIP WITH YOUR BOSS (OR BOARD)

When Hebrew National wanted to underscore the quality of its kosher hot dogs, it famously advertised that it "answered to a higher authority."

Similarly, one of the keys to success in any new job is establishing a productive working relationship with your boss. Whether you are moving into a position of expanded responsibility as a new manager or as a new CEO, how you establish and sustain that relationship will help shape your first hundred days and will be a crucial element in your ongoing success.

Because our research for this book concentrated on chief executives, much of our advice in this chapter will be targeted at new CEOs and how they can build a strong relationship with their higher authority, the board of directors. Given the central role of the board in a company's life (including selecting, reviewing, and compensating the CEO; evaluating strategy; approving new businesses, mergers, acquisitions, and divestitures; auditing the financials and controls; and overseeing the granting of stock awards for employees), it is valuable for any manager—especially an aspiring CEO—to understand board dynamics.* Moreover, it is not a big leap to understand how the essence of the advice pertains to any manager—direct report relationship. "Everyone has a boss," points out Steve Reinemund, chief executive of PepsiCo. "There are always checks and balances."

When Richard Parsons became a chief executive for the first time, at the Dime Savings Bank of New York, his predecessor gave him a salient—if slightly exaggerated—piece of advice. "Fifty percent of the CEO's job is managing the board of directors," he told him, "relating to the board, and keeping them informed, comfortable, supported, and united."

After four years at the helm of the Dime, Parsons became president of Time Warner in 1995. He became CEO of the company in 2002, adding the chairman's title in 2003—positions offering plenty of opportunities to test that lesson and confirm it many times over. The importance of "solidifying your relationship with your board cannot be overstated," says Parsons.

The CEO-board relationship is a delicate dynamic, a partnership defined by roles that are at once different and dependent on each other. You are in charge of developing strategy, while they are responsible for approving it; you execute the strategy, while they contribute their advice and counsel; you are immersed in the day-to-day operations of the business, while they provide a broader perspective. The professional-boss relationship is similarly mutually dependent in terms of setting and meeting objectives and aligning how various projects and responsibilities fit into the wider organization.

Each party in this partnership needs to know when to be hands-on and when to be hands-off, when to push and when to pull back. Sometimes these divisions are clearly delineated. More often the roles need to be redefined when there's a change in leadership, and often it is up to you to think through and surface that new definition. The process demands a diplomatic and deliberate touch to prevent the partnership from degenerating into a "you versus them" antagonism.

* If you feel that the board-CEO relationship is not germane to your situation, please skip ahead to Chapter 7.

Most CEOs today have more checks and balances than ever. Although the large majority of chief executive officers in the United States also hold the title of chairman of the board, over the past few years, as a result of more stringent corporate governance regulations, there has been a perceptible shift in the balance of power from the CEO to the board. It used to be that the CEO selected the board members, determined how much they would be paid, set the agenda, and in short, was in charge. Now the board is in charge.

As we noted in the Introduction, boards are more demanding of today's CEOs and less forgiving of poor performance, with continued increases in forced turnover. New CEOs are well aware that they are appointed, not anointed. As a result, it is to the CEO's advantage to ensure that the relationship with the board is launched on the right trajectory.

Most of the precepts are equally valid whether you are reporting to a board or boss: Align expectations; listen and learn about the main concerns affecting the business; explain and establish your modus operandi; delineate your authority; fit into and start to transform the culture; and constantly communicate the reasons for and results of your actions. While you've probably had plenty of experience throughout your career reporting to a higher authority, reporting to a board of directors is, for most new CEOs, a uniquely different experience altogether.

UNDERSTAND THE MOTIVATIONS OF YOUR BOSS (OR BOARD)

The best place to start establishing a productive working relationship with your boss or board is to understand the motivations of your higher authority. In the case of bosses, most will *say* that their driving goal is to grow revenues, control costs, develop strategy, make investments, and manage people. So too with board directors, who overwhelmingly believe that they are motivated by protecting and serving the interests of shareholders, selecting the CEO, and holding him accountable.

While these goals are usually true and a component of how bosses and boards think and act, our experience suggests that they have additional underlying motivations and preferences that, while less idealistic, turn out to be no less important.

When it comes to your boss, it is critical to consider your role from your manager's point of view. Your boss wants you to fulfill your responsibilities well and meet your objectives, but that is not all. David D'Alessandro, CEO of insurance company John Hancock, wrote in *Career Warfare* that "more than anything else, bosses want three things from their managers: loyalty, good advice, and to have 'their personal brands polished.' " There is nothing a manager disdains more than a subordinate who goes around his back. The rules of the game in corporate life support a hierarchy, so even if you are in the right on a particular issue, breaking the chain of command—or worse, betraying your boss—will cause other members of the management team to be concerned that you would do the same thing to them later on.

Bosses also want good advice, not yes-men or -women who offer insincere flattery, nor downers who only play the role of devil's advocate. All intelligent bosses instinctively separate the people they manage into three distinct categories: the sycophants, the contrarians, and the small percentage who are the balanced players. You want to be seen as one in the third group.

Finally, since your boss cares as much about his or her career as you do about yours, what managers *really* want is for you to make them look smart and successful. "Understand that it's your job to polish the boss's reputation," D'Alessandro states unequivocally. "Do not make yourself look good at the boss's expense."

Now, considering boards, the first place to look is at the directors' personal situations. They are generally already highly successful and prominent individuals with established reputations. They truly care about the success of the company on whose board they sit, but they will not get the credit for success since they are not management.

They are not compensated highly relative to most of their financial stakes. And they are invariably very busy with multiple commitments of running their own companies, serving on other boards, managing financial affairs, engaging in philanthropic interests, and often writing and speaking. All told, most directors care more about protecting the downside and their scarce time than about pursuing the upside. That's why, in the current governance and shareholder-activist environment, directors are deeply focused on avoiding scandal and conflicts of interest and on the propriety of financial accounts. They will therefore take swift action against a CEO if they gather even a whiff of concern in any of these areas. Conversely, as long as a CEO gains the board's confidence with a rock-solid picture of integrity and financial controls and puts this into the context of a sound strategic agenda, she will have the board's support, especially in the early days of her new role.

The other thing that grinds on directors is specially called board meetings and conference calls. Whether they are called to address an M&A proposal, an emergency succession issue, or some other crisis, evening and weekend sessions become irritating at first, frustrating later, and ultimately infuriating. When family plans are scuttled one more time, spouses of directors commonly ask when the interruptions are going to stop and why they are working so hard when they aren't being paid much for their time and service.

If CEOs ignore how directors really think about their role and how it fits into their lives, they risk establishing a tenuous relationship with the board. Conversely, if they keep both the stated and unstated motivations squarely in mind, they will be much more likely to establish an effective partnership.

AND NOW FOR SOMETHING COMPLETELY DIFFERENT

Although his responsibilities as president and CEO of the aircraft engine and lighting divisions at GE had given Jim McNerney plenty of experience in running a business, managing people, and setting vision and executing strategy before his arrival at 3M, he says that he had had only limited exposure to corporate governance and was not fully prepared for the relationship with the 3M board.

"You'd be amazed at how naïve I was about all that," he recalls. "I never knew that CEOs brought their operating management to board meetings until I left GE, and then I learned that most people do. I had to figure out how it all worked. So I asked a lot of questions: How does the committee structure work? What issues go where? I developed some close relationships with a couple of the guys on the search committee, and we had some of those discussions even before I showed up at 3M.

"I had a lot to learn and I'm still learning. I network with other CEOs who are friends. I network with our board. I've joined two other boards [Boeing and Procter & Gamble]. All these things help."

Paul Pressler was tossed in the deep end during his first week as CEO of Gap Inc. "I had been in Disney board meetings [when he was chairman of Disney's theme parks and resorts business] but only to present an operational update or business plan," he recalls. "I had never sat through a formal corporate board meeting; I really had no idea what to expect.

"In the first meeting I focused on people, observations about the business, and what I wanted from the board. At the end of the meeting I apologized for not being buttoned up."

As it turned out, Pressler's straightforward candor and disarming confession about being a neophyte was exactly the right approach. The board was thrilled at the prospect of starting a partnership based on mutual openness and respect. "Later, when I started to present strategy to them, they were very dynamic and engaged."

The analog for non-CEOs is that it is important to sit down with your new boss and ask how he or she would like to work. How does he like to establish priorities? How and how often does she want to be updated? Is he more comfortable with formal written updates or more fluid progress reports? Does she prefer e-mail or voicemail? What special rules are there for communicating outside the department or company?

In addition, talk to other people in the company who have experience working with your boss. What do they observe about what works well and poorly? How is your boss perceived outside her department? What kinds of results and initiatives would enhance your boss's reputation inside the company?

Develop your own point of view on how to make your boss successful. Come to an agreement on how she likes to work and what she expects of you. Then revisit this after a few weeks and see what needs to be changed or can be improved. Remember that no single person has more direct influence on your short- or medium-term career success than your boss. Figure out how she likes to work and how to support her success, and tailor your efforts accordingly. Doing so will create a lot of momentum for getting off to the right start.

WHO'S ON BOARD?

When a new CEO is appointed, he or she inherits someone else's board. Aside from conversations with the search committee—especially in the case of an outside hire—neither the board nor the new CEO have had many dealings with each other. Yet now they are going to be partners. If this is you, how do you lay the right foundation for a productive working relationship?

As in any business partnership, you always need to know who your partners are. "Boards are like any group or anybody," says Arthur Martinez, former CEO of Sears and a current member of the PepsiCo board of directors. "There are probably a third leading the charge, a third going along with the charge, and a third that are asleep."

The question is, which third is which? Which members are strong and experienced, and on which issues? Which directors are less engaged? Which are truly independent in their thinking? Which feel they owe their loyalty to the previous CEO, a dynamic that can cause considerable problems if the former CEO retains a seat on the board?

Complicating the matter, boards have their own culture, one that may or may not be similar to the culture of the broader organization. There can also be a jarring disconnection between the private thoughts of individual directors and the amalgamated opinion of the group. And even though many boards encourage independent opinions, they always have a natural inclination to move toward consensus.

Group thinking does not necessarily mean that the board automatically supports or opposes the CEO—either extreme can be dangerous. But the pattern of the board automatically agreeing with the CEO may be easy to fall into.

Bill Kerr, chairman and CEO of Meredith Corporation, explains why: "You go to these five or six meetings a year, and you generally don't have the knowledge base to truly challenge a part of the strategy in a line of business. You've got to trust management on a lot of stuff. And you might feel that to you it's the wrong thing. But the CEO says, 'Well, we've done X, Y, and Z. We have McKinsey's support. We don't see anything wrong. We think this is the right approach.' I think a lot of board members at that point back off."

At the other end of the spectrum, group thinking can skew the board's loyalty to what they know best: the board. The result is the erection of an intangible wall, a pin-striped code of silence shutting out the CEO.

Recognizing the culture of the board is an essential early step toward establishing credibility and building a healthy, productive relationship. Jacques Nasser, former chairman and CEO of Ford Motor Company, suggests that new CEOs, whether promoted from within or coming in from outside, conduct the same on-boarding process of mutual introduction with the board of directors that you would hold with your management team. "A change in leadership is a good time to have a fresh view of the board," Nasser states. "Interview the board. Talk to them about the things they like and don't like, some of the softer things, such as how information is communicated, and some mechanical things, such as the frequency of board meetings. It's an opportune time because you're flipping over a new page and people expect that."

In addition to getting a handle on the group dynamics of the board, it is also important to get to know the individuals who make up the group. The goal is to get past the point of asking, "Which one of you wants to help me?" to the goal of knowing who can and can't provide meaningful help on particular issues. "It's almost like evaluating the internal people," says Lew Platt, chairman of Boeing and former CEO of Hewlett-Packard and a highly experienced board member. "It just takes time to get to know them."

The CEO must be on the same wavelength as the board, yet many new CEOs are not aware of the board's complete set of interests, as described above. As a result, they risk failing to develop and maintain the broader relationships necessary for determining the best strategy and tactics for the company. That's why it is crucial for a new CEO to spend time getting to know the board members, listening to and analyzing their concerns.

What should a new CEO be looking for? George Tamke, former chairman of Kinko's, advises, "The first and foremost thing I would tell a new CEO is that it's very important that he understands who the 'team' directors are. Is there a lead director? It may not be names, but are there ones who act in that way? Who are the two or three top directors that really shape the board? You've got to get to know them. And you need to spend time with them. And you need to get from them their view of what's going on and where the company is and what's important. And find a way of interacting with them so as not to be a pain but to begin to form a relationship. That will be critical going forward."

Burl Osborne, chairman of The Associated Press, adds the following to his checklist: "You need to know what their business expectations are, what their definition of success is, whether they can accept failure in search of success. There should never be any big surprise conversations that start with the phrase 'Well, I didn't know you wanted me to do that.' Everybody must be able to speak the same language and hear it when it's spoken. A mismatch that way is very dangerous."

OPENING NEGOTIATIONS

Just as a CEO follows a process in aligning expectations and shaping his management team, a new CEO should do the same with the board of directors. Whether he has grown up in the company or comes in as an outside hire, the new CEO should pursue one-on-one meetings to listen and learn, which opens up communication, reveals insights about the company and the business, spotlights sources of wisdom, and identifies potential problems. An added bonus, says Art Martinez, is that "a deference for people's experience breeds enormous personal loyalty with the board of directors."

As detailed in Chapter 2, when Kevin Sharer became chief executive of Amgen, he made a point of inviting each member of his management team to air their insights and concerns to him by answering the same six questions (What are the five most important things about Amgen that we should be sure to preserve and why? What are the top three things we need to change and why? What do you most hope I do? What are you most concerned I might do? What advice do you have for me? Anything else you would like to discuss or ask me?). But he did not stop with just the top hundred managers. He extended these information-seeking—and bridge-building—conversations to include every one of the outside directors. "It was a big, big change from my predecessor," Sharer stresses. "I basically asked, 'How do you want the board to work? What did you like about the way it used to be? What would you like that's different?' I had the benefit of having been on the board for seven years at that point, so I knew all these folks. But a new CEO ought to do that anyway. Listen to your board members."

Jim McNerney made a point of calling each director a few times before his first few board meetings, "just to make sure everybody was in the flow." Some of these conversations occurred on the telephone, while others were face-to-face over dinner or in more informal social settings where there were no time or business pressures. The point was to find common ground. "After that, communication became more issue-oriented rather than just communication-oriented," he recalls.

Individual board members can offer not only their expertise but an ear for private counsel. Many CEOs rely on a confidant in their management team. The confidant serves as a sounding board off of which to bounce ideas, a conduit through which to float themes to the rest of the company, an antenna to gather and test the thoughts and opinions of the staff, and when necessary, a stand-in for tasks that the CEO either cannot or should not perform. It can be very helpful to have someone—whether an independent board member, a lead director, or a nonexecutive chairman—play a similar role on the board.

George Tamke took on that responsibility when Gary Kusin became the CEO at Kinko's. As Kusin recalls, "The prior senior leadership in this company had to deal with each discrete board member. The board members were literally setting meetings with director-level people without telling the CEO. George and I sat down and agreed on the front side that this wouldn't fly. I told him he had to run interference with the board for me. We had to stop the board members from dipping into the company without me knowing about it. And I did not have time to do the work I needed to deal with the board since I was going to go out and hit all the markets."

Tamke laid down the law to his fellow board members: "From my point of view, I felt many of them were overstepping their bounds as a board member and their role versus line management's role. I had a conversation with two gentlemen specifically about that point. I started the conversation by saying, 'I understand why you may have felt in the past that because management wasn't getting the job done properly, or wasn't communicating with you effectively in a timely manner on what the major issues were, that maybe you felt like you had to behave in a particular way. Well,' I said, 'those days are gone. If you're not happy, if you don't feel like you're getting the information you need or want, you call me and we'll talk about it and we'll find a way through that problem. But from this point forward, it is unacceptable for you to drill down into the organization without my knowledge. I don't want the people to be confused about who's running this place.' Although they told me they were going to behave, they didn't. I called them on it once and I said, 'Next time the conversation is going to be very short.' "

Over dinner with one of the offenders, Kusin reiterated Tamke's warning: "I knew this guy was known to call and dip into the company. We talked about it, and I told him that I didn't need that done anymore, and I hoped that he would appreciate and respect that. He said he absolutely would. Then the next day he called a director-level person." Kusin called Tamke, Tamke called the offender, and as promised, the conversation was very short. The man resigned from the board that very day. Muses Kusin, "That's what I mean by running interference."

Through one-on-one conversations with a confidant and individual directors, a new CEO can not only learn about board members' perspectives and areas of expertise but recast his relationship with the board. This becomes the first step in subtly shifting the dynamic so that the board becomes the new CEO's board rather than that of his predecessor. The questions he asks, the way they are asked, and the answers that are supplied all demonstrate that the new CEO is not just stepping into someone else's footprints; he is ready, with the help and support of the board, to make his own mark.

MAKING YOUR MARK

Upon arrival, the new CEO has a window of opportunity and leverage to address board issues and composition, with help, ideally, from the lead director or nonexecutive chairman. Most new CEOs will have a different relationship with the board than their predecessor—and most agree that this is a good thing. Certainly Meredith's Bill Kerr agrees.

"The CEOs who came before me had a more guarded approach with their board," Kerr says. "Part of that came from a time when boards were less inclined to be independent executives or CEOs were less inclined to want their boards to be too independent. My predecessor, Jack Rehm, grew up in the shadow of his predecessor, and Bob Burnett, who was a longtime CEO, had his own way of doing things with the board. Jack had only one model to observe and that was Bob's model, one that sought not to make the board active colleagues in what was going on but rather to have the board approve what Bob wanted to do.

"You may be able to get away with this in a strong environment where everything is going well," he continues. "But business cycles are business cycles, and there are going to be times when not everything is clicking on all cylinders. That's when you really want that board involved in the process of wanting to help make the business a success rather than them saying, 'You never told us about that.'"

Kerr is convinced that his relationship with the board benefited from his being an outsider. Not only did he have a wider range of experience to call on than that of his predecessor, but his perception had not been shaped by years of observing a strong-minded superior. Conversely, the board probably regarded Kerr as less intimidating than Burnett and felt more confident about offering their counsel and opinions.

Insider Kevin Sharer also deliberately recast his relationship with Amgen's board of directors. For inside candidates, that sort of shift is especially significant, sending a message that everyone's roles and responsibilities are about to change—not just the new CEO's but also the board of directors'.

"I changed the way the board meetings happened," says Sharer. "I start every board meeting with a two-hour executive session where I'm totally open with the board about what's going on, so I don't leave them in a position where they're saying, 'Gee, I wonder what Kevin's thinking.' They're obviously my boss, but I also treat them with complete openness. I let them know everything that's going on in the company to the degree that you can in a board session. And that establishes an open dialogue that carries over into the more formal part of the board meeting. I've mentioned this approach to a few other CEOs, who now do it at their companies, too.

"Particularly when you've got a change agenda, you want to get the board behind you," Sharer stresses. "If you're not totally open with them, it's hard for them to give you the full base of support you're going to need because there are going to be bumps." Sharer has called upon the Amgen board's support for major strategic initiatives ranging from an innovative convertible finance offering to major acquisitions, including Immunex Corporation and Tularik Inc.

Not unexpectedly, the CEO-board relationship also changed after one of the most-watched regime changes in a decade. Although he was groomed by outgoing CEO Jack Welch, GE's Jeff Immelt was well aware of the tectonic shift about to take place. "You've got to recognize what you've inherited with the board and yourself," he says. One of the things he inherited was the question of whether he would manage the board the same way as Welch did. Immelt, however, was determined to be his own man from day one.

"I've always said, 'I'm no Jack Welch.' I don't mean that I'm not worthy. I'm better at a lot of things. But leaders can fall into the trap of saying they've got to be like the last guy. That's pretty stupid. The biggest mistake I could have made with our board would be thinking that I would get the same latitude that Jack got. That's insane. I assumed I would have to earn my way."

As part of recasting his relationship with the GE board, Immelt realized that he needed to change the nature of their discourse. "The agenda had been a review of operations. My view was if I'm telling you about operations, it's already too late.

"One of the things on my list when I became CEO was to take the board through an education of where the company was at that time and our relationship to the new environment we were working in. Consider the luxury our board had—they had the best CEO in the world at a time of unprecedented tranquillity and prosperity. I knew that the board was really job number one, because I knew I needed these people to be with me through the tough times. We needed, for example, to discuss the challenges we were facing in our reinsurance business. You could see the storm clouds on the horizon, and I said, 'I'd better get these guys up to speed incredibly quickly.'

"So starting with my third board meeting, we restructured what the board looked at. We picked ten areas that we thought would be risk areas for the company, areas like reinsurance, like transparency, and we dug in deep. The result was they knew about reinsurance a year before they had to take a charge against earnings [for insurance losses]."

ESTABLISHING YOUR CREDIBILITY

As a new CEO begins to make her mark, she has to demonstrate to the higher authority that they made the right selection, especially in the early days after the appointment. Over time business results will hopefully speak for themselves. But in the first hundred days, and even over the course of the first year, the reported results of the business may well have very little to do with a new CEO's own efforts directly. She will be making decisions now that will translate into revenue growth and profit improvement in the near future. As a result, the key focus in the early days must be on establishing relationships and building credibility. Again, this point is equally valid for a CEO or a department manager.

Establishing your credibility takes a variety of skills, primarily: having a sound strategic agenda, being on top of the details of the business, listening and learning from your boss or board members, communicating clearly, building a strong and committed management team, and maintaining a certain amount of humility.

A good board will endorse the sentiment of Satchel Paige, the famous baseball player, who said, "Don't look back. Someone might be gaining on you." Bob Campbell agrees. This former chairman and CEO of Sunoco had headed up the search committee charged with finding his successor at Sunoco in 1996, and in 2002 chaired the search committee that brought Richard Lenny in as the CEO of Hershey Foods. He recalls: "In both instances, I told the incoming executive, 'Don't spend one minute looking over your shoulder at where the board is on any of these questions. We are a thousand percent behind you. You are going to have so many issues dealing with the existing organization that you don't want to spend any time at all looking over your shoulder. You have our complete support.' If we told them that once, we told them a dozen times."

While many CEOs have that support, Immelt cautions, "You got there because a bunch of people raised their hand one night. You've got to have a couple of members who are loyal to you. You're not going to have them all, but you need some whose first loyalty is to your success. They all say they're loyal, but they have to say that. Don't assume you have the credibility your predecessor had."

Our view is that you should keep both pieces of this seemingly conflicting advice in mind. You do want to be trusting, optimistic, and confident about your boss's or the board's support of you; they will actually respond to your positive energy in kind and follow your lead. But it is also wise to hone in on the thought leaders in your department or on the board, really get to know them, and secure their support to develop what you might think of as "high-leverage loyalty."

Before he took over AOL, Jonathan Miller had spent plenty of time learning how to work with and establish credibility with boards. Having both served on boards and reported to company boards, he realized that the surest way to credibility is through a disciplined management process. "My experience as a board member," Miller states, "is that they're looking to see if you, the CEO, have a handle on the business. It gives them the confidence that you will do what you say and deliver what you promise. As a board member, you're not there day to day—that's not your job. But it is your job to make sure you apply the necessary checks and balances and ultimately have confidence in the CEO. That comes down to confidence in the person and the process and the outcomes. The most important thing is that the board sees that you're doing it the right way, and that strategy is baked into the process, and there are outcomes you—and they—can have confidence in."

SHARING THE SAME REALITY

As Chapter 7 will detail, communication is an absolutely key layer in the first hundred days pyramid. This is true in all aspects of your process, from planning during your countdown period, to aligning expectations, to building and communicating your strategic agenda, to shaping your management team, and most certainly to working effectively with your higher authority. One of the greatest dangers for a CEO in making any kind of major change is that of not sharing the same perception of the business with your boss or board. Yet it is astonishing how many executives neglect to keep board members in the loop.

"I've been surprised at how thin the reporting is from the CEO to the board members in a formal sense and how anecdotal it remains at times," notes Jeff Killeen, CEO of GlobalSpec, who currently sits on three boards and has sat on five others during his career.

"Your success with the board is due in part to the communication protocol you set up with them. Similar to many early-stage companies, we do regular monthly meetings, as opposed to quarterly. While this puts an enormous burden on my financial staff—and the directors' calendars—early-stage companies have a lot to talk about. Beyond the meeting frequency, I follow one other communication practice that I have not seen too frequently. I write what I call my Monthly Comment Letter. It takes me around three hours on top of the board package to craft, but I do it because I think it's the right way to communicate with the board. The letter is six to eight pages of succinct and expressive narrative of what I'm worrying about and what I think the initiatives and priorities are. It has proven to be a wonderful forum between myself and the board. We're all engaged with the same vocabulary, and it keeps us tight, tight, tight." GlobalSpec board director Peter Derow concurs. "Jeff's monthly letter is very useful, particularly the section in which he notes his primary concerns. This is consistent with what he continues to do extremely well: dedicating a considerable and appropriate amount of time to two-way communication with the entire staff."

At Kinko's, Kusin and Tamke prepare a similar package for every board meeting, summarizing the current state of business in every functional area of the organization. Even more important, the package lists the questions and issues raised at previous board meetings and describes what has been done—or is being done—to resolve them. "As a result of that," Tamke says, "if they read this—and I believe they all do—there isn't any board member who can look in the mirror and say with a straight face that they don't know what's going on. It's not possible."

This same practice of communicating at regular intervals in written form can be applied to keep your boss informed about what you are working on and what you see as the primary challenges of your business. Having made this investment in time to write up the state of the business for your boss, you can then readily repurpose the content (with the benefit of word processing) and communicate your priorities and insights with your staff. High-performing professionals thrive on this kind of information and context so that they can understand how their own responsibilities fit into the broader progress of the organization. It also creates a productive way to solicit feedback from your team.

"When you move into a new organization and you don't know the people well," advises Jacques Nasser, "one suggestion I would always offer is to make it comfortable for people above you and those who work with you to give you informal feedback, both on your progress and on other matters, like style of work."

More and more new CEOs are also asking their boards for feedback. With so little slack allowed in performance these days, it's not just advisable but imperative that a CEO and board learn to make course corrections to avoid squalls before getting into trouble. And it's important to form a means of getting some indirect feedback fairly quickly. Paul Pressler and the Gap Inc. board are such fans of feedback that they schedule time for it in the agenda. They also make sure the feedback goes both ways: The discussions cover not only whether Pressler's performance meets the board's expectations but how the board can make its participation more valuable. "We do feedback at the end of every board meeting," Pressler says, "my feedback to them about what they could do better and theirs to me. It's a great way to get a sense of their expectations about what they like and what they don't like."

"We work hard at getting better," adds Steve Reinemund. Feedback helped him and the PepsiCo board measure their joint performance on a variety of issues and identify the capabilities that were lacking. It provided a new—and refreshingly apolitical—method of looking for new board members. "As a result, we went out for our two new board members and had the perfect conditions met based on the needs we identified in this process."

FORCE YOURSELF TO BE A LEADER

Even if you don't build feedback into every board meeting, force yourself to get a dialogue going, advises Gillette's Jim Kilts. He emphasizes being open and honest; no board likes to get the sense that you're pulling the wool over their eyes, and they're probably experienced enough to recognize it anyway.

That's why Kilts had no qualms about stating that he didn't have all the answers—and even fewer qualms about advertising that fact right off the bat. "I gave the board a presentation two days after I got here on what I saw as the key issues, how I would spend my time, and asked for their thoughts," he says. "It was even better that I spoke to them so soon because I could stand up and say, 'I've only been here two days and I obviously don't know a lot' " (although he did have an unusually productive countdown period).

"The first chance you get—even before you think you're ready—tell them, 'Here's what I'm going to work on, here are my priorities, here are what I see as the success drivers for the next two months. I'll come back in two months and report to you.' Your board appreciates it when you have the courage to stand up and disclaim what you don't know. But they also appreciate it when you tell them what you think, so force yourself to be a leader."

Another key element of being a leader is when a CEO encourages the board to talk openly among its members without the CEO being present. Executive session, as it is called, is a form of reciprocal respect. Just as the CEO wants the board to trust him enough to stay out of the day-to-day managerial details, he should have the confidence to let the board be an independent working group. What makes this work is open communication. After an executive session, the best practice is for a nonexecutive chairman or presiding director to sit down without delay with the CEO and share the feedback from the discussion, which should keep the CEO on track and help him prioritize the many competing demands and possible areas of focus.

GETTING THE BOARD ON BOARD

Five months after Jeff Immelt officially took charge at GE, he held a board meeting at which he asked all the board members for their commitment to put in the time needed to develop a deeper understanding of the risks the company faced in the current business environment. The time was February 2002, in the middle of the Enron debacle, when the bankrupt energy company's board of directors was accused of ignoring the signs of the impending implosion.

"I told our board, 'We're going to go through a lot of changes. It's going to be a tough time. You're going to have to know more, you're going to be in a lot more places, and you'll be on the hook for more. I'm going to give you thirty days to think about this on your own time. If you want to stay, tell me. If you want to leave, you're free.' " In the months after that meeting, five director changes were made to GE's sixteen-person board.

THE WAY IT SHOULD WORK

In an open, collaborative relationship, the board becomes an extension of the CEO's management and support team, an aid, a source of wisdom and counsel, an extra set of eyes, and an independent but supportive sounding board. Assuming the board is ready, willing, and able, how are CEOs putting them to best use?

At GE, Immelt relies on the board to take the pulse of the company, to gauge whether the business is humming along smoothly or there are glitches that need attention. "I ask each one of our directors to visit the GE businesses twice a year," he says. "You're never going to know the intricacies of this company. There's too much mass. But you can get a feel of the culture. So when they go to GE Aircraft Engines or GE Medical Systems, I want them by themselves [without corporate management], so they can make their own assessments—maybe we're pushing too hard or maybe we're not pushing hard enough."

At The Home Depot, all directors were required to visit eighteen stores every year and spend two hours on each visit speaking with employees and customers. When he became CEO in 2000, Bob Nardelli continued that tradition and enhanced it: "I pair two board members with every division president and every functional leader for a full day. I look for their advice and counsel. These are CEOs and experienced men and women in their own right. I took advantage of their experience. Rather than being intimidated by it, I reached out and said, 'You go in and assess, give me your view of the individuals and their staffs.' So the board is helpful."

At PepsiCo, Steve Reinemund uses his board to maximize his effectiveness in a variety of ways. It helped that as an internally promoted candidate, the board already knew him. "They had a pretty good understanding of my strengths and weaknesses," he says. "I've used them as a sounding board for advice collectively and individually since starting off. I've used them most on strategy and people issues.

Several of our directors have been through tough issues as CEOs themselves, and that has been helpful as we talk about change."

Like Immelt, Reinemund has found ways to integrate directors into the business and interact with corporate managers. Soon after becoming chief executive, for example, Reinemund conducted an executive-development program for forty middle managers at the University of Virginia's Darden Graduate School Business (where he had earned his MBA), and he invited PepsiCo's board members to attend, not just to address the group but to sit in on classes, participate in breakout sessions, and share their views.

While he's not at all hesitant about asking the board for feedback on what areas he should focus on or how he can improve his performance, Reinemund is also not shy about drawing a boundary between his sphere of authority and theirs: "I don't want the board to be involved in the day-to-day details. They don't want to be, and I don't want them to be. But they have a strong involvement in my success, so they're going to give me their advice."

DRAWING THE LINE BETWEEN OLD AND NEW

The distinction between the purview of the CEO and the board and the careful delineation of where the two intersect is key to maintaining a productive working relationship. But it is not always easy for a new CEO to draw that line when the former chief executive is still sitting on the board.

On the one hand, the former leader can be a valuable source of information and experience and provide necessary continuity to make the transition run more smoothly. When Chris Lofgren became the first nonfamily member to head up Schneider National, he encouraged and appreciated the continuing input from previous CEO, Don Schneider, in helping other board members get used to the change in leadership. "We had to become comfortable going from it being Don's board with me interacting with them inside of the meeting to it being my board with the opportunity to interact on a much broader basis," Lofgren says. "With Don being there, everyone pays him a great deal of deference. On the one hand, he's looking at me and saying, 'How would you like to handle that?' It's an evolutionary process."

On the other hand, while the former CEO can make valuable contributions, his or her presence can also hinder change. Other board members may be hesitant to openly discuss new strategic directions that might be construed as criticism of the old strategies. Such sensitivity is a function of the individuals involved, but it's also a function of where the company is at any point in time.

PepsiCo board member Arthur Martinez recalls how the board instinctively deferred to previous chairman and CEO Roger Enrico: "With the best of intentions, people would cue off Roger's body language—the way he looked down his nose or raised his eyebrows. It made it difficult for Steve [Reinemund] to articulate his business."

As for arch-rival Coca-Cola, much of that company's troubles from 1998 through 2004—the turmoil in its executive suite and its criticized succession process—have been attributed to the power and influence wielded by former Coke president and chief operating officer Don Keough. The energetic and charismatic Keough had been the company's number-two executive for twelve years until his retirement in 1993, but he has remained a force to be reckoned with ever since, first as a close adviser and confidant to the company and later as a corporate director.

There are clearly two sides to this story, which with the May 2004 appointment of former longtime Coke executive E. Neville Isdell as CEO is still being written. On the one hand, some insiders cite Keough's lingering resentment at not having been named CEO in 1981, when the board elected instead the elite Cuban-born chemical engineer Roberto Goizueta, as the underlying cause of his intense influence brokering. On the other hand, many see Keough as Coca-Cola's guardian angel and the man who worked behind the scenes since Goizueta's October 1997 death to keep the company on course. As longtime director James B. Williams told *Fortune* magazine, he is so experienced and valuable to the company that "you want as much of Keough as you can get."

On the whole, however, most CEOs and board members agree with Robert Campbell, former CEO of Sunoco: "In my mind, you should not have the former chief executive remain on the board as a director, period. When I took over at Sunoco, two predecessors were on the board, mine and the CEO who had served before him. That's not a good situation. The new CEO is brought in to achieve change. You don't want to spend your time looking at the body language and facial expressions of the predecessor sitting there. When I turned the reins over to the new CEO, I wished him godspeed, good luck, and then immediately got off the board."

At GE Jack Welch did the same thing, stressing that for him to stay around would only impede the new CEO's ability to assume leadership. He learned that lesson personally twenty years earlier from his own renowned predecessor, Reginald "Reg" Jones.

WHEN SUCCEEDING A FOUNDER

Jeff Killeen had a different challenge in establishing a productive working relationship with his higher authority. When he became CEO of GlobalSpec, a specialized search engine and online data resource for the engineering and scientific market, he had to forge a connection with its lead founder. When Killeen first met with the board of directors, he says, "I didn't know a flow sensor from an accelerometer. But whatever this domain was, I knew that these guys were doing it very well. It was the deepest, best-executed connection of buyers and sellers I had ever seen."

Killeen liked the company, he liked the board, and the board liked him. But there was a potential fly in the ointment. GlobalSpec was a founder-operated company, and after holding top executive positions at spin-offs of two other founder-operated companies—Forbes.com and Barnes&Noble.com—Killeen was understandably leery.

"The request I made to the search committee," he says, "once I was at the 'ninety-degree temperature mark' in terms of interest, was to do a different form of due diligence. I wanted to do all the traditional diligence—review the historical financials, go in depth on the audit, look at the business plans and the underlying assumptions—and then I wanted to spend deep time with all four founders who were still there, particularly with the lead founder, John Schneiter."

It wasn't difficult for Killeen to identify the core operating issue. "These guys did the best job I'd ever seen at the product and systems design element of the business, but there was a low level of scale in the sales organization and very limited marketing capability," he recalls. "Whoever came into this job would have to leverage the founders' expertise in engineering but would also have to reinvent the marketing and sales functions of the business."

The DNA of the company was engineering, dedicated to perfection, and suspicious of slick-talking salespeople and glossy marketing plans. Killeen realized he had to create a common understanding and language, to reassure Schneiter and gain his acceptance as a relevant successor: "I realized that if I couldn't convince John Schneiter that my coming in was a good idea and that we could work together, there was no sense in taking this job.

"John had a limited perspective on how big of an opportunity there was with this company," Killeen continues. "I had to absolutely convince him that I wouldn't screw up his baby—and then that this business could be even larger than his aspiration. And I had to do that in a way that didn't insult his aspiration. You can't accomplish that in an interview. You have to do that the way you go about creating a partnership or a business development deal, with lots of conversations at lots of levels."

Through what turned out to be ten several-hour one-on-one conversations with Schneiter, Killeen heard about his dreams, his goals, and his frustrations. Killeen also had meetings with each of the other founders and at least one meeting with every officer of the company, and he plowed through five hundred pounds—"literally"—of reading material over six weeks. "When we shook hands at the end of the process, I said, 'I know we're philosophically there, but the work is ahead of us. We just agreed to agree.' And John said—and this was a huge thing for an accomplished GE design engineer, a forty-five-year-old MIT Ph.D.—he said, 'Jeff, here's the deal. Train me to be a world-class general manager, teach me to be a CEO, teach me how to deal with the board, put me in the right slot.' What he was saying was, 'I'm still the founder and president, but mentor me.'

"That would not have happened if we hadn't spent those ten meetings together," Killeen concludes. "And the more confidence John placed in me, the more that worked back to the board and gave them more confidence that the whole would be greater than the sum of the parts."

REMEMBER WHAT YOUR HIGHER AUTHORITY WANTS

Do not forget that your higher authority generally always wants things to work out just about as much as you do. If you keep at the forefront of your mind what your boss really wants from you—strong performance, loyalty, and good advice—and key off of his or her preferred work and communication style, you will maximize your chances of establishing a productive working relationship. If you are a CEO, the rules also apply for how you lay the groundwork for working with your board and building the relationship into a true partnership. Shaping a productive relationship with a new business partner, especially one who has the power to hire and fire you, is always a challenge. "It's got to be a relationship of complete trust and complete confidence," says Robert Tillman, retired chairman and CEO of Lowe's, "and also at the same time complete candor. I would never hide things from the board, and expect the same thing in return."

You can see that effective communication is a central theme in establishing a productive working relationship with your boss or board. In fact, this subject is so important to establishing a great first hundred days and to ensuring strong successive first hundred days, we've devoted the entire next chapter to demonstrating how leadership communication is the key to implementing your agenda.

CONCLUSION

TEN GUIDELINES FOR ESTABLISHING A PRODUCTIVE RELATIONSHIP WITH YOUR HIGHER AUTHORITY

1. Understand the stated and unstated motivations of your boss or board. It's not just about meeting your objectives and building shareholder value, it's also about making them successful and protecting their reputations.

2. If you are a new CEO, initiate an "on-boarding" process with the board similar to what can be done with new managers. Sit down with each board member and interview them to determine what they are looking for; ask questions about their experience on the board, and the areas and disciplines they are most passionate about and expert in. Gather their input about how the board should ideally work in terms of the committee structure, what issues go where, and board mechanics such as meeting frequency and information flow.

3. If you are not a CEO, meet with your new boss and discuss how he or she really likes to work, establish priorities, and communicate. For example, is he more comfortable with formal written updates or more fluid progress reports? Does she prefer e-mail or voicemail?

4. Try to explicitly assess which members of the board or the department are strongest and most experienced—and on which issues; look at which directors are less engaged, and which are truly independent in their thinking.

5. Diagnose the culture of the board, and tailor your communication and management styles accordingly. Is the board formal and relatively distant or more informal and hands-on? As you increase your credibility with the board, migrate the culture to what you believe is most constructive and what you are most comfortable with.

6. If you are a CEO, develop one or more confidants on the board, whether a nonexecutive chairman or a presiding director. Look to them to serve as a sounding board to bounce ideas off of, to help set board agendas, and in the early days even to help manage the board process while you are getting up to speed on the business.

7. Establish your credibility by having a sound strategic agenda, being on top of the details of the business, listening and learning from your boss or board members, building a strong and committed management team, establishing a sound management process, and maintaining humility.

8. Establish an effective communication protocol with your boss or board, including formal information flows such as monthly management letters, as well as an informal communication protocol, such as phone calls before each meeting and informal meetings or meals with your boss or individual directors.

9. Establish the discipline of regular feedback with your board or boss. In the case of the board, encourage an "executive session" as a part of each meeting, where the board discusses your performance in your absence, which can then be delivered in a synthesized and constructive way.

10. Involve the board members in the business so they become more knowledgeable and effective. Create forums for directors to interact with managers, visit customers and facilities, and dive deeply into key businesses. This will increase their ability to help assess and support strategy and perform their most important function, ensuring optimal succession.

SEVEN

COMMUNICATION

THE KEY TO IMPLEMENTING YOUR AGENDA

For forty thousand years Aboriginal Australians passed their culture and knowledge down through the generations by storytelling. Socrates similarly established the oral tradition in ancient Greece. So deep were the beliefs in the importance of verbal communication that, according to legend, Greek scholars resisted the innovation of writing for fear that young people would no longer have to use their memories. Napoleon, by contrast, was a big believer in written communication. It is said that he was so impatient to get his messages out (and was so intellectually gifted) that he would and could simultaneously dictate five memos to five different scribes hurrying to take down his thoughts. (He would say one sentence on one memo and move to the next four before coming back around to the first one!) For thousands of years, communication has lain at the heart of leaders' actions as they tried to change their world.

In today's business world, communication is no less important.

Howard Schultz, founder and chairman of Starbucks Coffee Company,* has created a global powerhouse with one of the world's most valuable consumer brands that has influenced the lives of millions of passionate customers. How was he able to cause investors,

---

* Schultz founded the modern Starbucks in 1987 after working for a predecessor company established in 1971 of the same name, leaving to found a coffee shop chain called Il Giornale, and then acquiring the original Starbucks in Seattle's Pike's Market.

employees, customers, and the media to suspend logic and create a new way to think about what had previously been largely a commodity (and pay $3.75 instead of 50 cents for a cup of coffee)?

In large measure via storytelling.

Schultz has built a distinctive corporate culture of partnership, one of whose core attributes is employee stock ownership and full medical benefits for the company's seventy thousand employees. He repeatedly shares the emotional tale of his father, a hardworking blue-collar laborer who got injured on the job. With no insurance or medical benefits and working for a company "with no soul," the elder Schultz was let go from his job. The family had to move to the projects in Brooklyn and barely scraped by. Schultz brings tears to your eyes when he describes how as a boy he witnessed and suffered through his father's loss of self-esteem and the crushing effect on the family of this series of unfortunate events. And then, as if by divine inspiration, Schultz one day vowed, "If I ever have the opportunity to be responsible for other people, I will *never* let what happened to my father happen to them."

Shortly after the modern Starbucks was founded in 1987, this story was the heart of Schultz's presentation to the Starbucks board of directors, along with his recommendation to establish full medical benefits and stock option ownership for all employees as long as they worked twenty hours a week. While the board initially dismissed the idea as unaffordable, especially for an early-stage company, Schultz's ability to use both analytical and emotional reasoning won the day. He argued that such a program would pay for itself in three years if it reduced by half the high employee turnover common to the specialty retailing and food service industry. And he pulled on the heartstrings of the directors by talking about the kind of company that he wanted to build, one that he wished his father could have worked for. In the end the board approved the proposal, and the Starbucks Bean Stalk program was born. To this day the program (which incidentally was so successful in reducing turnover that it paid for itself in *one* year) is at the core of the company's culture and organizational strategy. Nearly twenty years later, Schultz's implementing of this element of his strategic agenda in *his* early days should serve as a beacon for all leaders as they assume new leadership positions.

Communication skills are one of the most important attributes of effective leadership. It only makes sense. Vision and strategy largely reside in a vacuum until they are applied. Consequently, your strategic agenda counts for scarcely a thing until it is communicated to others and becomes operative for them.

Richard Parsons, another highly effective communicator, is thoughtful about what is required to convey important messages to everyone at Time Warner. "Let's take the issue of empowerment," says Parsons. "The problem is, if people don't have a sense of what the big picture is, how they fit into it, and what the mission is, they'll all go in different directions. I want them to say, 'Okay, I understand where this whole thing is supposed to go and how my piece fits in. Therefore I'm now empowered to go make it work within the concept of the big picture.' "

If your people don't know what the direction is, they won't know where to go. The result: Energy dissipates, momentum slows, morale plummets, and the company drifts. It's not a pretty picture. Making sure everyone sees the same picture and then understands what that picture means, Parsons says, requires "more contact with people, more opportunities to meet them, and more communication."

COMMUNICATING GOES BOTH WAYS

One fanciful notion of communication in a company is that of the leader who comes down, Moses-like, from Mount Sinai and delivers divine truth and wisdom. This may work for you if you have indeed been given the Two Tablets. For most of us working with more earthly tools, however, communication is better thought of as a continuous give and take, an ongoing conversation in which ideas are explored, assimilated, and adapted before being locked in. This is a process of listening and learning, of absorbing and synthesizing data, then sharing the results.

In other words, communicating is much more than promulgating a message. It is just as much the gathering of disparate thoughts and information that will help shape the message. That's why interactive forms of communication have become so popular. Town hall meetings with an open microphone for questions and answers, brown bag lunches with smaller groups, and regular round-tables all offer opportunities to have dialogue and talk about what's on people's minds. All of these are especially important during your first hundred days.

Enabling people to get to know you on a more informal basis serves another important purpose: It shows them what kind of a person you are. "People have to see demonstrated leadership ability if you want to get your agenda through," says Dave Peterschmidt, CEO of Securify. "You have to be able to communicate in such a way that when people walk away from a conversation with you, they feel, 'This person is a straight shooter. He is honest with me and he doesn't screw around.'"

"WHERE'S PAUL?"

Paul Pressler used a combination of e-mail, voicemail, company intranet sites, face-to-face encounters, and video presentations to communicate with Gap Inc.'s 165,000 employees worldwide when he became CEO. The communication plan had four objectives:

- Inspire employees' confidence in Pressler's leadership by establishing his credibility;
- Help employees feel better about working at Gap Inc. under its new leadership;
- Help employees understand that Pressler will spend his first

hundred days "listening and learning" before developing a strategic vision for Gap Inc.; and

- Do this in a way that will reflect Pressler's personal style, provide opportunities for feedback, and promote two-way communication.

Pressler started work at Gap Inc. on October 21, 2002. At the end of the day an e-mail went out to all his direct reports recapping his first day on the job and discussing his plans for his first hundred days. That Friday all employees received a voicemail recapping his first week on the job, reiterating his plans for his first hundred days ("Wherever I am, I'll be asking a lot of questions: What are the most important things about Gap Inc. that we should be sure to preserve and why? What are the top three things we need to improve? What do you hope I do? What do you hope I *don't* do?") and encouraging everyone to read his GapWeb journal.

The journal, called "Where's Paul?" was a series of seven first-person missives, complete with photos of highlights from Pressler's first hundred days as he visited company locations across the United States. The journal entries described what he was doing, what he was learning, and how this was important to the company and employees. It was an opportunity for him to recognize particular teams and employees, as well as for helping employees get to know him.

Here's a typical journal entry, from December 2, 2002:

> I have to start by congratulating all of our store associates on their focus and hard work over the busy post-Thanksgiving shopping weekend. It really paid off. I was very pleased with what I saw out in the field as I visited stores throughout the weekend.
>
> On Friday I worked at the Glendale Galleria Gap in southern California. I really wanted to step into every role that our store associates perform, so I had a long day—but I learned so much! Here's a recap of my day as a store associate:
>
> 6 A.M.—Arrived at the store with the regional manager.
> 6–6:30 A.M.—General manager gave me an overview of Brand Standards and the Conversion Improvement Project. The metrics these programs

have put in place not only get the team focused on the right business goals, but they really encourage everyone to work together as a team.

6:30–7:30 A.M.—Training with associate manager, prepping me for all of the roles I was to play throughout the day. Took a break from our training at 6:45 for the "1 Minute Meeting." (I always wondered if these meetings were truly only a minute. It actually went a little over.)

7:30–9 A.M.—Sales floor deployment with my "buddy" sales associate. Got customers to the fitting rooms and focused on selling women's sweaters (even beat my sales goal!).

9–11 A.M.—Stockroom scanning and replenishment with my "buddy" stock associate. We had a lot of fun. Stock replenishment was one of my favorite jobs.

11–12:30 P.M.—I went to the Gap Kids store in the Glendale Galleria and learned how to sell a Top 15 item with associate manager.

12:30–1:30 P.M.—I'm famished! Lunch with employees at the adult store. Spoke with employees about some of the challenges they face. Several store associates had some great ideas and suggestions for ways to address these challenges.

1:30–2:30 P.M.—Back to the Gap Kids store to learn the cash wrap. Store manager taught me how to keep the line moving and bag product. Getting those sensor tags off was a little challenging, but I eventually got the hang of it. I loved this job because it gave me the opportunity to ask customers all kinds of questions and at the same time make their "line time" feel shorter.

2:30–3:30 P.M.—From Gap Kids, I went to the Galleria Baby Gap, where I shadowed the manager on duty.

3:30–4 P.M.—Shared some of my key learnings from the day with store associates. It was quite a whirlwind, so I hadn't yet processed everything, but I definitely learned that "size, color, style" is the name of the game.

4–5 P.M.—After finishing my work at Gap, I visited the Glendale Galleria Banana Republic store. Store manager gave me a walkthrough of the store, which looked great.

Overall, it was a tremendous day, and I felt totally immersed in the store environment. I appreciated all the feedback I got from store associates and will look forward to hearing more ideas from people as I continue to make periodic visits like this one to our stores. I'll draw on people's suggestions as we continue to evaluate ways we can better serve our customers.

This week I'll be touring all of our distribution centers. I look forward to visiting New York Product Development next week for Gap, Old Navy, and Banana Republic fall product presentations.—Paul.

In addition to the "Where's Paul?" journal, a standard biography, and an "Interview with Paul Pressler" discussing his personal interests, GapWeb also posted an "Ask Paul" Q&A page, in which employees were invited to submit their questions and concerns about the business. The column was an important feedback tool for the corporate communication team to understand and address employee concerns. It also provided a forum for Pressler to discuss strategic direction and priorities.

In January 2003, at the end of Pressler's first hundred days, the corporate communication department surveyed three hundred employees of all levels from across the United States to evaluate the result of the communication blitz. Their response:

• 98 percent said they had confidence in Pressler as CEO of Gap Inc.

• 98 percent said they believed Pressler delivered on his promise to spend his first hundred days "listening and learning."

• 75 percent said they felt better about working at Gap Inc. now than they did before Pressler's first hundred days.

• Out of the communication vehicles used for this project:

    − 92 percent said GapWeb was an effective communication vehicle for delivering Pressler's communications.
    − 93 percent said face-to-face meetings were effective.
    − 86 percent said voicemails were effective.

Overall, employees said that GapWeb stories had helped them to get to know their new CEO and that they were motivated by his messages. A typical example of the record amount of e-mail feedback was: "I feel loyal to Paul as a leader, and I believe that it is because the video and the journal notes help me to see the example that the leader is setting."

Not every new leader feels as comfortable as Paul Pressler did about sharing his daily actions and learnings with the troops. Nor is it necessarily the only way to communicate effectively in the early days.

STRICTLY BUSINESS

Jim Kilts set a different tone entirely in the interview posted on Gillette's intranet after he took over in February 2001. Forget about finding out his taste in magazines or his favorite sports. A Kilts Q&A session is strictly business—in fact, the most personal exchange is a question of how Kilts got started in the consumer products industry. (Answer: "I was seventeen years old, fresh out of high school. I had decided to work for a year before going to college, and since I was a chemistry buff, I took a lab technician test at General Foods. I got a 100 on the test and was hired at General Foods' Kool-Aid plant in Chicago.") The tone is different from Pressler's, but the underlying expectation of outstanding performance is the same, as is the importance of clear and copious communication in achieving it.

Here is a sample of the Kilts Q&A:

Q: What do you think is important for Gillette employees to know about your career?

A: By far the single most important characteristic of my business career is that I have spent my life *building brands* [Kilts's emphasis]. I've done it with some of the world's great consumer product companies—General Foods, Oscar Mayer, Kraft, and Nabisco. My business passion is building brands. And that is what I intend to devote my time and energies to at Gillette— making this great company and its great brands even greater.

Q: What do you consider the greatest challenge to returning Gillette to consistent growth in sales and earnings?

A: It's really not possible to talk about either Gillette's greatest issues . . . or our greatest opportunities . . . until I have completed a thorough and rigorous analysis of all parts and aspects of our company, our competitors, and the marketplace. Based on that assessment, I will determine strengths and weaknesses . . . problems and potential. Then we'll develop strategies and action plans.

However, I can say with a high degree of certainty from my thirty years of past experience that, going forward, Gillette definitely will have a sharp focus on: building brands, building organization strength, and controlling costs in all areas and at all levels within our company. These are givens; other priorities will follow.

Q: The board of directors cited your "decisive management style" as one of the reasons you were chosen as CEO. Can you provide examples?

A: In broad terms, my management philosophy is to keep things simple. I want rigorous analysis and thoughtful assessments, but I do not want complexity. If strategies and plans aren't easily understood by everyone, they will be acted on by no one. So by keeping things simple, we will be able to act decisively . . . and communicate clearly . . . throughout the entire organization.

Let me give you one example. When I joined Nabisco in 1998, one of the major operating units, the Nabisco Biscuit Company, was struggling with a sales force that had undergone a flawed restructuring the year before. Efforts to tinker around the edges of the restructured sales force had tended to worsen the situation. I worked with the operating unit to assess the situation, developed a new organization structure . . . and then moved swiftly to implementation. Within a matter of months, positive results were evident. Within a year, Nabisco's sales force was back to its former preeminence as one of the most powerful selling organizations in the sector.

Q: Just a few days ago, when employees arrived at work, they found a letter from you even though it was your first official day on the job. Then, a few days later, you agreed to this interview. Is it fair to say that communication is important to you?

A: It's part of my philosophy. We need to communicate. For example, I have a weekly staff meeting every Monday morning, and a quarterly staff meeting where we discuss priorities, accomplishments, and the coming quarter's objectives. I believe in strong communication with my staff, as well as with the Gillette organization at large. It's part of my role to communicate through publications, speeches, meetings, and lunches—all the appropriate ways of reaching out to share news and understand what's on people's minds. And I believe it is part of my staff's responsibility to communicate with their organizations.

Q: What might be the most important idea you'd like employees to understand about you?

A: With me, what you see is what you get. And as I said, what you get is a genuine belief in building total brand value—that's the important message. I've said it everywhere I've been, and I really believe it. Our role simply is to build total brand value. That is what we are all about, and everyone at Gillette has a vital part in it.

LEVERAGE YOUR COMMUNICATION

Most leaders agree that employees should be told as much as possible about the state of the business, both its problems and its opportunities. If everyone looks at the business with the same facts, they are much more likely to pull in the same direction—operate with a shared perspective—which is essential in making the business a success. This is especially true for employees, but it also applies to shareholders, the board of directors, the customers, and the suppliers.

Make sure that everyone fully comprehends whatever situation the business is in, good or problematic. Share your facts with them in as much detail as is possible and appropriate for each audience. Let them understand the market conditions you face and the financial implications for the company.

"I tried to make sure all the dots stayed connected," recalls 3M's Jim McNerney. "I spent an inordinate amount of time both one on one with the people who worked for me and in broad groups of employees and retirees. I made a point of calling everyone on the board of directors a few times before the first few board meetings, just to make sure everybody was in the flow."

While it's true that you cannot overcommunicate an important message, it is possible to spend too much of your scarce time engaged in communicating. (Remember, you only have 1,204 hours to invest in your first hundred days.) It's a tough call. On the one hand, the more personal the delivery method, the more likely the message is to get through and stick. It's especially gratifying to talk with someone and know that you've gained another supporter. A lot of people find that adrenaline rush hard to give up. On the other hand, given your limited time, the longer you spend in the act of communicating, the less time you can devote to other important activities.

It comes down to how you can maximize the return on your time. "You need to do some one-to-ones, but to be effective and leverage your time, you need to manage one-to-many," says Intuit CEO Steve Bennett. "You need to find all sorts of forums and leverage points to manage one-to-many."

Finding those forums is especially important as you try to scale up your message to an ever-increasing number of listeners. "When you have ninety thousand people, you can't go to that many cocktail parties," says Time Warner's Parsons. "So you have to have some structured process to get the word out to the troops and for getting contact with the troops."

Whether you're leading a department, an early-stage company, or a company of multiple thousands of employees, establish a regular opportunity for purposeful give and take so that communication channels are familiar and open conversation becomes part of the organizational DNA. That's something Dave Peterschmidt sets up as soon as he moves into a new position, which he has done at three technology companies: Securify, Inktomi, and Sybase.

"In every company where I had responsibility," Peterschmidt says, "I made sure every Monday started with a seven-thirty A.M. operations meeting of all the critical managers to review the status of the business, what had gotten done the previous week, and what would be done the coming week. Because it's repetitive, it becomes a galvanizing event that ensures that communications are clear and that goals and objectives are understood. In a small company, we would do company meetings at the end of every month, when we would tell everyone what happened that month: Did we get funding, how short of cash are we? Even when we got up to fifteen hundred people at Inktomi, we held quarterly employee meetings to let people know what was going on. This became an expected forum for communication."

WHAT EMPLOYEES CARE ABOUT

Much of your effort at communicating will be wasted if you forget a key reality: How well you communicate is determined not by how well *you* say things but by how well you are *understood*. You have to take the measure of your audience—their background, their mood, and their readiness—then tailor your message so that it is not just appropriate but is well received and assimilated.

That's what Steve Bennett learned when he tried to deliver the same message to employees that he did to investors.

Six weeks after becoming the chief executive of Intuit, Bennett stood up in front of a group of investors and delivered the following message: "This is a company that's been doing fine, but with our assets and opportunities we should be performing at a much higher level. We're underperforming against the opportunity." Bennett explained, "It was meant to signal that I'm raising the bar and it's a new ballgame."

But when Bennett delivered the same message to the employees, he got a fast reality check. "Employees are not mobilized and energized by a new CEO coming in and talking about how we should deliver at a higher level for shareholders," he muses. "They just don't care about that."

Bennett went back to basics in his conversations with Intuit employees. He had much to draw on, having visited about twenty of the

company's office locations during his first month on the job and having held town hall meetings in which employees were encouraged to
air their questions and concerns. He had also talked with Intuit customers to find out what they liked and disliked about the product, the
service, and their relationship with the company. Upon reflection,
Bennett realized that he knew which message he needed to deliver to
motivate his people.

"If you're an employee, what you really care about is delivering for
customers," he says. "And you care about working with other great
people to do great things for customers. So the message we focused
on was creating a great place to work and a high-performing organization that delivers for customers." After all, he concluded, "if we have
great employees and they deliver for customers, we'll take care of the
shareholders."

ENGINEERS CAN TALK A DIFFERENT LANGUAGE

Jeff Killeen had a different dilemma. As the new chief executive of
GlobalSpec began to build a relationship with the company's founder,
John Schneiter, he had to find a common language that would bridge
the communication chasm between two totally different and often di-
ametrically opposed backgrounds. It turned out that this was just as
much an issue of corporate culture as it was of communication.

"I consider myself a precise communicator, but my DNA is sales
and marketing," Killeen says, "not component technology and certainly not design engineering to a Ph.D.-level executive. Because
John is a Ph.D. design engineer, I found that he would either not have
an experienced-based frame of reference or would ascribe a different
meaning to business phrases or concepts that I assumed to be univer-
sally understood. I learned right up front that we needed to talk
through basic conversations about media businesses and that I had to
do some remediation. When I referred to things in shorthand—for
instance, when we discussed financials and I'd say, 'Make sure you

fully accrue for that project'—John would understandably say, 'What does that exactly mean, and how does that work?'

"I found I had to be very precise and resist my natural temptation to use too many superlatives when describing the accomplishments in the business. John would say, 'You spin things all the time. You make everything sound good.' I'd say, 'John, that *was* good.' And he would say, 'But you make it sound like it's even better than it is. We're engineers. We don't use words like *terrific* and *outstanding*. We say, "You did your job." When you say that the team did a terrific job, they don't believe you.' We finally agreed that whenever he thought I was spinning, he would tell me. And whenever I thought he was underwhelming, I would tell him."

Killeen elaborates on how he learned to communicate in an engineering culture. "The perspective from which John comes to the business is obsessive in a wonderful way. He harks back to the philosophy that he's building a bridge and that a bridge cannot fail. I said, 'John, but we're not building a bridge, and failure is okay if we fail fast and incorporate that learning so that we can grow as fast as possible. It's preferable to me to get eight things done well and fail at two versus doing three or four things to perfection.' John said, 'We're not trained to accept a lot of failure or welcome it into the process.' I said, 'That's a management concept we have to work on.'"

With all of that give and take, Killeen, Schneiter, and the rest of the GlobalSpec staff established a common language and shorthand that describes the business in terms of metrics, drivers, and issues. In this case, you can also clearly see how the process of communicating is intertwined with the issue of fitting into and adapting to the corporate culture.

COMMUNICATOR, KNOW THYSELF

We would all like to stir a packed auditorium to a standing ovation with our skilled oratory. In our work to recruit a successor to Jack

Valenti, chief of the Motion Picture Association of America, we shared a podium with the eighty-three-year-old legend. In front of more than six hundred MBA students from the nation's most prestigious business schools, talking about leadership in the media and entertainment industry, the one-time speechwriter for LBJ wowed the young crowd with inspirational missives, engaging homilies, and anecdotes about the greatest leaders in the industry's history. Not everyone can be a communicator like Jack Valenti. But as he writes in his book, *Speak Up with Confidence: How to Prepare, Learn, and Deliver Effective Speeches,* everyone can improve their communication skills and effectiveness through diligent preparation and continuous practice.

You also have to be aware of your natural strengths and weaknesses in communicating. Be aware too of which settings are the ones in which you are most effective at delivering your message. Some people radiate to a crowd; others are at their best in smaller groups. Which is best for you?

When Steve Reinemund succeeded Roger Enrico as the CEO of PepsiCo in May 2001, the fifteen-year company veteran was self-consciously aware of the differences in their communication styles. "Roger is a terrific public speaker," Reinemund says. "So it's smart for him to capitalize on large audiences with major messages. That's not my strength. I can do it and I may be getting better at it, but it's not what I love to do. I think I'm more effective in discussions in smaller groups, where I can actually have a dialogue about the business and what's on people's minds, and just getting to know people on a one-on-one basis."

Reinemund points out that when you grow up in a company, it may be easier to be an effective communicator in small groups and one on one. As an insider, you are generally well known, especially compared to the outsider who only has a short amount of time to make an impression. Reinemund was given the confidence to play to his natural strengths in communication by one of the company's directors. "You didn't get here without having tremendous strengths," the director told Reinemund. "Use your strengths in this job, even though they may well be different from the strengths of your predecessor."

COMMUNICATING IN A CRISIS

Regular opportunities for purposeful give and take should become a habit at any company. It's especially important when the company is in trouble.

"In tough times, my advice is, 'Communicate, communicate, communicate,'" says Joseph Tucci, who became chief executive of EMC, a leading data storage company, when the bottom dropped out of the technology market. "And when you think you've done enough, communicate again."

In a crisis, communication law number one is to get the information out and quickly. In today's 24/7 world, you can be absolutely sure that all key information will find its way out, whether you like it or not. If you are not the one to bring it to light or if you are seen as sitting on damaging information too long, then you will have lost your opportunity to try to solve the problem. And you will very likely lose your job. Just look at what happened to the top three executives of behemoth Shell Oil. When it came to light in early 2004 that they had been reporting inflated oil reserves for two years, they were gone from the company in no time flat.

Once the information is out, it is essential to paint an accurate picture of reality, one that acknowledges rather than minimizes the challenges of the situation. Without this level-setting, you will have no credibility on which to build. But once you have it, you can focus on the continuous communication that needs to occur with your key constituencies: employees, the board of directors, customers, the financial community, and the media.

Let's take a look at some of the best examples of leadership in crisis communication.

Tyco International

Few people had a greater crisis than Edward Breen, who took over Tyco International in July 2002, as the scandal-plagued manufacturing conglomerate flirted with bankruptcy in the wake of strategic reversals, accounting concerns, and the forced departure of CEO Dennis Kozlowski, who was charged with personal tax evasion and looting the company. (Tyco shares jumped more than 40 percent following the company's announcement of Breen's appointment as CEO.)

"Communication with employees is a top, top priority," Breen says. "You have to put yourself in the shoes of an employee who is not close to the fire. They only know a fraction of what I know. Their tendency is to worry more. I talked to all the employees, and I was very open about the problems facing the company. I was up front about what the goal was, what needed to be improved, and that it might take some time, and people rallied around that. I showed an upbeat attitude about the company and said I wouldn't have come if I didn't feel great about the long-term health of Tyco.

"But I also said that we had a lot to work through. Significant change needed to occur and needed to occur immediately. I had an attitude that if I didn't change things radically, the status quo would set in, and then you can't change things."

When you're in a crisis, you also have to show confidence. You have to be visible and absorb the uncertainty that people feel. Think of your job as being a sort of shock absorber between the events swirling around the company and your employees' deep-seated desire for stability and security. This will help when people are constantly examining your every gesture and expression for hidden messages that imply that things might be worse than they already are.

Rudy

One of the most memorable examples of communicating in a crisis was New York mayor Rudy Giuliani in the immediate aftermath of the

9/11 attacks. You can still picture the images of him—fierce and determined yet empathetic; omnipresent in the midst of the rubble at the fire stations and at the daily press briefings; communicating with his team, the media, and the people of New York. This leadership and communication moment transformed the very image of Giuliani from a lame-duck public servant going through a public divorce into a national hero. It is important to realize that communication during a crisis has a magnifying effect on you as a leader.

Lucent Technologies

Henry Schacht also knows the importance of putting on a game face in a crisis. When the former CEO and chairman of Lucent returned in October 2000 after the forced departure of CEO Richard McGinn, the technology bust had vaporized many of its customers and slashed the spending budgets of the ones that remained. The financial analysis that Schacht had completed showed that Lucent could well run out of money in ninety days. Schacht's crisis communication plan and the way he communicated with his largest customers helped save the company.

"In the midst of a crisis, nothing is more calming than a calm CEO," Schacht says. "Nothing is less helpful than a frenetic CEO. If some smartass comes in and starts telling everyone what to do, half the people will be scared to death that they're going to be let go, and the other half will think he doesn't know what he's talking about. People want someone reasoned and thoughtful, who can say, 'We're okay, and here's why we're okay.' "

Schacht adds that even in a crisis you probably have more time than you think. "Companies don't go out of business quickly," he told employees during his earliest days, "and this one's not about to. We're going to sort things out, and be very clear with each other, and when we relaunch, we'll all know what we're doing."

What specifically did Schacht do? "On day one of my return to Lucent," he explains, "I went in front of the community with an all-employee broadcast. I didn't have any answers, and I didn't provide any answers. I said, 'This company has lots of assets. We're all going to gather together, and we're going to take a deep breath, slow things down, and make sure we're on the right track.'

"A frenetic approach just makes the company even more unstable. One, you're not likely to be right. Two, even if you are right, nobody knows what the heck you're doing. Three, you haven't bothered to listen to anybody, so you have strained relationships you want to cement. Now, if you're going to run out of money in five or six days, you've got a bit of a different story than if you're going to run out of money in ninety days. That's what I call the 'burning platform' problem. If you've got a burning platform, you don't have a lot of time, so you have to take things in two steps. You have to gather your team together and say, 'Guys, before we do anything else, we had better put this fire out. Then we'll take a deep breath.' "

During tough times, your customers can be some of your greatest allies. But if mistreated or misled, they can quickly become your worst enemies. This was an issue Schacht dealt with immediately.

"When I went back into Lucent," he says, "I divided my time almost fifty-fifty between the internal folks and our major customers. And boy, did I get an earful. Lucent had about ten customers that took eighty percent of the output, and they were all furious, because Lucent had made a conscious decision to set up their competitors and in their view we had neglected them completely. I walked in to each one with a notebook and said, 'What do I need to know?' It was like ripping a scab off the jugular vein. I was there four, five, six hours with each customer. And I said, 'Gotcha. I don't know how to respond, but I'll be back.' Three weeks later I went back and did it again, and a month later I did it again." In time this interactive process of engaging, listening, and responding settled things down and helped create enough stability to concentrate on other areas of the turnaround.

Adelphia Communications

William Schleyer stepped in to quench the fires of yet another 2002 corporate flame-out, this one at Adelphia Communications. The nation's fifth-largest cable operator made headlines when John Rigas, its former CEO, and two of his sons were accused of defrauding the company and driving it into bankruptcy. Behind the headlines, the operating situation wasn't much better. Adelphia ranked at the bottom of the cable industry based on most financial benchmarks. "I was as shocked at the underperformance of the company as I was by the alleged criminal acts," Schleyer said in an interview shortly after being appointed chairman and chief executive officer in January 2003. But he also declared, "I was brought in to clean up the company. My goal is to bring Adelphia out of bankruptcy intact.

"The most important issue was to calm down a company in massive crisis so the new management could focus on its operating and financial performance," Schleyer says. He explains how he set priorities and how important it was to be consistent and continuous in his communication. "First we had to get a $1.5 billion loan to make sure the company had access to capital. We had to convince all the financial constituents that their capital was worth investing on us. We had to get all the large bondholders, the financial advisers, legal advisers, pre-petition banks, and DIP [debtor in possession] lenders, to get on the same page. That required meeting after meeting. I spent most of my first three months in New York City, because that's where they were. I was working fifteen-hour days, five days a week, in meetings with banks and bondholders first thing in the morning and dinners at night to help them understand the world the way we looked at it. We told everyone the same thing—and more important, we told them that we were telling everyone the same thing. There was no difference in how we treated anyone. We went to each of these folks with a consistent story, rather than a story targeted to a certain person or constituency. That paid huge dividends. We gained a lot of credibility in the marketplace. Now all the constituents respect us and leave us alone, which gives us more time to focus on our operating performance and getting out of bankruptcy. And our financial performance is improving every month."

What advice does Schleyer offer to other new leaders coming into a crisis? "First, be as totally candid as possible. Don't stonewall. Tell them what you know and what you don't know. If I didn't know about the areas under litigation, I told them and said that I was looking into it. This buys you time because people know you're honest and are trying to do the right thing. Second, it's important not to set unreasonable expectations. That becomes a downward spiral, and you inevitably have to spend a lot of time mending the damage."

COMMUNICATING WITH YOUR BOARD

If you're a CEO, another critical piece of the communication puzzle, as we reviewed in Chapter 6, is the board of directors. It is essential to establish a protocol for communicating with them, one that, like many other facets of a new leadership situation, requires being tailored to the situation. Lucent's Schacht offers sound advice for the new CEO in a crisis:

"If I were a new CEO coming into a new company at a tough time, I'd have a deal with the board. I would tell them, 'I'm going to keep you informed every step of the way. But you're not my most important problem right now. You've asked me to come in and you've given me a good briefing and I thank you; now please give me a little room. I'll be back with a status report in two or three weeks, and if something else comes up, we'll be on the phone together. But right now my most important constituent is the internal folks and our customers.'

"That said, we had fifty-one board meetings the first year I was back. But this was a crisis—we were burning two billion dollars a quarter in negative cash flow. So virtually every Friday I reported back where we were, what I was finding, what the crisis issues were, what my assessment was, and the remedial action as we got to it."

Taken together, Schacht's seemingly simple advice and example offer valuable insight to how a new CEO works effectively with the board, as we detailed in Chapter 6. He set expectations that were linked to his assessment of the priorities; he underpromised and overdelivered; he kept his board informed every step of the way; and he set up a straightforward process of communication that would be as convenient for the board as possible, even in a crisis. These actions give a board confidence in their leader.

TALKING TO THE MEDIA

There are two predominant schools of thought about communicating with the media during a crisis. One holds that you shouldn't hide from the press. As we said earlier, if you have damaging information, it is imperative to get it out and communicate it immediately. Your accessibility is especially important during difficult times. After all, when you talk with the press, you have the opportunity to tell *your* story. You can use the occasion to try to have them share your perspective. If you are in a leadership position in a visible company, especially in a time of crisis, stories will be written regardless of what you do. Reporters have a job to do, and they will do it whether you like it or not. Treating them forthrightly, consistently, and with facts is considered best practice in crisis situations.

Intriguingly, Schacht, for one, is in the opposite camp. During Lucent's crisis, he recalls, "I did not talk to the press or the financial community. I just said, 'I haven't got anything to say. Talk to somebody else.' There was all sorts of stuff written about Lucent, but you never saw a quote from me in there because I wouldn't talk to them. The only constituents I took care of were the board, the internal folks, and the customers."

Whether you're talking to the press, the financial community, customers, or an internal audience, resist the temptation to paint a rosier picture than pertains in reality. Remind yourself that you're talking with serious-minded people on whom you are relying to execute your agenda. Show your respect for them by being straightforward, honest, and open-minded.

"You have to be able to articulate direction and vision without putting yourself in a position to make one of the worst mistakes a business leader can make—to overcommit and underdeliver," advises Bob Nardelli. "Don't try to come across as smarter than you are. You could get lucky—or you could be terribly embarrassed."

SENDING SIGNALS

There are both explicit and implicit methods of communication. Explicit methods are the messages deliberately articulated in memos, speeches, town hall meetings, open e-mails, and the like. Implicit methods are the subtle, unspoken signals sent by your actions. Often, as in the case of parents who ineffectively advise children to "do as I say, not as I do," the implicit signals carry the most weight.

In the early days, you will be sending signals with everything you say and don't say, everything you ask and don't ask, even facial expressions and hand gestures, and very certainly what you wear and what you don't wear.

Some sartorial signals are completely unconscious, but the response can actually be measured. Lou Gerstner described a classic signal that he unwittingly sent in his first meeting of IBM's corporate management board on his first day as chief executive of Big Blue. The meeting comprised the top fifty people in the company, and all the men were wearing white shirts—with the exception of Gerstner. His was blue, a major departure for an IBM executive. When the same group met weeks later, Gerstner recalls, he showed up in a white shirt and found everyone else wearing other colors. Gerstner's blue shirt made national news, and he commented later that he had wanted to send a deliberate signal about change.

IBM's shirt-switching was more culturally telling than strategically significant, but other sartorial signals mean a great deal. When Paul Pressler started at Gap Inc., he made a point of adding boot-cut corduroy pants to his wardrobe, which was previously dominated by Armani suits, and he publicized the fact on the company intranet.

A similar change of clothes took place at 3M when Jeff McNerney came in. In his case, the signal was sent by the 3M employees; McNerney picked it up the moment he walked into the company's headquarters. Most of 3M's eleven thousand employees had dispensed with coats and ties long ago, but starched shirts, jackets, and ties still prevailed at the top. The message was like a headline to the new chief executive: Senior management was out of touch. The suits soon went the way of discarded Post-it Notes, a return message from the new CEO that he was trying to repair the disconnect in the company.

Dave D'Alessandro, CEO of John Hancock, who happens to favor bright ties—somewhat unusual in the staid insurance industry—similarly observed that after he became CEO, the ties around the company became brighter.

In short, every move you make is being watched and analyzed. Because you don't have the history of actions on which people can fill in the rest of the picture, signals, even seemingly small things, will be magnified. In this way, communication—explicit and implicit—plays a direct role in cultural transformation, especially in the early days. Whether it is formal or informal attire, or messages about timeliness and respect for others that you send when you schedule and show up for meetings, or your use of e-mail versus voicemail, your subtle signals work their way across the entire organization. They communicate the new rules with regard to what is and what is not acceptable and expected under the new leadership regime.

THE MATHEMATICS OF FIRST IMPRESSIONS

Harvard University president Lawrence Summers has come up with a mathematical metaphor to describe the impact of first impressions. His insight helps explain the science behind the timeless expression *First impressions are lasting impressions.* "People form their impressions as an average," Summers says. "If they've had only two impressions of you and they get a third one, then it could move you as much as three halves. But if they've had ninety-six impressions so far and they get a ninety-seventh, it won't have such a big impact."

While choosing the color of your shirt or showing up to a meeting on time may not be an item that tops the chart of your agenda during your first hundred days, all of the decisions you make demonstrate whether you are willing to walk your talk. To ensure that your actions are consistent with your message, you have to be alert to whether your decisions amplify the message or cause dissonance in the signal.

FIRST PRIORITIES HAVE MAGNIFIED EFFECT

For an airline, nothing says more about the state of the company than the physical quality and appearance of the planes. Intuitively sensing this fact, Leo Mullin scored points soon after he took command of Delta Air Lines when he promised to refurbish the interior of every single Delta airplane within sixteen months.

"I remember flying down for my final discussion [with the board of directors] and finding that the seat in front of me had a big tear in it, almost like somebody had put a knife through the leather. Then I looked around: the carpeting was raggedy, and the seats were in terrible shape, and the spaces between them weren't clean. It was extremely reflective of the nonspend mentality that had prevailed there for about three years. As I listened to the flight attendants and to the airport customer service personnel, I heard a real sense of apology in their voices, as if they were saying, 'Gee, we're really sorry the plane looks like a dump.'

"I didn't realize it at the time, but that particular commitment turned out to be a really important symbol of a new phase at Delta. It said that we were no longer going to put the passengers in crappy seats, that we were really supposed to do something for the customer, and that that's why we exist. It was very symbolic. And it was not as costly as you might imagine."

WHEN HAVING ALL THE ANSWERS IS THE WRONG ANSWER

Sometimes you can have the greatest communication skills and the very best of intentions but still run into difficulties. During her early days at Hewlett-Packard, Carly Fiorina, one of the highest-profile women leaders in business and someone known for her gift of inspirational oratory, inadvertently raised hackles at introductory coffee talks for an ironic reason: There was no question she did not answer, according to company insiders. Never once, said an observer, did she say, "Gee, I didn't think about that" or "I'm not sure right now." Long accustomed to Socratic dialogue, HP people became concerned that Fiorina was not interested in learning about them, about their products, or about the processes by which the business is carried out. Fiorina, who in fact had done such an in-depth study of the company and the situation that she had many of the answers, probably meant to reassure people by her knowledge. But by not asking questions and by not failing to have some answers, she scared many of the employees. Fortunately, when this feedback was delivered and received, Fiorina adapted her active listening and allowed her natural gift for communication to flourish. This increased her credibility and at the same time deepened her insights into the company, its challenges, and its opportunities. When it came time therefore to "bet the company" by going after the acquisition of Compaq Computer, she had built up a reservoir of trust on which she was able to successfully wage the battle.

HOW AND WHERE YOU SPEND YOUR TIME COMMUNICATES YOUR EXPECTATIONS

Your actions, whether large or small, communicate your expectations. Obviously, moving the company headquarters is a hugely tangible indicator of a break from the past. But so are things like showing up two minutes early for every single meeting. "That says, 'I respect your time, you respect my time, and this is a disciplined company,' " says Dan Schulman of Virgin Mobile USA.

How you allocate your time can be an enormous signpost of change in a company. When Lou Gerstner came into IBM, he said that 50 percent of his time would be spent with customers. Another CEO, coming into a company that was notoriously internally focused, constantly questioned his management team about the process they used to gather customer insights. Knowing that no such process existed, he asked them to commit to start thinking about one.

Dan Kerpelman, president of Kodak's Health Imaging Group, declined an office in the corporate executive suite in favor of a fairly basic one closer to the troops. He thereby signaled more than simply how he wanted to spend his time. "As an outsider coming into Kodak, I wanted everyone to know from day one that I believe in teamwork and consider myself part of Health Imaging," he says. "What better way to do so than to locate myself closer to the rest of the team, in an office that is relatively modest. Relating to people early on is key to the success of any new leader. This symbolic gesture went a long way in that regard."

THE POWER OF THE PURSE

William Schleyer emphasized the change in the chain of command at Adelphia Communications when he passed on the power of the purse to his people. Against a long tradition of centralized decision making for everything, he delegated authority to make spending decisions. This action hit home precisely because it wasn't merely symbolic; it symbolized change and a new respect for employees in the everyday course of doing business.

"We wanted to shorten the chain from management to people in the field and put decision making as close as possible to our sub-scribers," he says. "This was a huge change from a centralized organization, where just a few people made decisions, to more of a decentralized environment where decisions could be made at a local level. In one case, we were trying to get a rebuild done in a certain town, and they were waiting for approval for a particular vendor. I said, 'Just do it. I'm holding you accountable for the P&L, not some guy in corporate headquarters with fourteen things on his desk.' In the data business, the manager was grousing about how he couldn't get a circuit. I said, 'If you can't get it done internally, go out and buy it yourself. Buy it from MCI, if necessary. We're holding you accountable for results, so you're free to make those decisions on your own, within a certain range.'"

YOUR ORGANIZATION STRUCTURE AS A COMMUNICATIONS TOOL

Steve Bennett is a big believer in flat organizations and the messages about accountability and customer focus that such a structure communicates. He is also a believer in listening first and reorganizing later. But these two beliefs quickly came into conflict after he became the chief executive at Intuit in January 2000.

"My original plan when I came here was to take three months before I made any big changes," he recalls, "because I didn't want them to be knee-jerk reactions. But the fact of the matter is, as I traveled around and met with the staff and the employees and saw how we were running things, what had to be done was so clear and compelling that I reorganized the company the fifth week I was here.

"It used to be that we as a company thought the whole game was building great products, not the total customer experience. We were very business unit–centric. The whole service and support was owned functionally. But running a business didn't mean owning the total customer experience, and my view is that to run a business, you have to be responsible for the end-to-end customer experience.

"When I first got here," he continues, "I was down in Tucson, Arizona, talking to the people who provided technical support for Quicken. They told me a story of somebody in Mountain View, California, where Quicken was run, who decided to add a new feature button on Quicken.com that you could press for help. And in their infinite wisdom, they added the feature—but they never told anybody in Tucson that they had done that. The next day Tucson got nine thousand telephone calls. Nobody even knew they were coming. And the attitude of the Mountain View group was, 'What's wrong with you guys in service?'

"When I reorganized the company, I used that story as an example. I said, 'This change won't fix the problem of the product people adding a new feature without telling the service people, but at least I'll make one person responsible because they own it end to end.'

"That was a big signal. The other thing I did was eliminate a layer of senior vice presidents. I'm a big proponent of de-layering. Layers are like sweaters. If it's twenty degrees outside but you're wearing seven sweaters, you have no idea what the temperature is. The fewer layers between me and the front-line employees, the better, because layers generally dilute an organization's effectiveness. We used to run the company with the same eight white males that just kind of rotated from job to job in a good old boys' network. If you asked them, 'What's your job?' they would say, 'It's to help Bill [Campbell, the former CEO and now the chairman of the board] run the company.' As opposed to saying, 'I run such-and-such business.' I de-layered that whole bubble of eight people and had all the people who were running the businesses work directly for me. I went from eight reports to fifteen or seventeen. Of course, that made everybody say, 'How could anybody manage fifteen or seventeen direct reports?' But my theory is that if you have six direct reports, you spend all your time meddling in their business, because you've got no job. But if you've got seventeen direct reports, you'd better make sure you've got the right people because you can't baby-sit them all. So de-layer, get great people, tell them what you expect, figure out what you can do to help them, and get out of the way."

GET DIRECT INPUT

One of the most surprising aspects of taking on a new leadership position is the torrent of information that comes at you. Many people try to cope by establishing proper channels of communication. While doing so has possible benefits in terms of time management and control of messaging, giving and getting direct input from the field has manifold countervailing benefits. Handling this information requires a significant effort and time commitment on your part, but it's an investment that will pay off—in credibility, in trust, and in stakeholder engagement.

That's what Gary Kusin found when he became the new chief executive of Kinko's in June 2001. "In the first six months, I had town hall meetings in every one of the twenty-four markets in the United States," he says. "The fewest number of people at the meetings was about a hundred fifty. I took questions from everybody, and I visited stores on the graveyard shift, on the weekends. I hit three hundred fifty stores in six months and met eyeball to eyeball with about five thousand of our twenty thousand employees.

"I took my case directly to the people and told them what we had to do if we were to survive. I didn't to it through middlemen. And I started writing company-wide newsletters about every two weeks that were streams of consciousness about what I was seeing in my travels, what I was learning, what I thought we did well, what I thought we didn't do well. I called it like it was, and I got very positive feedback from the rank and file."

Kusin also invited direct feedback. "I gave them all my e-mail address—all twenty thousand people in the organization—and said, 'You let me know.' And you know what? They did let me know with about a hundred e-mails a day. The way I respond is becoming part of the lore around here.

"I'll give you an example," he continues. "A technology guy in Kansas City sent me the absolute nastiest letter you've ever seen, but it had a really good germ of an idea in it. The whole thrust of the letter was, 'This company isn't listening to the people who built it, and if this is such a smart thing to do, why don't we do it?' I happened to be going to Kansas City, so I wandered into his store and introduced myself. I thought he would faint dead away. Then I said, 'Let's get some coffee,' and we sat down and talked. We have since implemented his idea, because it was the right thing to do.

"I cannot overstate the importance of getting direct input from the rank and file about their thoughts about the company and what it needs. It is very easy to become way too insular in the ivory tower of a corporate environment and not clearly grasp the issues from the 'factory floor.' The first hundred days is a political campaign. You have to win the hearts and minds of the electorate, and you can't do that when you're sitting in a conference room with a consulting firm."

• • •

Communication is a central aspect of leadership and indeed all human activity. It has a magnified effect during your first hundred days. Take care to do it well and do it often, which requires active listening, tailoring communication approaches both to your natural strengths and to the situation, and giving and getting direct feedback. It will help support your strategic and cultural agenda; it will also help you avoid many of the most common pitfalls that threaten new leaders as they try to get off to the right start. And that is the topic of the next chapter.

ONCLUSION

TEN GUIDELINES FOR EFFECTIVE LEADERSHIP COMMUNICATIONS

1. Know your audience so you can tailor your message and your style to their readiness and to what *they* care about.

2. Tell stories to establish an emotional connection to your point.

3. Effective communication is more than promulgating a message, it is a continuous give and take in which ideas are explored, assimilated, and adapted before being locked in.

4. Use and reuse your communication in various forums and formats both to reinforce your message and to leverage your time.

5. Communicating is intimately intertwined with corporate culture; adapting an organization's language and shorthand—or introducing a new and agreed-upon language—will help transform that culture.

6. Know the communication settings that you are most comfortable in—be it stirring a large crowd to action or working in small groups—and play to your natural strengths.

7. In a crisis, get the information out as quickly as possible. Acknowledge the challenges of the situation to establish credibility, then act as a "shock absorber" between the uncertainty of the situation and the employees' deep-seated desire for stability.

8. Be conscious of the signals you are sending. In the early days, every move you make is being closely watched, and communication, both explicit messages and implicit signals such as your manner of dress, your allocation of time, your mode of communication, and even your organizational structure, play a direct role in the cultural transformation.

9. Having all the answers is usually the wrong answer. People need to see you listening and assimilating their information. If you don't pause to ask questions and circle back when you have more data, you will lose credibility and trust.

10. Get direct input from the field; while this requires making a significant time investment, it will pay back multiple-fold in enhanced credibility, trust, and stakeholder engagement.

EIGHT

RESISTING TEMPTATION

AVOIDING THE TOP TEN TRAPS FOR NEW LEADERS

For years, entertainers and sports heroes had a lock on the popular consciousness. Madonna, Britney, Oprah, Shaq, and Tiger were all you needed to say, and instantaneous recognition was the result. But over the past decade businesspeople have approached that first-name notoriety, both in fame (Jack, Warren, Bill, and of course The Donald) and in infamy (Martha, Bernie, and Dennis).

Perhaps it is not so far-fetched, then, to imagine the following scene:

> It is 11:45 P.M., the television is tuned into CBS, and David Letterman bellows, "Ladies and gentlemen, we have a very special treat tonight. Straight from our field reporters along the perp walk, at the courthouse, and in secret boardrooms across America, we have tonight's Top Ten List—The Top Ten Causes of CEO blowups.

Well, perhaps this is a stretch, but the fact is that many seeds of destruction for new leaders are sown in the first hundred days. The goal of this chapter is to identify and help you avoid the most common pitfalls that seduce and trip up new leaders so that you can not only establish the right foundation in the first hundred days, but build on the momentum in your next hundred days and the next hundred days, all the way to achieving your ultimate goal: enduring great performance.

If the actions detailed in Chapters 1 through 7 are the right ones to follow to get off to the right start for long-term success, then the flip side is also true: You can seal shut the valuable window of opportunity represented by your first hundred days and actually create the underpinnings for failure during the same period. In fact, just as enduring success does not occur in the first hundred days, neither does definitive failure. While many of the leadership collapses that are punctuated by high-profile ousters seem to be sudden, the reality is that in almost every case the metaphorical water has been heated to the boiling point for some time. The goal in a new leadership role is to be aware of the longer-term problem areas and to be vigilant in preventing the seeds of destruction from getting planted in the fertile soil of the first hundred days.

What are the longer-term problem areas? Author and Dartmouth Tuck School of Business professor Sydney Finkelstein completed the largest research project ever on leadership failure, for his groundbreaking book, *Why Smart Executives Fail*. According to Finkelstein, true failure—"spectacular failure"—is the result of a series of destructive behaviors (seven, to be precise) that executives in failing companies exhibit:

1. They see themselves and their companies as dominating their competitive environments, even if this view is out of step with reality.

2. They identify so completely with the company that there is no clear boundary between their own self-image and interests and the company's image and interests.

3. They think they have all the answers, often impressing others with the speed and decisiveness with which they deal with significant issues.

4. They make sure that everyone is 100 percent behind them, ruthlessly eliminating anyone who disagrees with their views.

5. They are the consummate company spokespersons, obsessed with managing the image of their company and themselves, often devoting the largest portion of their time to image management.

6. They underestimate fundamental major obstacles, treating them instead as temporary impediments to be simply removed or circumvented.

7. They stubbornly rely on what worked for them in the past, clinging to the strategies and tactics that made them successful in the first place.

Most executive failures, then, are not the result of commonly cited causes, such as insufficient intelligence, questionable motivations, dishonesty, or even lack of leadership capabilities. Most top executives actually have the intellect, skills, and experience to lead their companies through the inevitable challenges they encounter. It turns out that "softer" issues, such as communication mishaps, misaligned expectations, the need to be loved, and the notion that you have to be the savior are more often than not the real culprits, especially in the early days.

In *Why CEOs Fail,* David Dotlich and Peter Cairo discuss eleven personality traits that their research showed can derail a career. Arrogance, excessive caution, volatility, and melodrama can indeed all be causes of failure, as the authors convincingly point out. In our research, however, we were interested in spotlighting the pitfalls that occur on a day-to-day basis in the earliest days of leadership *as a result* of these characteristics.

In our interviews, we asked CEOs and board directors to identify their most common dilemmas in their early days and the forces that tempted them to do certain things. We went out of our way to interview not only the most successful protagonists in CEO successions but some of the least successful as well. We complemented this process by reviewing a wide array of third-party research on executive failure, leading us to recognize the common pitfalls for the first hundred days.

Many of the traps are interconnected. Take, for example, the syndrome of "The Emperor's New Clothes," which we will detail later. When you create an environment of intimidation such that no one has the confidence to give you honest feedback, you won't be able to make well-informed decisions. And the desire—or even the need—to feel good about yourself in the media and in front of Wall Street analysts can lead to unrealistic expectations that force you to untenably borrow from the future to deliver in the present.

So without further ado, let's turn to the top ten traps for new leaders. Once we have identified them, we hope you will be able to avoid them.

1. SETTING UNREALISTIC EXPECTATIONS

"The most universal trap for a new leader is wanting to do so much so fast that you overpromise and overcommit," says Jeff Killeen of Global-Spec.

Setting unrealistic or unsustainable expectations is one of the most seductive and common pitfalls for new leaders. Real pressures lead to this, such as the all-too-human need to impress your higher authority—the board or your boss—or the media, to demonstrate that you are in charge. Some executives secretly dream of getting that long-sought-after *Fortune* or *BusinessWeek* cover story. Others legitimately want to energize the organization based on the belief that setting tough targets drives results. Often executives think that if they impose stretch objectives and reward managers for hitting them, and penalize or let go those who don't hit the numbers, they will achieve the growth they desire (or have already promised).

The problem is that if you allow these stretch goals to turn into expectations, they then become the baseline against which you and the organization will be measured. Serious problems arise when these targets are not rooted in the underlying realities of the market and the company's position. A suffocating pressure develops to do whatever is necessary to hit the current quarter's numbers, even at the expense of doing the right things for the business over the longer term.

Such pressures are often the root cause of serious problems, such as trade loading, which Jim Kilts confronted when he took over Gillette, or revenue recognition issues, such as those that helped force Sanjay Kumar from the CEO position at Computer Associates in April 2004.

We believe that Jeff Killeen is right when he describes the *best-case* consequence of setting unrealistic expectations: "You find that you have to become superhuman and make things happen that ultimately are good for the business but probably are running your life and your company's life at a pace that is just not sustainable."

Not all companies whose leaders create unrealistic expectations succumb imminently to destructive behaviors. But their doing so can undermine their leadership and create unhealthy cultures. Failure to meet expectations, once set, can also result in relatively harmless but nonetheless negative reactions. Killeen warns, "When you get behind the curve, you have to use up political capital when you then have to reforecast."

More serious instances of expectations mismanagement can cost you your job. Witness the case of Durk Jager, the Procter & Gamble executive who was appointed CEO in September 1998. He was given the nod to take over from beloved CEO John Pepper, based on his perceived ability to drive rapid growth at the world's largest consumer products company. Unfortunately, Jager had an inauspicious start: the company's stock plunged 10 percent on the day he was named CEO. What doomed him, however, was that he promised revenue and earnings growth, only to continually miss those expectations. After failing to reach expectations in his first year, he shocked investors and analysts in early 2000 by *pre-announcing* lower-than-expected third-quarter earnings. The stock immediately crashed *30 percent!* On the ensuing conference call, Jager soberly promised, "We will not disappoint you again." But then in June 2000 he was forced to tell investors to expect flat fourth-quarter earnings compared with the previous year, whereas analysts had been led to expect a 16 percent profit increase for the period (which was actually down from the original projection of 22 percent growth). To no one's surprise, three strikes and Jager was out after only seventeen months at P&G. He was succeeded by A. G. Lafley, who has met or exceeded expectations in every period since.

There are other pernicious examples of the perils of overpromising. Former CEO Richard McGinn was notorious for his optimistic growth story at Lucent Technologies. Once he articulated the expectations externally, he created debilitating pressure internally to hit the targets, even while the storm clouds were rapidly gathering over the telecommunications equipment industry. His growth story worked only so long before the fundamentals of the business diverged so significantly from his message that his credibility was destroyed. After he repeatedly promised—and failed—to restore Lucent to profitability, disgruntled board members lost patience with him and forced his resignation in late 2000.

McGinn's permanent successor (after Henry Schacht served as interim CEO), Pat Russo, was a study in contrast, making sure to be absolutely realistic about the state of the business and setting appropriate goals, no matter how gloomy they seemed, in an effort to restore credibility. Her more grounded approach translated into setting expectations that were both appropriate and realistic. Like Lou Gerstner at IBM, Russo felt that the last thing Lucent needed when she became CEO was a bold new vision. The company needed to survive. Russo came to recognize that the central question facing Lucent in 2002 was not the grand long-term vision but rather how to navigate the company through an unprecedented time, one of precipitous decline that was unanticipated, either in depth or duration. The challenge and the imperative was to make it through the downturn and emerge leaner, stronger, and able to create value going forward. In the questionable industry environment, she developed and communicated a simple but powerful message to employees: "My vision for Lucent during this period is to make it through the down cycle stronger, leaner, and more customer-focused than it was coming in." This simple message helped secure the support and shared commitment of Lucent's remaining 62,000 employees. And coupled with painful but necessarily aggressive cost reduction, sophisticated balance sheet management, focused product line rationalization, and attentive customer service, this approach gave Lucent the time to ride out the difficult market and work its way back to a smaller but healthier positioning.

How do you avoid the pitfall of setting unrealistic expectations?

"The best way to avoid that trap," according to Gillette's Jim Kilts, "is to tell the organization what you know from the outside world's point of view but don't take ownership of it yourself right away. This way you can communicate that you have a knowledge of the company without giving an answer before you feel you have an answer." When Kilts came to Gillette, the company had not made its numbers for five years and had missed expectations fourteen quarters in a row. Kilts concluded that "our decision was to not talk to analysts until we were ready. That took four months, which was very tough for the Street to swallow."

Remember also that setting expectations is a delicate balancing act that is difficult to get right, especially for a new manager. "If you keep missing on the high side, people will say you're out of touch with reality," says Steve Reinemund, CEO of PepsiCo. "But if you set them too low, you may be worse off than if you set them too high. If you set them lower than what the organization thinks it can do, you're going to disappoint high-potential people who want to achieve strong results."

In short, keep in mind that while setting expectations is an important part of your responsibility set, in the end you will be judged by your results. "As long as you're doing a good job of openly communicating where you are in your evaluation and change process, it is what it is," says Sears CEO Alan Lacy. "If people think that's too slow, that's what it is. You can only have people work so many hours for so many days. As long as you're getting at it as aggressively and proactively as you can, and you're keeping people informed of where you're at and where you want to get to, that should be enough."

2. EITHER MAKING RASH DECISIONS OR SUFFERING FROM ANALYSIS PARALYSIS

One dimension of your clout in the first hundred days is your permission to—more often the expectation that you will—take bold action. This is fine if you make the right moves. "If you can get something resolved quickly that is absolutely appropriate, you should get along with it," advises Alan Lacy, CEO of Sears. But if you act just to act, or make premature pronouncements, you can set yourself back. Adds Lacy, "If a promise can't be met or if you don't have the knowledge to know what to do, don't try to bluff it. Take the time you need to figure out what to do. Don't be rushed into making commitments. The cost of reworking them is very high."

The flip side of acting too quickly is succumbing to analysis paralysis. The current environment certainly encourages prudence; newly aggressive boards, vocal shareholders, and watchful regulatory bodies are imposing greater scrutiny on managers who already have to analyze potential competitive threats, new technologies, cash flow requirements, supply chain interruptions, and all the other factors that can trip them up. It's no wonder that you want to be absolutely certain before you make a decision.

The major problems with overly cautious behavior are that it eats up time and sets the example of risk aversion. Fear of making the wrong decision may lead you to seek reassurance in one more study, one more task force, or just a little more data. But by the time you've found the perfect answer, the problem has spiraled out of control or the opportunity has been missed. Your own caution can cause the very failure that you sought to avoid.

Seeking the perfect answer is as major a pitfall for new leaders as is rushing to judgment. But while we actively encourage listening and seeking input, you can't engage in a study for too long or postpone a tough decision indefinitely. You've got to pull the trigger while the target is still there, especially if your company is in a crisis situation. "If you don't make changes quickly, it's not fatal, but boy, it gets tough," says Ed Breen, who faced one of the gravest crises in corporate America when he took over at Tyco in 2002. "Gather the facts as quickly as possible, but never worry that you don't have all the facts in front of you. You're never going to have them all. Get enough to feel comfortable, then make a decision and move on. People who sit around for too long analyze and reanalyze, and that's a pitfall if you're in a crisis."

Most new leaders want to seize the moment and make a decision or a promise right on the spot, but making premature assurances is as dangerous a pitfall as overpromising. "You will be constantly tempted and tested by senior members of the team," says Killeen. "Resist being impulsive. Don't make promises without the facts. You should force yourself to be boring. Say things like, 'That sounds like a great idea, but I have been here for just a week, so I'll have to think about that. Meanwhile, keep those ideas coming.' During the first hundred days and beyond, you can always go back to the issue and do something about it, but you can't repeal a promise without great collateral damage. You have only so many chips, so don't waste them by being impulsive, most of all at the very beginning."

We've been taught to admire the dynamic leader who juggles multiple crises simultaneously, makes a dozen decisions a minute, and takes only seconds to size up complex situations that have stumped everyone else. The problem with this picture, according to Syd Finkelstein, is that it is a fraud.

Leaders who settle issues *too* quickly limit their opportunity to grasp the ramifications. One of the most dangerous traps is failing to solicit the input of others on the team. Not only does this mean that you most likely won't have all the information, but you will be absolutely certain to disenfranchise your colleagues. "It is close to fatal to decide or pronounce before you listen," says Henry Schacht. "And in crisis situations, I think you exacerbate the problem as opposed to moving toward a sound solution. Even if at the end you come back to exactly the same decision you would have made, how you get there is as important as getting there."

Trust your own judgment while soliciting input and feedback. That will maximize your chances of making the right decisions in the right time frame—neither rashly nor indecisively.

3. BEING A KNOW-IT-ALL

Another serious pitfall in the early days is believing that you have all the answers. Leaders who make rash decisions are generally people who are *so* sure of their views that they don't gather input from knowledge-able sources. But the reality is that know-it-alls typically don't know what they don't know. By not recognizing or admitting that you don't have—and can't possibly have—all the answers, you shut out new perspectives, as well as the possibility of getting the valuable information and input that may lead you to new discoveries and answers.

Being a know-it-all also invariably leads to quickly alienating your colleagues and employees. They will see you as someone who shoots from the hip, who is impulsive, potentially inconsistent, and probably insecure. One top executive we know may have worked himself out of the chance to run one of the world's most admired companies by "having to prove in the first five minutes of every meeting that he is the smartest guy in the room," according to a member of his senior management team.

An even worse part of jumping to conclusions is that it can set you up for the vicious cycle of overpromising and underdelivering—the serious number-one trap described above. "If you've been in the position for only a month or two, you can't possibly understand how everything really works," says Jeff Killeen.

Even someone who has been promoted from within a company or was there before should take heed. Pat Russo knew Lucent well when she came in as CEO in January 2002. After all, she spent the vast majority of her career at the company and its predecessor, AT&T. Including her ten-month stint as president and COO at Kodak, she had been away from the company for less than two years. "When I came back to Lucent, I made a conscious decision to assume that I knew nothing," Russo says. "This was evidently a surprise to many people, who expected me to come in and dictate what needed to be done. But I believed that before I made my own determination about what had changed most and least, the right thing to do was to be intentionally quiet and listen. Then I got my team together and reviewed all the input and finally got our top five issues together."

The key takeaway: Spend a large portion of your first hundred days listening rather than talking, learning rather than preaching, observing rather than jumping to conclusions, and inviting input rather than promulgating the gospel according to you.

4. FAILING TO LET GO OF YOUR PAST IDENTITY

What's past is prologue, according to Shakespeare. But for many leaders who stumble early in their tenures, what's past is still very much present. Leaders who have been trained and have made their reputations ascending the ranks of market-leading companies often cling to the mores of those institutions. Sometimes without even realizing it, they simply talk about it too frequently, creating the impression that their former employer is better than their new one, or that they have buyer's remorse. In so doing, they disenfranchise their new organization or simply annoy people, undermining their ability to be effective in the first hundred days.

The failure to let go of a past identity manifests itself in a variety of ways, none of them positive. Some leaders bring all the accoutrements of their prior office to their new one, causing people to disdainfully view their new digs as a mausoleum. This happened in a major media company, when a top executive joined from a position at the White House. Fellow division chiefs made sarcastic quips about how the new individual wasn't comfortable unless he was in front of a picture of himself shaking hands with a U.S. president or a foreign head of state. Of course, behind most jokes is a hint of truth. In this case, the remarks were indicative of how this man's colleagues had come to view him—as a self-promoting opportunist hungry for power and prestige. To no one's surprise, the executive was pushed out of the company within the year.

A much more benign example is the case of Larry Johnston, CEO of Albertson's supermarket chain. Two years into his tenure at the helm of the $35 billion company, an article in the *Wall Street Journal* described his office as a memorial to his twenty-nine years of achievement at GE: a framed magazine ad behind his desk touting a GE medical business that he helped revive, photos of him smiling at GE awards banquets, and so on. While both common and understandable, lauding his former employer rubbed some of his Albertson's employees the wrong way. Reacting to the feedback, Johnston increased his sensitivity to the signals he was sending in continually referring to GE and soon decreased such references markedly.

More important than how you decorate your office is how you take the experiences of your prior company and tailor them to the unique circumstances, culture, language, and ways of doing business at your new one. Of course, at a top-level position it is largely your prior track record that positioned you for your new leadership role. But a sure way to blow out of your new position is to inflexibly apply the processes and jargon of your previous organization now.

To illustrate the point: We can't tell you how many times we've discussed the risks of hiring a new CEO straight from some of the best-known "academy companies," such as GE, PepsiCo, P&G, and American Express. Many boards and hiring managers prefer not to recruit a long-term executive from one of these companies directly, but to recruit their alumni, who have already left to join a second company, so that they are less likely to try and impose their old ways on the new organization lock, stock, and barrel.

One former leader who did not fall into this trap was Dan Kerpelman, who left a seventeen-year career at GE to become the president of Kodak's $2.4 billion Health Imaging Group. He was very conscious of GE's long shadow and did his best to minimize it.

"I promised myself that I would not mention GE more than once a week," Kerpelman says. "I allowed myself to do it many times in the first week because I knew people would ask comparative questions, but after that I adhered to my promise. I chose not to be GE. I wanted to be Dan, and I wanted to be Kodak as quickly as possible. I tried to instill the confidence I had about coming to Kodak: I talked about Kodak's great R&D, our intellectual property, our global brand, the legacy of our hundred years in the medical imaging business. I spent a lot of time trying to communicate that I respected Kodak and that I wasn't here to turn the Health Imaging business into a GE clone." This led to a tremendous jolt of pride and energy from the Health Imaging team, which has remained ever since.

Another way to live in the past is to get stuck in your predecessor's history. Still another way is to accept a legacy financial plan or strategy without being able to get out of it quickly enough.

Financial legacies are the most damaging, warns Jeff Killeen. "Don't get trapped into adopting someone else's budget," he says, "even if the board puts pressure on you to lock down a plan. You need several months to assess assumptions, and budgets are products of assumptions, thoughtfully drafted. You need time to think about the right metrics and business drivers, and then you need time to think about the talent and resources necessary to pull it all off. By letting yourself compromise on this point," he concludes, "you give up a slice of your credibility. God forbid you adopt someone else's plan, knowing you want to revisit their assumptions. Six months later when you do that and you have to reforecast, the board won't remember that that's what you said you were going to do."

5. SPORTING "THE EMPEROR'S NEW CLOTHES"

Everyone knows the fable about the emperor who declared he would have a gorgeous set of robes created out of *nothing*. As he modeled each imaginary item to the court, no courtier dared disagree. It was only when the emperor went out of the palace to parade his new "suit" to the public that a young boy uttered the truth, exclaiming, "But the emperor isn't wearing any clothes!"

The "emperor's new clothes" malady can happen in any enterprise and to any leader. The fact is that the higher up you go in an organization, the less likely other people are to give you the straight scoop. At the top, your insights are somehow brighter, your jokes funnier, and you are routinely considered the fount of all wisdom—at least to your face. This insulation can prevent leaders from obtaining a clear reflection in the mirror.

Worse, it prevents them from getting honest feedback. As early as infancy, when we wailed for our mother's attention, individuals have always sought a leader's approval and have tried to avoid his or her displeasure. As a direct consequence, many people are reluctant to disagree or pass along bad news. When it is passed along, the bad news is diluted and delayed so that by the time it reaches the end of the chain, its significance and urgency have been diluted. The result: The leader is often the last to know what's going on.

"I was one of the last to understand the implications of the Pentium crisis," Andy Grove wrote in *Only the Paranoid Survive*. To his chagrin, the former Intel CEO discovered that like most CEOs, he lived in the center of a fortified palace, and that news from the outside, where the action was, had to percolate through layers of people. "It took a barrage of relentless criticism to make me realize that something had changed—and that we needed to adapt to the new environment," he recalls.

"Everything isolates you in this job," notes Amgen CEO Kevin Sharer. "You're surrounded by people who want to make you happy. The people who work for you at least partially got there because they're really great at managing their bosses. And you often don't get the nuance of what's going on. So if you don't fight against isolation—by insisting on going out in the field on Friday with a sales rep, for example—you're going to be isolated. You have to be the one to break this down."

No one wants to be associated with bad news when meeting the new boss. But if you don't get accurate feedback and honest advice, you will not be able to develop the best strategy. Jim Kilts suggests the only real solution to this deep-seated problem: "You have to preach that you'd rather get the bad news than not get it. And promise that they'll get a gold star for delivering it to you a day before you have to deliver it to someone else."

6. STIFLING DISSENT

In *The Five Patterns of Extraordinary Careers*, Jim Citrin and Rick Smith wrote about the "benevolent leader," who is as focused on the success of those around him as on their own success. Our research showed that 90 percent of extraordinary executives are benevolent leaders, compared with only four percent who put themselves first.

One of the top traps for leaders—both new and not so new—is

the failure to understand and use this success pattern. While the majority of pitfalls for new leaders reviewed in this chapter are indicators of nonbenevolent leadership styles (such as what we call "The Pirate" and "The Mercenary"), perhaps the greatest pitfall of all is creating a work environment that stifles dissent.

Executives who smother dissent cut themselves off from the chance to see and correct problems as they arise. They create an environment of fear and control that turns off the most talented employees and eventually drives them out the door. Hesitant employees are given a draconian choice: "It's my way or the highway." Usually only the mediocre talent ends up submitting to work in such an atmosphere.

One of the most visible examples was Mattel's Jill Barad. She was described in a flattering May 1998 *BusinessWeek* cover story as "glamorous and radiant" and seeming "more Hollywood than corporate." And the many people who worked either with her or against her in the marketplace would agree that she was a ferocious competitor with a keen sense of popular culture, style, packaging, and marketing. They would also agree that in her rise up the ranks, from a $38,000-a-year product manager in 1981 to her appointment as CEO of the $4.8 billion company in January 1997, Barad demonstrated that she was as tough inside the company as she was in her dealings with competitors. With her pointed communication style and combative nature, Barad thrived in Mattel's aggressive culture. One of her former bosses told *BusinessWeek* that Mattel was "always a place where people were pitted against one another—a shark pond. You throw people in and see if they can swim fast enough to stay alive. For Jill, it was a fit."

In 1990 CEO John Amerman appointed Barad a copresident of Mattel's U.S. operations and then promoted her to COO in 1992. She soon went back to him demanding to succeed him as CEO. When she finally took over, the transition has been described as rocky. Barad imposed her will on the company and her managers by eliminating contrasting views and by terrifying employees. One former marketing manager described a meeting in which Barad asked for a glass of water. When a secretary brought one, it is said that Barad looked at the glass and snapped, "This better not be *tap*." More ominously, according to the research done by Dartmouth's Finkelstein, Barad removed her senior executives if she thought they had serious reservations about the way she was running the company. She fired several executives at a moment's notice and ultimately drove six direct reports to resign "for personal reasons."

Such stories became routine, and after the financially disastrous acquisition of The Learning Company—an action that Barad had pushed through—the Mattel board finally had had enough. Barad was forced to resign as chairman and CEO in 2000.

7. SUCCUMBING TO THE SAVIOR SYNDROME

In the Gilbert and Sullivan operetta *Iolanthe,* the Lord High Chancellor introduces himself with a song whose message will seem very familiar to some CEOs:

> The Law is the true embodiment
> Of everything that's excellent.
> It has no kind of fault or flaw,
> And I, my Lords, embody the Law.

Nowadays leaders are under so much pressure that they often fall prey to feeling that they are carrying the weight of the business on their shoulders. They are responsible for the employees under their watch, their livelihoods and morale; they are responsible for strategy, operations, and finances. They have all been brought up to believe in Harry Truman's famous phrase, "The buck stops here."

All this is well and good and not at all incorrect. But if these responsibilities are not kept in context, a new leader can wander into the morass of the Savior Syndrome.

A savior believes that he or she is the embodiment of the institution and is personally responsible for its success. At the extreme, the line between their identity and the identity of the business blurs. And in some cases they come to believe that they are above the rules—or even laws—that bind everyone else. While this affliction is not likely to occur in the first hundred days, one of its early causes—believing that it's all about you—can lead to ruinous results. Witness the infamous case of Dennis Kozlowski, who is charged with (but has not been convicted of) defrauding, together with his chief financial officer, more than $600 million from Tyco, mostly by getting the company to pay for their personal expenses. The most blatant example, of course, was the birthday party that Kozlowski threw for his wife in Sardinia, where the company paid half of the $2 million bill. Kozlowski's lawyers claim that business was getting done at the party, so it was fitting that Tyco paid.

Even in the vast majority of cases when no malfeasance occurs, trying to do it all alone is still a serious trap. If you operate as a lone wolf who refuses to ask for help or involve others, you will cut yourself off from valuable input and feedback. Even if you are on the right track, you will invariably burn out, which will only further hurt the organization. Furthermore, you will only make your managers feel disenfranchised, alienated, and impotent. After all, as Jim Kilts of Gillette points out, "You can lead, but ultimately it is the people in the company who have to deliver."

8. MISREADING THE TRUE SOURCES OF POWER

One common attribute of the most successful business leaders is a sensitivity to the unwritten rules of an organization, an empathy Daniel Goleman popularized with the term *emotional intelligence*. An essential aspect of this skill is the ability to accurately diagnose where the true source of power lies.

Roberto Goizueta, Coca-Cola's highly regarded CEO for sixteen years until his death from lung cancer in October 1997, had an uncanny ability to manage the true source of power at the company. It is said that each and every day Goizueta made phone calls to Warren Buffet and Herbert Allen, two of Coke's largest shareholders and thought leaders on the board of directors. He gave them an update on several key performance metrics compared to arch-competitor Pepsi. This simple habit kept Buffet and Allen fully informed and in so doing maintained the legendary investor's and powerful financier's support.

Sometimes a large investor or even the whole board can appear to give you a mandate, but if the true power lies elsewhere, you need to take care not to try to do too much too soon. As described in Chapter 5, the board of the U.S. Olympic Committee hired corporate turn-around executive Norman Blake to institute a radical restructuring plan in advance of the 2002 Olympics. Despite his best efforts and following the action plan for which he had been hired by the board, Blake's failure to marshal support among the athletes, their parents, and their coaches undermined his efforts severely and led to his res-ignation after a matter of months.

Gauging the true source of power is critical in the early days, but it is also important to keep refreshing your assessments as you go forth. Consider the case of Thomas Middelhoff of Bertelsmann, the giant German media conglomerate, who was appointed CEO in 1996. Middelhoff earned his reputation and vaulted to the top role largely based on his prescient decision to make a major investment in upstart America Online in 1994. As the investment came to be worth billions of dollars—its 50 percent stake in the joint venture AOL Eu-rope *alone* was later sold for $7 billion—it put the company and Mid-delhoff on the map as being cutting edge and one of the few global media companies to figure out how to harness the power of the Inter-net. Middelhoff built on this success with a series of other deals (both buying and selling assets) and bold strategies to centralize the fa-mously decentralized company and continue its march into the digi-tal age.

In a move that shocked the media world, on July 28, 2002, the Bertelsmann board accepted Middelhoff's resignation at an extraordi-nary board meeting and installed a corporate veteran, Gunter Thielen, at the top. This move was initially surprising, as the company was thriving and Middelhoff was seen as responsible for many of its successes. But Middelhoff had become increasingly disconnected from the true source of power in the company. As one of the world's most celebrated CEOs, Middelhoff had come to think that he was the source. But in reality Bertelsmann was still a family company and still a very German one at that. The Mohn family, headed by patriarch Reinhard Mohn, owned 75 percent of Bertelsmann, and they became increasingly concerned about Middelhoff's bold new direction, especially his push to take the long-privately-held company public in an IPO. Middelhoff shared his view on German television that "management has to have enough flexibility to continue the group's development through an IPO." The Mohns had evidently watched what had happened to publicly traded media companies (whose stocks were under severe pressure at the time) and therefore wanted to put a halt to the IPO plans. It was also widely reported that Middelhoff's push to make the company more "American" and visible had always been disdained by the Mohns, who prefer traditional European values. Middelhoff summed up the reality best when he said, "Our shareholders had mid- and long-term development prospects that were different from mine. In this context, I had no choice but to resign."

9. PICKING THE WRONG BATTLES

Chapter 4 focused on crafting a strategic agenda as one of the key processes for achieving a great first hundred days. Your strategic agenda is all about setting a framework and identifying the right priorities that will guide you and your team in the short time that you have to get off to the right start. One of the major traps for new leaders, however, is to select the wrong priorities—or, more colorfully stated, pick the wrong battles.

Lawrence Summers, president of Harvard University, learned this lesson the hard way. "I would say the number-one lesson I've learned is, force no gratuitous battles," he says. "As an example, say the dean of the Divinity School wants to hire somebody to be his administrative dean whom I would guess is inept. He comes and tells me about it. Two years ago [in Summers's early days] I would have been prone to say, 'He's inept, it's a big mistake, I don't want you to do that.' And he'd go off unhappy and talk to other faculty members about it, and there'd be another wave of gossip that the president's a jerk. Today I'm more likely to say, 'I wouldn't do that if I were you. But you are the person in charge, so if that's what you want to do, go ahead and do it.'

"I wouldn't say that I've taken the pressure off on the things that I care about. But I would say, pick your battles, engage in no gratuitous battles, *and* put goodwill in the bank whenever possible."

New leaders tend to want to focus on the problem areas and figure out how to solve them. That's commendable, but not if it comes at the expense of sustaining your success in existing areas of strength. Dan Kerpelman, who skillfully avoided that trap after joining Kodak, offers some helpful advice: "If you come in and discover that one of your growth businesses is struggling, give it big-time attention. But don't ignore your cash cow, which may also be struggling. The key is to keep all the plates spinning simultaneously. In other words, devote ample time to all the key businesses to ensure greater success."

The same warning applies to people. It's natural to concentrate on getting your bottom people up or out, but you must remember to focus on retaining, motivating, and developing your top people, too. Spend as much time on your winners as on your problem children.

A corollary is, concentrating on the big things at the expense of the little ones. The little things may turn out to be not so little after all. Summers confesses that when he became president of Harvard, he gave short shrift to little things like being on time, answering letters from important people quickly, and returning phone calls. "There's a tendency in the beginning to think that it's more important to be visible and out at functions rather than taking care of business," he says. "But it can be a black hole for a person who's new. Truth be told, if I'd been sitting at my desk answering my mail, I probably would have been more effective."

10. "DISSING" YOUR PREDECESSOR

Whether you are succeeding a sitting incumbent or, even more important, if you are taking over from a founder, the tenth and final common pitfall for a new leader is to disparage—or "dis"—your predecessor. Under all circumstances, our advice is to be respectful and sensitive of their position and tenure, regardless of how you feel.

"There are lots of dumb mistakes that new CEOs can make," says Lew Platt, former CEO of Hewlett-Packard. "But one of the most common is to blame your predecessor for everything that's wrong. It's probably human nature to do that, but it's a very bad thing," he adds. "People forget that just about everyone who is there when the new CEO arrives has worked for the old CEO and probably has some degree of loyalty to him or her."

One of the best founder-to-CEO transitions of all time was Meg Whitman taking the reins from eBay founder and chairman Pierre Omidyar in February 1998. In addition to the power of the company's online marketplace auction business model, its superior brand building, innovative customer feedback ratings system, robust technology platform, category expansion into high-ticket items such as autos and real estate, and disciplined international extension, one of the key factors to Whitman's success at eBay was her "embrace" of Omidyar. Rather than succumbing to the all-too-common thinking that a new leader needs to push out the founder, Whitman made sure to become Omidyar's partner. In so doing she built on the company's founding cultural and strategic DNA.

Similarly, in May 1998 Reader's Digest recruited Tom Ryder to join the company as the fifth CEO since its founding in 1921. The company was in dire straits: The stock had fallen nearly 40 percent, profits had shrunk by over 80 percent, and revenue growth had stalled over the prior two years. Ryder took over from interim and former chief executive officer George V. Grune. Grune was the third

CEO in the company's history, originally appointed in February 1984, he had given up the role to James P. Schadt in August 1994, then resumed it in August 1997.

In addition to many of the standard competitive, financial, strategic, and organizational challenges that the new leader of a troubled company faces, Ryder had one more issue to contend with: one of the most complex and criticized corporate governance structures of any company in the United States at the time. This governance deficiency was the result of the company's history as a family-owned and -operated enterprise under founders Dewitt and Lila Wallace, who died with no heirs and as a result put all of their ownership into a powerful trust known as the Wallace Funds. Its ownership of Reader's Digest generated millions in annual dividends, which allowed the Funds to be among the most important benefactors to the New York cultural community, bestowing largesse on the New York Public Library, the Metropolitan Museum of Art, and the New York Philharmonic. While the company was doing well during the 1980s and early 1990s, the governance approach had worked fine, but when growth stalled and the stock price slid, the pressures from the governance system came to the forefront. The Wallace Funds controlled three seats on the company's board of directors, but the most problematic issue was the influence over the company of former CEO George Grune, who was also chairman of the Wallace Funds itself.

Not surprisingly, during the outside search for a permanent CEO in early 1998, most candidates said, "My interest in coming into the company is contingent on George Grune stepping off the board and off the Funds board." But Tom Ryder had a different point of view. He told us at the time, "First of all, anyone who thinks that they will be able to come into Reader's Digest and oust George Grune is sorely mistaken. Not only are they kidding themselves, but they would be dead wrong. My strategy will be to embrace George."

At the four-year anniversary of Ryder taking over as CEO, he recalled that this was one of his wisest decisions. He said, "George has been fabulous. He knows this business cold, cares deeply for its success, and has been totally supportive."

For a manager, a related problem arises when the person who previously held the job is still on the premises. Every suggestion you make, every change you propose, gets interpreted as an implicit criticism of their work. That's what one division president confided in us after he joined a *Fortune* 100 company: "When you say, 'I think we need to change these things,' what the predecessor hears is, 'You're saying I didn't do it right, is that it?' "

Finally, a little tact goes a long way—and the inverse is also true. When one *Fortune* 500 company appointed a new high-profile CEO with a history of making bold moves, everyone knew to expect big changes. But beyond the kinds of cutbacks and new marketing strategies that people had been braced for, the new leader made a blunder that showed disrespect for the company's founder. In a move that galled employees, this CEO wanted to signal a break from the past by replacing the portrait of the founder hanging in the boardroom with his own.

While we cannot say that hanging your own portrait is one of the *most common* pitfalls for new leaders taking over, we hope you will agree that this certainly qualifies as one of the top ten blunders for new CEOs.

A FINAL PITFALL: A GREAT FIRST HUNDRED DAYS DOESN'T GUARANTEE ENDURING SUCCESS

Even if you successfully avoid the entire top ten list, you still need to remain aware of a final pitfall that can beset a new leader: A great first hundred days in no way guarantees long-term success.

C. Michael Armstrong had a spectacularly successful start when he came in to head up AT&T in October 1997. In our interviews with Armstrong a year into his tenure, he shared the specifics of his early plans and actions. He had done significant due diligence on the company and the top executives before he joined, which enabled him to embrace the existing management team and catalyze the development of a strategic agenda. He did *not* come out with any bold public pronouncements right away, but rather met with his management team continually for ninety days to develop strategy; no one outside the company, with the exception of key clients, saw him, and there were no press conferences, speeches, or meetings with securities analysts. The team made some correct fundamental assumptions and predictions on which their plans were based, such as the coming industry and technology convergence in information, entertainment, and communications, the commoditization and pricing erosion of long-distance calling, consumers' desire for simplicity in purchasing and billing for services, and the power of the AT&T brand. When he was ready to share the vision about using cable lines to sell customers a bundle of television, Internet, and local phone service, the plan was bold and easy to understand at all levels, from Wall Street to the company's far-flung employee base. Then he followed up decisively and quickly with bold transforming transactions, such as the acquisition of cable giants TCI Communications and MediaOne Group. Investors responded enthusiastically, doubling the company's stock price by May 1999 and adding $92 billion in market capitalization.

But rather than sailing off to the happy ending of enduring success that looked likely and that Armstrong had surely expected, the strategy proved flawed, execution turned out to be marginal, and the company paid too much too soon for the series of deals, including $12 billion for Teleport Communications, $48 billion for TCI, and $54 billion for MediaOne, all within a year of Armstrong taking over. The *Wall Street Journal* wrote in mid-2004 that Armstrong "steps down as a widely discussed case study of a failed CEO." So while his performance is still being debated, especially taking into account the argument that AT&T was overpowered by the extraordinary fraud at arch-rival WorldCom, which allowed them to pump up their numbers and put pressure on AT&T, Armstrong's ultimate legacy is that he is the CEO who was humbled into breaking up (for the second time) the venerable company.

NEXT STEP TO ENDURING SUCCESS

THE NEXT HUNDRED DAYS

One thousand two hundred and four hours. That's 72,240 minutes, or about four million seconds.

What should you accomplish in this exceedingly finite period that comprises your first hundred days in a new leadership position? How should the adrenaline-stoked sprint of this phase fit into the marathon that makes up your longer-term plan? Our hope with this book is that having built up the layers of the first hundred days pyramid one by one, and by knowing the pitfalls to avoid, you will be well prepared to create sufficient momentum for your first hundred days, the next hundred days, and the hundred days after that.

Amgen's CEO, Kevin Sharer, puts the early days of a new role into proper perspective. "The first hundred days is just a start. You really can't get that much done." After all, barely three months—just one quarter—is not much time to assess and make changes to your management team; to learn enough about the business, customer base, and competitive reality to articulate a strategic agenda; or to fully evaluate, much less change, the culture; let alone accomplish all these things.

So what have we learned from our three years of research into more than a hundred of the highest-profile leadership transitions, including some of the best and some of the worst? That while there is

256

no single playbook to follow that will guarantee success, there are common principles, strategies, and actions to follow that will enable a new leader to capitalize on the unique window of opportunity that makes up the first hundred days.

For some leaders, the focus of their early days is all about maintaining momentum. Looking back, Sharer, who succeeded to Amgen's top post in an orderly inside transition, says, "I think my first hundred days were B-plus/A-minus. I wouldn't do anything different that I can think of right now. And we've done everything that we said we would do. The top team has come together in a way that is a delight to me and to the rest of the company. We've continued to bring in great new talent. We made a major acquisition that we successfully integrated. We'll see how it's going to play out financially. The board is open and strong. I think we've still got the momentum, and I don't think we're going to lose it." But then again, Sharer pointed out that during that early period, given the company's strong shape and long-lead-time R&D-based drug development, there was only so much that could reasonably get done.

For other leaders, the focus of the first hundred days is on setting standards and establishing expectations. "Just about everything you do matters in one way or another," suggests Outward Bound USA CEO John Read, who had previously headed up a series of manufacturing companies. "In a manufacturing plant, when you walk the shop floor, it's the body language and eye contact that matter as much as what you say. The same holds true here. At the end of the first hundred days, if I were to approach people inside the organization, they should pretty much know what I was going to ask them. It could be, 'Is your program safe? Are you making money in this department? Is the quality right? Is the customer of your work happy with what you're doing?' And you want people to think, 'Here comes Read. He's going to ask me this, and I'd better have an answer.' "

For still others, it's about having enough of a handle on the organization to be able, as GlobalSpec CEO Jeff Killeen says, "to make commitments and boldly sign your name." He continues, "Clearly, you should have made an assessment of your management team relative to its strengths and weaknesses and where you need to move to up-grade your human capital. You must be able to make those calls because it drives everything else. You should have personally vetted the financials, including, if need be, revisiting core assumptions relative to growth, outlook, and risk. If you need to recast assumptions, outlook, or guidance, that first hundred days is the best period you'll have. You should be in an advantageous position to make commitments and do so with confidence.

"At the end of the first hundred days," Killeen goes on, "you should be able to fully articulate and express your aspiration for the company. That can run the gamut from a bold vision statement to more practical 'this is our work, these are our points of view, and these are our critical success factors going forward.' It could be rich with strategic imperatives or focused on blocking and tackling. It's hard to say that after the first week, but after fourteen weeks you clearly should be able to say that."

It all comes down to the fact that there are so many possible things to focus on and so little time. The essence of leadership is finding a way to take all the strands of possible activity and be an integrator, prioritizer, synthesizer, direction-setter, motivator, and executor. Doing so well necessitates that you accurately assess your situation from all dimensions and tailor your plan accordingly.

What you do will vary greatly depending on the situation. Speed, visibility, and decisiveness may be the right course of action if, like Ed Breen, Jim Kilts, Bill Schleyer, or Terry Semel, you are coming in from the outside to settle down a crisis and turn a company around. But if you are promoted from within into a relatively healthy situation, such as was the case of Jeff Immelt, Kevin Sharer, Mike Eskew, and Steve Reinemund, then you may have to be more deliberate in nudging the organization forward, changing the management team, striking a new strategic direction, and transforming the culture. The bottom line is that by following the thoughts and actions detailed throughout this book, you will get off to the right start and create the momentum for long-term success.

There is no question in our minds, or in those of the many CEOs, board directors, and other executives with whom we spoke over the course of our research, that the first hundred days are crucial. When you are moving into a new position of responsibility, you have only one chance to make a first impression, and that impression stays with people for a long time. But even in your same position, as Jeff Immelt says, you are bound to experience multiple first hundred days. Every time you are confronted with a major change in your operating environment, whether it is a new competitor appearing on the scene, a new regulation that changes your industry landscape, or the application of a new technology or business system, you have an opportunity to demonstrate fresh leadership and action.

"The organization is sitting there trying to assess you," recalls Gap Inc. CEO Paul Pressler. "They're evaluating your every move and every word that you say. In the first hundred days you set a strong tone about how you want to run the business. I'm not sure that if you stumble in the first hundred days it's fatal, but it's going to take you a lot of time to recover."

What you do during that first hundred days has the potential to establish your foundation as a true leader. Even if you have the time to take only the early steps of what you will ultimately achieve, people will make judgments and decisions about whether they choose to follow you.

But it is also important to remember that this period *is* just a step. Jeff Immelt points out not only that he had a lot of first hundred days over the course of his GE career, but also that he has had many first hundred days since becoming CEO.

Every CEO, and every manager, and every professional is going to have many first hundred days, simply because of the world we now live in. You will have to prove your credibility again and again. But like fine steel, each tempering will make you stronger and more flexible and better able to handle the challenges of the first hundred days, the next hundred days, and the hundred days after that.

We wish you all the best on your path to enduring success.

THE SPENCER STUART 8 POINT PLAN FOR THE FIRST HUNDRED DAYS

Maximizing the window of opportunity represented by the first hundred days of a new leadership position, and building on the momentum to achieve enduring success.

GREAT PERFORMANCE

Building On the Momentum

The Next 100 Days & Beyond

8. Avoid Common Pitfalls

7. Communicate

6. Manage Your Board/Boss

5. Start Transforming Culture

4. Craft Your Strategic Agenda

3. Shape Your Management Team

2. Align Expectations

1. Prepare Yourself During the Countdown

Building Your Foundation

GREAT FIRST 100 DAYS

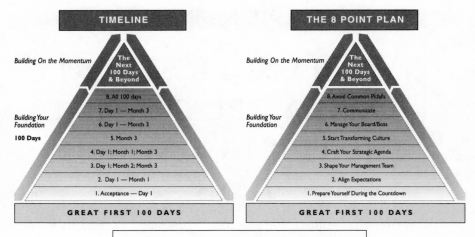

Several of the steps occur simultaneously and many take place continuously.

EXECUTIVE SUMMARY

- Follow our 8 Point Plan to get off to the right start in a new leadership position and create the momentum to help you achieve great long-term performance and enduring success.
- Use the pyramid model as your guide for the major activities you should accomplish during the first hundred days.
- Flexibility is critical during this period, so make sure to tailor your plan to the situation.

POINT 1: PREPARE YOURSELF DURING THE COUNTDOWN

Action Items	Comments
Plan effectively; get set to learn.	Do your homework; review the company, industry, and competitor press, financials, and marketing materials.
Determine what questions to ask key constituents and meet with the smartest observers possible.	The best questions yield the best answers.
Meet with top management, board/boss, employees, alumni, customers, suppliers, analysts, trusted confidants, and investors.	Lay the groundwork for strong relationships with your key constituents and future colleagues, and gather valuable input.

Construct your First Hundred Day Plan with tasks and rough timing.	Once you start your new job, the rush of information and activities will make it difficult to think and plan.
Assess your own knowledge, skill, or experience gaps.	Determine what functional expertise or specialized training you will need to succeed in the new job.
Prepare family and/or personal support base for the intense ride ahead.	Minimize personal disruptions within your control; create the ability to immerse yourself in your new role in the first hundred days.
Plan to keep track of how you spend your time.	Stick to priorities; resist the temptation to personally solve the first problem to arise. Even with six fourteen-hour days a week, you only have 1,204 hours to spend.
Start a diary and keep it for the first hundred days.	Some of your freshest ideas will come to you when you are new to the organization; if you do not capture them now, they will be lost forever. Review your notes in the future, when you feel in equilibrium.
Get in good physical shape.	There is no time like the present. Do not defer or neglect your conditioning and fitness— your stamina is about to be tested.

"The days up to the point when you actually start your new job are some of the most important to being successful. Day one on the job better not be "day one" where you're putting your action plan into place; it should be well under way by the time you get there."
Dan Schulman, CEO, Virgin Mobile USA

POINT 2: ALIGN EXPECTATIONS

Action Items	Comments
Truly understand the hiring manager's or board's objective for the position you are coming into.	Make sure you find common ground about key goals, both during the hiring process and throughout your early days.
Introduce yourself to the management team. Most employees will be wondering, "Is this new boss going to be good or bad for me?"	Prepare to answer these questions: Who am I? What's my background? Why did I join? What do I hope to accomplish? How do I hope to work together?
Communicate your management philosophy, professional background, operating principles, and expectations.	Use your early management meetings to do more than meet and greet; set the tone for the weeks to follow.
Ask a lot of questions. Listen. Repeat.	Don't be a know-it-all. You cannot have all the answers on day one or throughout the first hundred days.
Create an agenda for active listening; engage in one-on-one meetings to pose key questions.	Be a receiver as much as a broadcaster. Listen and learn. People appreciate being listened to and heard.
Synthesize learning and provide feedback to the organization and those with whom you've met.	Begin developing your agenda by sharing what you have learned through memos, intranets, presentations, etc.

PROVEN "ACTIVE LISTENING" QUESTIONS

Prototypical questions to use in one-hour sessions with each senior manager:

- What are the most important things (top five) about the company that we should be sure to preserve and why?
- What are the top three things we need to change and why?
- What do you most hope I do?
- What are you most concerned I might do?
- What advice do you have for me?

Take careful notes; synthesize your learning, and communicate it back to the management team/organization.

> *"As the new guy, I realized that every first encounter with a Mattel employee had the potential to be fraught with tension, and I felt it was my responsibility to do everything possible to reduce it. Surprisingly, I found that in each situation, recognizing my own lack of knowledge about the company's people and culture—in effect, allowing the employees to be 'the boss' in certain situations—actually helped me lead."*
> Bob Eckert, chairman and CEO, Mattel

POINT 3: SHAPE YOUR MANAGEMENT TEAM

Action Items	*Comments*
Determine whether you have a strong enough management team to reach your aspirations.	Establishing a strong team is the best first step a manager can take toward implementing and executing the strategic agenda.
Build a team of people with similar values and passion, but complementary skills.	The composition of the team should match the company's challenges, enable you to do your best, and reflect the values and standards that you want to prevail throughout the enterprise.
Unless the company is in utter crisis, avoid making critical personnel moves immediately.	Recognize that people have enormous capacity if you give them a chance, set clear expectations, and hold them accountable.
Develop a confidant.	You will need someone trustworthy, discreet, and with superior judgment with whom to brainstorm.
Articulate objectives and desired outcomes; encourage frank and open conversations.	Your early team meetings will set the tone for the meetings to follow.

Recognize the power of your predecessor; acknowledge and in some cases embrace your predecessor.	While it may be tempting to push out or vilify him or her for the challenges you've inherited, doing so will likely create unnecessary ill will.
Seek awareness regarding how each individual is motivated.	Great leaders tailor their management styles to the recipient rather than approaching the team from a one-size-fits-all perspective.

"The whole team should start with a clean piece of paper. The good people should have to prove themselves all over again, and the ones that may be on the bubble should get a brand-new chance. Find a way of critically assessing the talent around you in the first couple of months. Don't be rash, but decide whether you have a team that you have confidence in, because you can't get it done by yourself. Ultimately, you've got to have the right players around."

George Tamke, partner,
Clayton, Dubilier & Rice, and former chairman, Kinko's

POINT 4: CRAFT YOUR STRATEGIC AGENDA

Action Items	*Comments*
Build the strategic agenda in a joint effort with your team, not in a silo. Limit the number of themes and priorities so they can easily be remembered by the organization.	Find the right balance between creating a compelling picture of where you want the organization to go and not becoming prematurely locked into a plan.
Diagnose the company's (or department's) problems starting with the customer perspective and continuing with a grounded view of what the company stands for.	Use this diagnosis and your constituents' feedback to start building your short-term strategic agenda; make sure to underpromise and overdeliver.

Define the operating mechanism/ process—the meetings, documents, and report formats to conduct the day-to-day business.	Incorporate these processes and build an explicit plan to address cultural issues and barriers to change.
A strategic agenda is by definition a work in progress; use it to help you and the organization make decisions, see how they work, and make adjustments as needed.	Expect pushback on your agenda, but rather than resist, coalesce that input in a positive way to maximize buy-in.
Secure some early wins.	Look for flaws in the organization and fix them quickly to establish your credibility as a leader.

"At Gillette, I only felt comfortable about a year after I walked in that we knew exactly what we would need to do over the next five years. . . . A leader must take action immediately to fix obvious problems. But developing an insightful strategic plan will take at least three to five months."
Jim Kilts, chairman and CEO, Gillette

POINT 5: START TRANSFORMING CULTURE

Action Items	*Comments*
Identify how "things work around here": Work to understand the culture of the new organization; diagnose how much of a change is required.	Many new leaders fail because they could not make headway against an intransigent culture, pushing too hard in the wrong ways.
Go on the hunt for the knowledge networks, key influencers, decision-making protocols, and the unwritten and unspoken conventions that are the nervous system of any organization.	The place to start assessing a culture is to look for physical evidence and to listen and learn. Within most appearances and generalizations there lies an inner core of truth.

Solicit views about the culture from members of the board, the management team, and employees, customers, and industry analysts.	As you learn more, keep sharpening and improving your questions.
Create the conditions for cultural transformation. Adopt new measures of success; set new expectations; establish new operating processes; empower change leaders; and lead by example.	Be sensitive to the fact that even when you have a change mandate from your board or boss, it may not be enough; understand where other sources of power lie.
With a truly obstinate culture, you may need to make structural and people changes, but do so with the bought-in support of the key power center, and establish a concerted program to address the cultural legacies of the organization.	Make your first moves count. In your early days, people are the most open about change, but remember that too much change can break the culture. So pace yourself, continually assess the tolerance of the organization, get feedback, and adapt along the way.

"This culture is powerful. It grows from the inside out and has the ability to spit out leaders who don't fit into it. . . . I went to business school to learn how to keep the club in the closet until needed. In this job, there's no club and no closet that I can locate."
John Read, president, Outward Bound USA

POINT 6: MANAGE YOUR BOARD/BOSS

Action Items	Comments
Understand the stated and unstated motivations of your board or boss.	It's not just about building shareholder value; it's also about their reputations and schedules.

Initiate an "on-boarding" process with the board similar to what can be done with new managers. If you are not a CEO, establish priorities with your new boss.	Sit down with each board member or your boss and determine the most critical issues and what they are looking for.
Establish your credibility by having a sound strategic agenda, being on top of the details of the business, and establishing an effective communications protocol.	Understand how your boss really works or diagnose the culture of the board; tailor your communication and management style accordingly.
Listen and learn from your board or boss; establish the discipline of regular feedback.	In the case of the board, encourage "executive sessions" where the board discusses your performance in your absence.
Create forums for directors to interact with managers, visit customers and facilities, and dive deeply into key businesses.	This will increase their ability to help assess and support strategy and perform the board's most important function, ensuring optimal succession.

"I changed the way the board meetings happened. I start every board meeting with a two-hour executive session where I'm totally open with the board about what's going on, so I don't leave them in a position where they're saying, 'Gee, I wonder what Kevin's thinking.' They're obviously my boss, but I also treat them with complete openness."
Kevin Sharer, chairman and CEO, Amgen

POINT 7: COMMUNICATE!

Action Items	*Comments*
Know your audience so you can tailor your message and your style to their readiness and to what they care about.	Tell stories to establish an emotional connection to your point.

Effective communication is more than promulgating a message; it is a continuous give and take in which ideas are explored, assimilated, and adapted.	Be conscious of the signals you are sending. In the early days, every move you make is being closely watched; both explicit messages and implicit signals will have an impact.
Use and reuse your communications in various forums and formats.	This will reinforce your message and leverage your time.
Know the communication settings that you are most comfortable in, and play to your natural strengths.	Communicating is intimately intertwined with corporate culture, the way you present your message will affect the culture.
In a crisis, get the information out as quickly as possible.	Acknowledge the challenges of the situation to establish credibility. Act as a "shock absorber" between uncertainty and employees' desire for stability.
Having all the answers is usually the wrong answer. Get direct input from the field.	While this requires significant time investment, it will pay back multiple-fold in enhanced credibility, trust, and stakeholder engagement.

"Communication with employees is a top, top priority. You have to put yourself in the shoes of an employee who is not close to the fire. They know only a fraction of what I know. Their tendency is to worry more. I was up front about what the goal was, what needed to be improved, and that it might take some time, and people rallied around that."
Ed Breen, chairman and CEO, Tyco International

POINT 8: AVOIDING COMMON PITFALLS

Action Items	Comments
Don't set unrealistic or unsustainable expectations; in the end, you will be judged by your results.	Serious problems arise when the targets against which you are measured are not rooted in reality.
Don't allow yourself to suffer from analysis paralysis; don't be a know-it-all and make rash decisions.	Overly cautious behavior eats up time and sets the example of risk aversion; know-it-alls typically don't know what they don't know.
Don't fail to let go of your past identity; don't stifle dissent.	What's past is prologue. Leaders who smother discord cut themselves off from correcting problems before they arise and create an environment of fear.
Don't misread the true sources of power, and don't pick the wrong battles.	Gauging the true source of power is critical during the early days. Select the right priorities—little things may turn out to be not so little after all.
Don't succumb to the Savior Syndrome, and avoid "dissing" your predecessor.	You are not the embodiment of the institution. You are not above the rules that bind everyone else. Be respectful and sensitive regarding your predecessor's position and tenure, regardless of how you feel.

"If you can get something resolved quickly that is absolutely appropriate, you should get along with it. If a promise can't be met or if you don't have the knowledge to know what to do, don't try to bluff it. Take the time you need to figure out what to do. Don't be rushed into making commitments. The cost of reworking them is very high."
Alan Lacy, chairman and CEO, Sears

FINAL THOUGHTS

> The 8 Point Plan condensed:
>
> - Listen and learn.
> - Underpromise and overdeliver.

"I've had a lot of first hundred days since becoming CEO. I had the first hundred days of dealing with global terrorism, the first hundred days of global discourse and government intersecting with business as it never has before, the first hundred days when I was CEO-designate, and the first hundred days as CEO. Every manager and every CEO is going to have a number of first hundred days, simply because of the world we now live in. . . . Leadership is an intense journey into yourself, particularly if you want to go all the way. It's how far you're going to go, how fast you're going to learn, how much you can improve. You never get the top job because of what you know. It's all about how fast you learn, how much you can adapt."

Jeff Immelt, chairman and CEO, General Electric

GARY KUSIN'S FIRST HUNDRED DAY PLAN FOR KINKO'S*

APRIL 2001

OVERALL OBJECTIVES

Key Items

In my first hundred days on the job, I would expect to:

- Introduce myself to the company and its stakeholders
- Communicate my expectations, and those of others, for the performance of the company
- Take steps to ensure that the core business is operating at its full potential
- Design the plan for future growth and profitability
- Communicate the plan for future growth and profitability to the company and its stakeholders
- Begin implementing the future plan

Executive Summary

- This document outlines the major proposed activities I would hope to accomplish in my first hundred days with Kinko's.
  - Top-level objectives
  - Major tasks and accompanying rationale
  - Information required, tied to each major task
  - Rough timing and resource issues

- Flexibility is a key success factor during such a transition period, so the proposed timing may be subject to change

---

* Developed when Kusin was a finalist candidate for the CEO position in April 2001. Reprinted with permission.

— But I believe that the outlined objectives should be viewed as relatively firm goals.

- I believe that there is the potential for significant value creation at Kinko's and that my first hundred days offer a unique opportunity to reshape the company

Phases, Goals

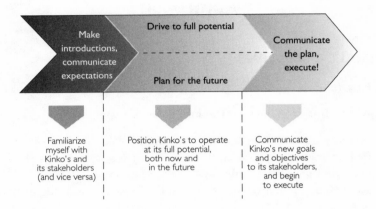

Familiarize myself with Kinko's and its stakeholders (and vice versa)

Position Kinko's to operate at its full potential, both now and in the future

Communicate Kinko's new goals and objectives to its stakeholders, and begin to execute

OBJECTIVE DETAILS

Phases, Key Tasks

- Review of general company, industry, competitor materials
- Face-to-face meetings with top-level management, largest customers, investors, and other Kinko's stakeholders
  - Two-way communication of respective short-term expectations, "hot-button" issues
  - Communication of operating principles, expectations

- Analysis of field "manufacturing" structure
- Analysis of Kinko's overhead structure
- Analysis of product-line profitability and identification of best demonstrated practices
- Analysis of Kinko's footprint, development plans
- Analysis of management information systems capabilities
- Analysis of marketing strategy/structure

- Redefinition of Kinko's mission, objectives
- Analysis of new product, new customer opportunities
- Analysis of international operations
- Formulation of new strategic and operating plans

- Face-to-face meetings with top-level management, largest customers, investors, and other stakeholders
  - Communication of new Kinko's direction, structure, strategies
- Begin to execute

Make Introductions, Communicate Expectations
(Action Items, Rationale)

Action Item	Rationale
• Review of general company, industry, competitor materials	• Become expert on business services industry, key competitors

• Face-to-face meetings with top-level management, largest customers, investors, and other Kinko's stakeholders
  – two-way communication of respective short-term expectations, "hot-button" issues
  – communication of operating principles, expectations
	• Build relationships with key Kinko's management and other stakeholders
	• Level-set expectations of Kinko's management, customers, investors, and other stakeholders as to expected performance and operating principles

Make Introductions, Communicate Expectations
(Desired Information)

Desired Information

- Any information compiled on Kinko's general industry and competitive position
- Data on typical customer profile, typical transaction economics, typical/target employee, center economics
- Kinko's capital structure breakdown
- CapEx spending breakdown over time
- Background information on rationale for and status of relationships with investors/partners (e.g., AOL)
- Current organization chart
- Biographies and evaluations/ratings of top level managers
- List of top 25 customers by revenue
- Customer satisfaction ratings over time
- Results of customer surveys conducted
- Employee satisfaction ratings over time
- Kinko's current mission statement, operating principles, etc.

Drive to Full Potential
(Action Items, Rationale)

Action Item	Rationale
• Analysis of field "manufacturing" structure	• Determine optimal center operating hours, test out "magnet center" concept
• Analysis of Kinko's overhead structure	• Determine optimal corporate overhead structure, staffing levels
• Analysis of product-line profitability and identification of best demonstrated practices	• Identify top/bottom performing products, top/bottom performing centers; drive to root cause of performance, make "pruning" decisions
• Analysis of Kinko's footprint, development plans	• Develop city/market strategies in consonance with manufacturing structure
• Analysis of management information systems capabilities	• Determine ability to support customer/operating metrics reporting requirements; ability to introduce, manage Web-based products
• Analysis of marketing strategy, structure	• Understand, review brand strategy, value propositions, sales organization structure

Drive to Full Potential
(Desired Information, 1 of 2)

Desired Information

- Global and market-specific footprint maps
- Center revenues by hour of day
- Machine utilization by hour of day
- Data on cost/machine, Kinko's cost/page, typical center operating costs, etc.
- Breakdown of corporate overhead expenses by location, department, job type/title
- Breakdown of field overhead expenses by location, department, job type/title
- Data on layers and spans of control in the field management structure
- Details of employee incentive plans, stock/option ownership, etc.

Drive to Full Potential
(Desired Information, 2 of 2)

Desired Information

- Ranking of products by revenue, fully loaded costs, profitability
- Ranking of products by (fully loaded cost) ROI
- Ranking of centers by revenue/sq. ft., by profitability/sq. ft., by sales growth year over year
- Global, market-specific footprint maps
- Development strategy/plan documents
- Lists/sample of types of customer data collected
- Description of center data collection capabilities
- Sample of periodic metrics/management reports generated
- IT road map document
- P/L statement for Web-based businesses
- Current marketing strategy/plan document
- Breakdown of sales organization structure, metrics, historical performance

Plan for the Future
(Action Items, Rationale)

Action Item	*Rationale*
• Redefinition of Kinko's mission, objectives	• Broaden thinking about the definition of Kinko's business, competitors, competencies
• Analysis of new product, new customer opportunities	• Compile new product candidates, screen to prioritize
• Analysis of international operations	• Determine whether to prune or grow international operations
• Formulation of new strategic and operating plans	• Focus Kinko's on most leveraged opportunities, provide resource allocation framework, translate to budget, operating targets

Plan for the Future
(Desired Information)

Desired Information

- Kinko's mission statement, objectives, current strategic plan
- Kinko's five-year operating plan
- New product screening criteria, process plan
- List of new product proposed for consideration in last 18 months
- Percent of revenues from products <12 months old
- New customer sales effort reports
- Percent of revenues from new customers (<12 months as Kinko's customer)
- P/L statements for international operations by country
- Competitor analysis by country
- Strategic plan for international centers

Communicate the Plan, Execute!
(Action Items, Rationale)

Action Item	*Rationale*
• Face-to-face meetings with top-level management, largest customers, investors, and other stakeholders – Communication of new Kinko's direction, structure, strategies	• Ensure all employees and other stakeholders clearly understand, support, and are aligned with the new direction for Kinko's
• Begin to execute	• Let's get started!

TIMING, RESOURCES

Phases, Timing

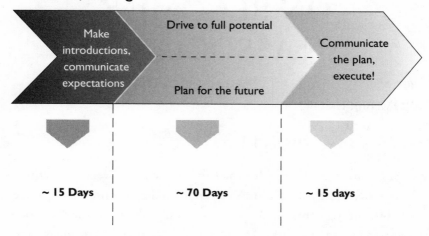

- This hundred day plan is designed to (potentially) redesign the company strategically, operationally, and structurally
  - Or at a minimum, answer whether such redesign is required

- Will be relatively resource-intensive
  - Substantial data mining, analysis leading to many important decisions in a short period of time
  - Must continue to operate the business in the meantime

- May consider enlisting outside consultants to assist with some of the analysis that will be required during the hundred-day transition period

"ON BECOMING AN ASSOCIATE"*

TO: New Associates
FROM: Ron Daniel
DATE: April 1979
ON BECOMING AN ASSOCIATE

It has been traditional for the firm's managing director to write to all new associates. It is difficult to personalize such a communication, but through this memorandum I would like to add my welcome to you as you join the firm. My purpose is to convey a few ideas that I think are important. These ideas are largely personal, not matters of firm policy, and are offered for whatever value they may have for you.

The first concept has to do with a basic attitude that I believe can significantly affect the satisfaction and fulfillment you will derive from your work. I urge you to think of yourself from this day on as a member of our firm, not as an employee of it. This is your firm, and you should assume a proprietary state of mind toward it. In many ways, the kind of firm McKinsey & Company is five years from now will be the result of your interests, your convictions, and your energies.

Secondly, recognize the necessity of getting off to a good start in the firm. Your first few engagements are critical. During these studies, you can establish an internal clientele for yourself—that is, by

---

* Former McKinsey managing partner Ron Daniel's April 1979 memo to new professionals joining the firm is reprinted with permission. We have included this memo in this book because twenty-five years after it was written, it is still as valid and vital as ever, not only for McKinsey but for any professional firm. While we are both McKinsey alumni and Ron's words hold special significance for us, we believe that this letter contains essential advice for any professional starting a new job. It is also a role model of how any leader has the opportunity to inspire their team when it comes to getting off to the right start.

performing in an outstanding way, your reputation will be quickly established in your office and even the firm. If you are successful, you will be sought out by your colleagues when new engagement opportunities come along. New responsibilities will flow to you. You can overcome a poor start, of course, but it takes considerable time and effort—and obviously it is better not to have to rebuild professional standing but, rather, to continuously add to it.

Our firm has a long history that, among other things, has left us with a well-established value system. The professional approach, the one-firm concept, and a commitment to quality are all essential values of the firm that I hope you will soon understand and support. There are written materials about these topics in your office. I hope you will read them and discuss them with your office manager, your teammates, or any member of the management group. Another part of our value system is the expectation—indeed, the responsibility—for even the newest associate to speak up, to come forward, to contribute from the very beginning, to understand his or her role in an engagement team, to be clear on and supportive of our arrangements and commitments to a particular client, to bring to bear facts and evidence that challenge the thinking of the engagement director and engagement manager, and to be convinced that we have placed our clients' interests first. While this kind of behavior implies a strength of character and the courage of one's convictions, and while the firm expects this from even our newest associates, we don't expect you to be all-knowing and able to prove your superiority in every situation.

Men and women who join this firm are invariably achievement motivated and ambitious people. Most have egos of generous size. But another key aspect of the firm's value system is the concept of collaboration. Reach out for help. Establish the habit of teamwork early. When you don't know, ask. When you're uncertain, ask. It's ironic that it is our strongest performers, our most effective consultants, who most often reach out for help from their colleagues. In the process, the strong get even stronger.

Finally, I urge you to regularly establish some perspective on your firm, on your work, and on yourself. Step back once in a while and take stock of things—not every day, not every week, but perhaps every six months. Are you still learning and being challenged? Are you getting personal satisfaction from a life that essentially involves serving others? Are you growing personally? Is the word *professional* coming to have any special, personal meanings for you? Have you experienced the benefits of our one-firm concept? Have you enjoyed the stimulation, the congeniality, the support of your colleagues? Can you—like the Nobel biologist Albert Szent-Györgyi—run to work most of the time out of enthusiasm for what you are doing? Have you exercised the control that only you can exercise to maintain a reasonable balance between your professional work and your personal life? For over twenty years I've been able to answer yes to most of these questions, most of the time. During this time I've believed it to be a genuine privilege to be part of this group of high-talent people of diverse talents, varied backgrounds, and wide-ranging interests who comprise our firm.

I wish you good luck as you begin, and hope that you come to feel the same measure of excitement, stimulation, support, warmth, and fun that I've enjoyed.

BIBLIOGRAPHY

Books

Citrin, James M., and Richard A. Smith. *The Five Patterns of Extraordinary Careers.* New York: Crown Business, 2003.

D'Alessandro, David. *Career Warfare: 10 Rules for Building a Successful Personal Brand and Fighting to Keep It.* New York: McGraw-Hill, 2003.

DePree, Max. *Leadership Is an Art.* New York: Doubleday, 1989.

Dotlich, David L., and Peter C. Cairo. *Why CEOs Fail: The 11 Behaviors That Can Derail Your Climb to the Top and How to Manage Them.* New York: Jossey-Bass, 2003.

Finkelstein, Sydney. *Why Smart Executives Fail: And What You Can Learn from Their Mistakes.* New York: Portfolio (Penguin Putnam), 2003.

Gerstner, Louis V., Jr. *Who Says Elephants Can't Dance? Inside IBM's Historic Turnaround.* New York: Harper Business, 2002.

Grove, Andrew S. *Only the Paranoid Survive: How to Exploit the Crisis Points That Challenge Every Company.* New York: Doubleday, 1999.

Sartain, Libby, and Martha I. Finney. *HR from the Heart: Inspiring Stories and Strategies for Building the People Side of Great Business.* New York: American Management Association, 2003.

Valenti, Jack. *Speak Up with Confidence: How to Prepare, Learn, and Deliver Effective Speeches.* New York: Hyperion, 1982, 2002.

Watkins, Michael. *The First 90 Days: Critical Success Strategies for New Leaders at All Levels.* Cambridge, Mass.: Harvard Business School Press, 2003.

Articles and Journals

Hsieh, Tsun-yan, and Stephen Bear. "Managing CEO Transitions." *The McKinsey Quarterly,* March 1994.

Lucier, Chuck, Rob Schuyt, and Junichi Handa. "CEO Succession 2003—the Perils of Good Governance." Booz Allen Hamilton, 2003.

Morris, Betsy. "The Accidental CEO." *Fortune,* June 23, 2003.

Wiersema, Margarethe. "Crisis in the Boardroom: Lessons from CEO Dismissals." Graduate School of Management, University of California, Irvine, White Paper, November 2002.

ACKNOWLEDGMENTS

This book was motivated by a question that many of our Spencer Stuart top executive placements ask us after they accept a new leadership appointment. With attorney-client-privilege-style intimacy, the leaders often ask us, "Okay, so I'm about to be in charge. Now what?" To answer this critical question, on which their success—and ours— depends, we wanted to go beyond anecdotes and mere common sense to identify the truly best *and worst* practices for how to get off to the right start in a new leadership position. This is our second book collaboration. We enjoyed our first joint publishing effort, *Lessons from the Top* (released in 1999), so much that we decided to join forces and do it again.

We are deeply appreciative of everyone who helped make this book a reality. Most especially our clients, with whom we work each and every day, and the hundreds of executives and board members we interviewed, who shared the lessons from their own leadership transitions and those they have been involved in. Their candor about both the successes and the setbacks was an essential element of this book. We would also like to thank the ongoing support and partnership of our Spencer Stuart colleagues, who together form the most professional and enjoyable firm in our industry.

Let us single out a few from among these groups who made exceptional contributions:

We would first like to thank Jordan Brugg, a Spencer Stuart knowledge manager in Washington, D.C., who enthusiastically, intelligently, and selflessly led much of the data gathering and analysis that formed the foundation of this book. He also led the development of The Spencer Stuart 8 Point Plan for the First Hundred Days, taking all the learnings from the book and synthesizing them into a framework that we hope will be of practical use for readers and our future placements for a long time to come. We are grateful for his valuable contribution.

Aki Naito, a Spencer Stuart associate in the Stamford, Connecticut, office, also provided analytical, data, and graphical support to the book over its entire project life. Aki worked to help us structure the research and ensure that everything that needed to be found or reviewed was completed efficiently and intelligently.

We are also deeply thankful to Roger Fransecky, CEO of The Apogee Group, one of the preeminent top executive coaching firms in the United States. Roger helped us form the intellectual foundation for the book as well as critical advice to make it as practical as possible.

We would also like to thank our firm, Spencer Stuart, for its support of this project from its initial conception to completion. Specifically, we would like to recognize David Daniel, Dayton Ogden, Kevin Connelly, and Manolo Marquez, who provided critical management support. In addition, we benefited greatly from the efforts of Alastair Rolfe, editor of Spencer Stuart's website. Finally, there is no more important thank-you than to our administrative partners, Karen Steinegger and Deborah Alton, who served as tireless sounding boards and logistical captains for this entire effort.

Turning such an ambitious project into an entertaining and readable book is rarely the result of the authors alone, and such was the case with this book. We would like to thank Catherine Fredman, an exceptional writer who previously collaborated with Andrew Grove on his best-selling book, *Only the Paranoid Survive,* and who coauthored *Direct from Dell* with Michael Dell. Catherine helped us formulate the structure of the book and draft each chapter. She also scrupulously transformed more than a thousand interview transcript pages into a logical construct and helped tighten them into various drafts of the manuscript. Her contribution to distilling and organizing our thinking was crucial to getting our arms around the hundreds of potentially disparate ideas we had considered. Another one of Catherine's important contributions was having the divine stroke that allowed her to come up with the title, *You're in Charge—Now What?*

We would also like to thank John Mahaney, our editor from Crown Business. We've heard many stories from other authors bemoaning the fact that editors don't really edit anymore. Happily, this is not at all the case with John. After raving about John to a professional in the publishing business, he said, "Make sure to tell him how you feel." Well, this is the best way to describe how we feel about John: It is as if we give him a big lump of clay, and through his edits he shows us exactly what to cut, what to add, and what to put where, and when we do, our lump magically takes the form of a beautiful sculpture. When we may have been content to stop, feeling satisfied with our work, John would push us further, inevitably leading each time to breakthrough new thoughts, frameworks, and presentation. We also appreciate the work of John's extended Crown team, including Tara Gilbride and Shana Drehs, who have been outstanding partners in this process.

We would also like to thank our friend and confidant Rafe Sagalyn, of the Sagalyn Literary Agency, who has been our literary agent for eight years and is simply the best in the business. His candor, open and honest feedback, incredible depth of experience, and true partnership have served as invaluable resources throughout this project. We are proud to be in his stable.

Finally, we would like to thank our loving families—Gail, Oliver, Lily, and Teddy Citrin and Sally Neff and David, Mark, Brooke, Bailey, and Scott—for their unwavering support of our work. With demanding executive search practices, the vast majority of the creation of this book has taken place at nights, on weekends, and during vacations. We are indebted to the contribution, love, and support that our families have provided us over these three years.

INDEX

ABOUT THE AUTHORS

Thomas J. Neff is chairman of Spencer Stuart in the United States and has been with the firm since 1976. He managed the worldwide firm from 1979 to 1987. His consulting practice focuses on CEO and other top-level recruiting, board of director searches, and succession counseling. He founded the Board Services Practice in the U.S. as well as the firm's U.S. Advisory Board of prominent CEOs. He previously served as leader of the firm's Professional Practices Committee for ten years.

Neff, hailed by the *Wall Street Journal* as "The No. 1 Brand Name in CEO Searches," has been the subject of numerous profiles, including cover stories in *BusinessWeek* and the Sunday Business section of the *New York Times*. He has also appeared on CNN and CNBC, among many others.

Neff is coauthor, with James M. Citrin, of *Lessons from the Top: The 50 Most Successful Leaders in America—and What You Can Learn from Them* (New York: Doubleday, 1999), which has been released in seven languages.

Prior to joining Spencer Stuart, Neff was a principal with another executive search firm. Previously, he was the chief executive officer of an information systems company and also held a senior marketing position with TWA. Earlier, he was a management consultant with McKinsey & Company in the New York and Melbourne, Australia, offices.

He serves on the board of directors of ACE Limited, a NYSE Bermuda-based insurance company; Hewitt Associates, Inc. (NYSE), a leading human resources and outsourcing firm; and the Lord Abbett Mutual Funds. He previously served on the board of Macmillan, Inc., for eight years until it was acquired. He also served as a trustee of Lafayette College for twelve years and previously served as chairman of the board of the Brunswick School.

Neff's notable searches include the CEO for Albertson's, AT&T, Campbell Soup, Federal Reserve Bank of New York, Gillette, Hershey Foods, Honeywell, IBM, JCPenney, Lucent Technologies, Merck, New York Stock Exchange, Prudential Insurance, Reader's Digest, and Weyerhauser.

With an MBA from Lehigh University and a BS degree in industrial engineering from Lafayette College, he served as an officer and aide-de-camp in the U.S. Army.

James M. Citrin leads Spencer Stuart's global Technology, Communications & Media Practice and is a member of the firm's worldwide board of directors. He is also a member of the firm's Board Services Practice. In his eleven years at Spencer Stuart, he has completed approximately three hundred executive and board searches in the media, entertainment, publishing, high-technology, Internet, telecommunications, and education industries, as well as in consumer products and hospitality, with a particular focus on chief executive officers, presidents/chief operating officers, and board directors. Notable placements include the CEOs and/or presidents of: Yahoo!, America Online, Motorola, Motion Picture Association of America, Vodafone, Gartner, Reader's Digest, Gruner + Jahr, Primedia, Eastman Kodak, Panavision, Reed Elsevier, Reed Business Information, Penguin Publishing, L.L. Bean, TV-Guide, Ziff Davis, Kinko's, NTL, Six Continents, Hotels & Resorts, Westin Hotels & Resorts, and Outward Bound. He has also advised the governments of Mexico and the European Union as well as more than two dozen global corporations on leadership, management, and career success.

Jim is coauthor of the international best-selling book *The Five Patterns of Extraordinary Careers* (New York: Crown Business, 2003) and is the author of *Zoom!: How 12 Exceptional Companies Are Navigating the Road to the Next Economy* (New York: Doubleday, 2002). He is also coauthor with Tom Neff of *Lessons from the Top: The 50 Most Successful Business Leaders in America—and What You Can Learn from Them* (New York: Doubleday, 1999), which has been released in seven languages. In addition, he has published numerous articles on leadership and corporate governance in the *New York Times, Directors and Boards,* and *Strategy and Business* and has also been interviewed on these topics by NBC, ABC, CBS, CNN, CNBC, NPR, and the *Wall Street Journal.* He has been profiled in *Business-Week, Fortune, Fast Company,* and *Business 2.0,* among others.

Prior to joining Spencer Stuart in 1994, Jim was director of corporate planning at The Reader's Digest Association. Before that he spent five years with McKinsey & Company in the United States and France, serving as a senior engagement manager. Earlier, he was an associate with Goldman, Sachs & Company and spent three years as a financial analyst with Morgan, Stanley & Company.

A 1981 Phi Beta Kappa graduate of Vassar College with a BA in economics, Jim serves as a member of the Vassar board of trustees. He earned an MBA from the Harvard Business School, graduating with distinction in 1986. He is on the board of the Harvard Business School Club of New York.

THE 8 POINT PLAN